THE COVETING CHRISTIAN

THE COVETING CHRISTIAN

You shall not covet. . . anything that is your neighbour's
(Exodus chap.20 v.17 [RSV])

Covet. . . the best gifts
(I Corinthians chap.12 v.31 [AV])

Richard Eldridge

Published by Henry Cauline
16, Polwell Lane, Barton Seagrave, Kettering NN15 6UA

Date of Publication
January 1998
Reprinted July 1998

Published by:
Henry Cauline
16, Polwell Lane,
Barton Seagrave,
Kettering NN15 6UA

Printed by:
ProPrint,
Riverside Cottage
Great North Road
Stibbington
Peterborough PE8 6LR

ISBN: 0 9532058 0 0

CONTENTS

FOREWORD

Human nature is clearly physical; equally, vast numbers of people see it as fundamentally spiritual. One crucial contemporary issue is the way these two views are related in daily life.

About the first assertion there is no argument. From the moment we wake up we are faced with material concerns - clothes, food and drink, work, money and the like. On spirituality there is much less agreement. This is partly due to confusion about what the word means. Nevertheless, experiences which relate to the spirit of a person are real enough.

As soon as we meet with others we are affected by the vague and subtle sides of personality. 'Cheery soul;' 'She has plenty of ability, but there's no 'go' about her;' 'Quiet type, but a great fellow when you get to know him;' 'Our boss is a workaholic; she's got no soul;' 'They're marvellous neighbours - salt of the earth.' Remarks like these are commonplace. They may have little to do with wealth, brains, achievements, social standing or culture. But such comments touch a chord in us; they point to realities other than the straightforward mental or physical aspects of human nature.

Similar reactions crop up amongst groups of people. In almost any involvement with others a spirit, good or otherwise, can be sensed. We can 'feel' it in a home, in an office or factory ('You could cut the atmosphere with a knife'). It is present in dramatic societies and sports clubs, board-rooms and trade unions. Spirit may stem from quiet dependable mutual support, it may be an electrifying sparkle; it can be plain dull. It can be divisive, destructive and deadly. In ways like these, experiences where 'spirit' may be sensed are real, widespread and central in human experience. Many go further and see spiritual features as being of the essence of human nature.

Clearly a spiritual view of life continues to have a powerful appeal all over the world. People today, as throughout history, turn to all sorts of spiritual outlooks and practices for comfort, guidance and strength. The Christian Faith has exercised a huge influence on the countries of the Western world. It has undergirded and inspired the quest for truth and the free flow of truth, and the significance of impartial justice. It has stressed the supreme value of personal relationships, and the importance of care for those in need. Times have changed. To an increasing number of people in the West the Christian Faith seems unrelated to present day life. It is, in any case, just one among a great number of beliefs. Books and magazines, tapes and videos, radio, television and the internet present a bewildering variety of other options.

However, a sizeable proportion of people in the West still accept Jesus Christ as the key to their understanding of God and His purposes. Scores of millions join in Christian worship. Many clearly regard their Christian faith as central to their lives. Yet church life and worship are widely regarded as jaded and feeble, especially by adolescents and young adults. Individual Christians are still to be found who attract others and command respect. But the churches as a whole seem weak and ineffective in the face of powerful challenges to civilised life. Christians themselves are caught up in present day all-consuming greed, the breakdown of family life, indifference to world-wide human need and environmental problems.

Christians don't have to look far for one pointed insight into the cause of Christian weakness. In the parable of the sower, Jesus spoke of seed sprouting well, but being choked by thorns. This seed, He said, represents those whose belief is choked by the 'cares of the world, and the delight in riches, and the desire for other things.'(1) Their belief does not mature and brings no benefits; it is sterile. Nearly two thousand years later, covetousness, banned by the tenth Old Testament commandment and denounced in the New Testament,(2) is still widespread, even among Christians. Covetousness still damages faith.

Men and women must eat. No-one can avoid worldly cares and material problems. Full-blooded Christian belief provides the ground for dealing comprehensively with such material matters within an overall spiritual vision. But Christian truth and experience is to govern the whole of life. It is not just a matter of adding a form of spirituality to a conventional life-style. There must, as a consequence, be a thoroughgoing understanding of the relationship between Christian belief and everyday working life. This understanding has constantly to be reworked as technology and communications develop and circumstances change, both locally and world-wide.

It is essential for Christians to get to grips with this central issue of the interrelation between Christian belief and the material world. Otherwise the Faith will become less and less relevant to the practical issues of community life and to those of the world at large. So the relevance of Christianity to personal issues will be further questioned and that Faith will be further marginalised.

This book is an attempt to review and sketch out the relationship between spiritual and material matters, in the light of Christian truth. In a sketch significant aspects are emphasised, while much detail is left aside. The pattern of this work is similar. I hope it will be of value both to Christians and to those looking for a practical faith for daily life.

Richard Eldridge

ACKNOWLEDGEMENTS

There is nothing new under the sun, as the Preacher said long ago. So it is with this book. Its notions have emerged from tutors, family and friends, from books, supremely through reflection on the Scriptures; also from the much maligned media - newspapers, periodicals, radio and television. The script has been read, between drafts, by numerous friends. So my thanks are due to all who have helped in any way, not least by simple encouragement. It would be invidious to try to name them, with one exception. My wife has provided healthy criticism and stimulus, with much patience, over many years. It is to her that the book is dedicated.

DEDICATION

To

Inez

CHAPTER 1

INTRODUCTION

Jargon

Jargon easily slips into language. Any subject soon develops its special terms. Jargon can be helpful for those familiar with it; but for others it creates difficulties. In this book some of the technical terms of Christian belief have already been used. Others will follow. It will be important to clarify the meaning of words used in Christian thought, as they occur. But there are good reasons for tackling one or two of them at the outset.

Words like 'spirit' and 'faith' have special Christian meanings, as well as their everyday senses. There is bound to be confusion when words like these are used by Christians unless their meaning is clear. For example, does 'Holy Spirit' have anything in common with 'spirit' as used in describing the atmosphere at a football match? ('There was a marvellous spirit amongst the crowd at Wembley on Saturday.') Does faith in Christ have anything in common with 'faith' as exercised by the business man? ('He's got great faith in what he's doing; he's sunk all his savings in the business.') We cannot get very far when considering Christian belief, quite apart from commending our beliefs to others, unless it is recognised that questions like these need to be addressed.

There is a further point which underlies the importance of clarification. Everyday practical illustrations, in the form of parables, have been used for thousands of years as means of throwing light upon spiritual truths. When Jesus said 'I am the good shepherd'[(1)] He used the everyday sense of the word 'shepherd' to help people understand His own work and purposes. So today the everyday sense of a word may help in understanding what it points to in Christian use. 'Spirit' and 'faith' are two such important words.

Spirit

Although this book will focus on visible actions and physical and material matters, the spiritual truths of Christian belief are primary.

The word 'spirit' is so important that its meaning needs to be made clear.

In considering the ways in which people are involved with each other, the physical senses are basic. Sight, speaking and hearing are primary. Touch, smell and taste may also come into play. Other factors are also involved. Various terms are used for them, for example, mood, atmosphere, spirit, temper or vibes. These extra factors are often just as important, and sometimes more so, than those of the first set. ('The meal was fine, but the evening was spoilt by the atmosphere between Jack and Jill'). Such factors also occur in connection with the world around us as, for example, when we are affected by the beauty of a sunset.

Here is a working definition of spirit -

Spirit is a reality
evident in human interaction
with the self, with others,
with nature, with God,
which may not, at present, be able to be measured,
or even discerned, by physical means.

The word spirit is quite neutral. It simply refers to a key aspect of human nature. Some people may be spoken of as fine-spirited, others as mean-spirited; a few may be felt to be evil-spirited. As we view those with whom we come into contact - family, friends, colleagues and acquaintances - people rarely fit neatly into these categories. No doubt each of us may appear warm at one time, but selfish at another. In many, there may be flashes of a mean or unpleasant spirit. There is a continual ebb and flow of spirit, and this flow occurs wherever people are in any form of contact with each other.

Spirit varies enormously in the way it shows in individuals. In some it may be so obvious that others are brought almost magnetically under their spell. The charismatic person - literally meaning 'one with a gift' - is able to exert a powerful influence over individuals and crowds, as with an actor, entertainer, musician, or orator. The same quality has also been seen in powerful cult leaders. Spirit may be developed; it may be manipulated. It may be used for good and upbuilding; it may be used for evil and destruction.

Sensitivity to spirit varies greatly from one person to another. Some remain almost untouched by spiritual experiences which exert a powerful influence on others, as is clear from the different ways in which people react to art and music. Equally, people may remain unaware of the way in which they are affected by long-term spiritual influences, good or bad.

Spiritual experiences are clearly not just individual matters. A group of people may reflect warmth or selfishness, excitement or laziness, generosity or meanness. Experiences like these can seem erratic or illogical. A crowd at a sporting occasion can change from elation to fury in seconds. In the armed services there can be a fine spirit amongst a body of men trained for material destruction or even human killing. An artistic or scientific team with high aesthetic or intellectual standards can be a seed-bed of discontent.

There is clear significance and strength in these everyday spiritual experiences. Every human being shares in them, whatever their standard of intellectual ability, cultural background or material wealth. Human nature is essentially spiritual. Where there is continued good spirit in the family, in the work place, or recreational club, there is clear positive effect. It can make a real difference to the development of a child; it affects the performance of a sports team and the productivity of a business. A good spirit is enhanced by the way in which each person is drawn into the common concern. It will grow as people give wholeheartedly of themselves and as they remain open to new experiences. As individuals are ready to use their gifts in fresh ways, so they find themselves producing fresh talents and abilities.

It is important to emphasise certain characteristics of spirit. The rules of arithmetic and measurement, whether in size, power or location, do not apply here.To take an obvious example, many spiritual experiences grow as they are shared. Teaching, whether at home or school, brings the delight of seeing another person grasp knowledge and understanding. To experience beauty of nature or art with other people similarly increases one's personal awareness and enjoyment.

Spirit may not have a simple relationship with time. Visions of the future can excite or frighten a person, as is obvious over the prospect of promotion on the one hand, or death on the other. An unforgiving grudge can be carried for years, long past the immediate effect of the incident which upset the relationship. National spirit, whether in pride or resentment, can be even more persistent, extending over centuries, as is evident in many places today.

Spiritual matters can seem tantalisingly elusive. In speaking or writing of them, even to add 'a' or 'the' to the word spirit can restrict the reality. But spiritual matters are real, and can be more important than physical life itself.

Faith

As with the word 'spirit,' 'faith' has a variety of meanings. Here is a working definition of faith as experienced in everyday life -

Faith is belief formed out of incomplete knowledge.

Having faith and using faith are universal necessities, for everyone is subject to two great limitations. In spite of all the abilities available to the human person, we cannot know, with certainty, what the future holds, even in the short term. And in spite of the brain's immense abilities, we cannot know everything which may be of personal importance to us. All human beings use faith, in order to plan ahead and to cope with uncertainties and crises, as well as for daily living.

It is obvious that in many instances in daily life deliberate faith hardly plays a part. Often we can assume that what has happened in the past will happen today, tomorrow and on into the future. So we have faith in the people who supply us with food and drink, and in those who keep postal and telecommunication systems working. Significant faith does, however, have to be exercised in many matters, for example in planning a holiday, or buying a house, where it is often not possible to have enough information before making a decision. Faith is even more significant in facing changes in which other people are closely involved, as in family life or business arrangements. Where a decision has to be made in collaboration with others it is rarely possible to know all that we might wish before making up our minds.

The two factors, incomplete present knowledge, and ignorance about the future, intertwine in life. Consider the common event of a person starting a commercial or professional enterprise. He or she believes in skills which have been acquired and developed, is already experienced, and has made careful plans. But there can be no certainty of success. After the launch, things may go well, with opportunities increasing and the enterprise growing. On the other hand a variety of misfortunes may result in a long struggle. In many such ventures, the person concerned has staked considerable material assets. Both the initial faith in launching the project, and the continuing faith, have been real. Such faith is an invisible human quality worked out in material ways in a physical world.

No-one goes through life without disappointments or being hurt. These experiences may be physical, mental or emotional, affecting life at home, at work, or both. They may result from the breakdown of deep personal relationships. Some of the worst crises occur when someone in whom we trust lets us down, or when a dearly loved person is hurt, or dies prematurely.

Reaction to a crisis is one of the acid tests of personality. One may lapse into dull resignation, or into bitterness, cynicism or selfishness. Another may be determined to rise above the crisis. Hurts may be accidental or intentional. Yet bad experiences may be turned to good effect. Crises can uncover previously unrecognised resources from within. Many a person has come to echo the old truth - 'It is good for me that I have been in trouble.' (2) Out of these experiences abilities can develop and wisdom can increase, for wisdom stems in part in learning from one's own problems and from those of others.

Surmounting a crisis may result from sheer dogged determination. For most people however, the path of their recovery is shaped by their outlook on life. Whether they admit it or not, they are crucially affected by their faith and by the faith of their friends.

Faith is an inescapable part of everyone's life. The one who professes to have no religious belief generally has convictions which centre on personal influences, abilities and resources. Everyday faith is often vested in a relative, a friend or a professional adviser. However, it is one thing to consider particular situations where faith is needed; it is another to suggest that there may be an overall body of belief which can relate to any eventuality. Yet experience, and the history of beliefs point in this direction.

Time and again practical matters lead to basic questions. The man or woman struck by repeated misfortune cries out 'What is the purpose of living?' The emotionally bruised lover asks whether it is possible to love or trust again. The wrongly judged individual shouts for perfect justice for himself, and for those who appear to get away with crime. The everyday 'It's just not fair' and 'Why should this happen to me?' point time and again to questions about the meaning of life.

An all-inclusive body of faith must be able to cope with fundamental questions. It has to embrace the whole of life, including one's inner thoughts as well as one's outward actions. It needs to take in our involvement with the material world as well as dealings with all people. If one spur to faith is the need for hope for the future, it must also enable one to cope with the past, with all its failures. All of this serves to warn those who affirm an all-embracing belief. They must take care to grasp something of its whole scope and how it actually applies to their own life.

Faith does not necessarily have anything to do with religion. It is exercised by the rationalist, who declares his mind to be supreme in all things. So too it is exercised by the materialist and by the atheist. It is important that those with a religious faith should recognise that the outlook of a materialist, a rationalist or an atheist may deal with large areas of human experience with a real degree of comprehensiveness.

All are spiritual; All exercise faith

From the considerations of this chapter it should be clear that every person is a spiritual being. Every person exercises faith and has some belief which underlies personal actions. So it is not surprising that bodies of belief, in the form of philosophies, world views and religions, abound. Some, covering restricted areas of life, such as financial and political doctrines, are constantly proclaimed as if they are central to human life, which they obviously are not. In a shrinking world, the variety of religious faiths which claim to be all-embracing in scope becomes more and more apparent. Some have been in existence for thousands of years. Adherents of one or another belief assert that theirs is the truest, most relevant and most satisfying of faiths. Before drawing out the relevance of Christian faith, we must therefore sketch the outlines of Christian belief. For we shall, at various points in the book, point to particular aspects of this belief to make clear the fundamentals on which our assertions are based.

CHAPTER 2

CHRISTIAN BELIEF AND CHRISTIAN LIFE

Belief in God

Few people deliberately work out a philosophy of life, but vast numbers assume that God exists. At the great turning points in life and at other crucial times, many people in the West still look towards God. For some there is simply a whispered 'Thank God' or a cry of 'Oh God.' Some turn to organised religion, perhaps merely following family routine or general custom. But as they move towards God, they grope towards a being bigger than themselves from whom they may gain help. Then they are likely to find themselves caught up in an act of religious worship. They may have little knowledge or understanding about any god and may have all sorts of questions about the service in which they are asked to take part. But on balance they accept it.

A wide variety of reactions and emotions come to the surface at times of crisis. For example, in the approach to a baby's baptism, part of what is being expressed is the family's gratitude for the safe arrival of the child. Often, too, there is a sense of wonder at the whole experience of childbirth and parenthood with a feeling that there is more to life than can be rationally understood. There may be concern at the responsibilities to come, with a desire for strength and guidance for the days and years ahead. A similar variety of feelings occurs at the time of a death. At many a funeral there is a cry of 'Why should this have happened?' At the same time a feeling persists that after death we return to God.

These feelings are not only personal. Some members of a local council may regard participation in an annual religious service simply as part of their duties. Others may be seeking for wisdom to guide them in their work. Still others will be deliberately looking to God as the origin of their wisdom and the source for their guidance. Within all such services lies the belief that human authority operates under the rule of God.

But who is God, and what is He like? In these questions lies a huge problem. If God has relevance to life as a whole, He must be greater than all that can be known of Him. Imperfect human minds (and this includes the greatest intellects who have ever lived) cannot take in His whole nature. It follows, therefore, that all statements concerning God must fall short of completeness. However, in everyday experience with people, clues as to what a person is like are found in what he does. So it is with God. We may know Him and understand something of His nature as we discern His actions.

Time and again individuals have been convinced that they have been directly affected by God. They have said that they were aware of His speaking to them, that they had been called to particular work by Him, or simply that they had been influenced or changed by Him. However, because God cannot be described in any full sense, and because His qualities are so diverse, different people see God in different ways. The poet expresses his awareness through his own particular gifts. The historian chiefly sees God through the development and movement of people. The moralist may sense God's truth as he watches everyday actions of men and women. Ordinary people use everyday words and ideas to convey their own experiences. All down the ages, in all cultures and religions, there has been variety in the ways in which divine action and truth have been perceived.

It is obviously difficult to put ideas about God into the restricting form of words. So the use of picture language, parables and analogies is inevitable. Words such as revelation and vision are to be found throughout religious writing. Revelation points to the conviction that the source of the truth or experience lies outside the rational abilities of the writer. Vision points to awareness which clearly goes beyond normal experience.

God in the Old Testament

The 39 books of the Old Testament present us with a library concerning faith. They were set down by a variety of writers from the Jewish community over a period of centuries. They were not finally gathered into one volume until early in the Christian era.

Within these books there is history of the peoples and countries of the time.[1] Failures are not glossed over, yet there is a sense of divine providence which pervades the lives of individuals and of whole communities. There is drama, as in Job; there is poetry, supremely in the Psalms; there are whole books, Proverbs, for example, devoted to wisdom. Laws and guiding principles are laid out, dealing with even the details of everyday life, particularly in Exodus, Leviticus and Deuteronomy. There are great declarations concerning God, His nature and purposes.[2] There are passages of unequalled praise and worship, such as Psalms 95-100 and 145-150.

The Old Testament books were set down by human hands. Yet constantly the writings point to a divine origin, and carry a sense of divine authority. From these records God is seen as the one and only supreme divine being. He has created all things. He sustains all things.[3] He is perfectly just and righteous and these qualities are to be reflected in all people by their behaviour.[4] He upholds justice in the world, bringing retribution on people and nations whose behaviour falls below His standards.[5] Yet love and mercy are at the heart of God.[6] So He is seen as a redeemer, one who brings good out of evil.[7]

One of the great words used to indicate the nature of God is that He is holy.[8] Within this word lie concepts of perfection and purity, with a sense that He is distinct from the material universe. Yet He is involved in this world, both in creation and redemption. He is supreme over all things. As such He is to be honoured above all else.[9]

Nevertheless, within the Old Testament there are to be found notes suggesting unfinished business. More remained to be revealed of God's unfolding purposes[10] and of His judgement upon people and nations. There are indications that a particular and special servant of God, a new Saviour, would, at some time in the future, appear on earth.[11]

Jesus of Nazareth

Into this heritage and into the Palestine of two thousand years ago came the person of Jesus. He grew up as a normal member of a Jewish family. He worked as a carpenter.[12] It may well be that, as the eldest son, He had for a time to shoulder responsibility for the whole family, for little is heard of His father Joseph after Jesus was twelve years old.

When Jesus was about thirty His public ministry started. He chatted with individuals and taught in small groups.[13] Huge crowds followed Him and listened to Him, even forgetting their hunger.[14] Tough fishermen were prepared to give up their livelihood to join His inner group of disciples.[15] Fearless in front of the country's rulers,[16] He had compassion and understanding for the outcasts of society, whether fraudsters or prostitutes.[17] Women were attracted to Him.[18] Children gathered round Him.[19] His own religious practices were steeped in tradition,[20] yet He was scathing and ruthless with those whose concerns with rules obscured their devotion and obedience to God.[21] His own life was so saturated with a sense of complete and perfect relationship between Himself and God that the disciples sensed in Him a perfect and visible holiness. This was to be seen in His total submission to God, His total honouring of God and His complete one-ness with God.[22]

With Jesus there came a fresh understanding of the old concept of righteousness. The word indicated perfect fairness and right dealing between God and man, together with perfection in all human attitudes and actions. The Hebrew prophets had thundered against all human unrighteousness in the name of a perfectly righteous God.[23] Jesus had been nurtured in these teachings[24] and did not depart from them, but He spoke with deep insight into the truth of God with an authority quite unlike that of other religious leaders.[25] It came to be understood that any person who trusted in God's forgiveness and love as shown through Christ was counted as righteous by God. With this privilege came a new motive and power for expressing righteousness in daily life.[26]

By His attitude and by His words Jesus challenged many of the traditionally assumed social divisions of the day - man and woman, master and slave, adult and child, resident and foreigner.[27] He made clear that the divisions were not merely to be abolished. They were to be replaced by a transformed and creative concern. Jesus' words, care and actions lifted to new levels the way in which human relationships were to be seen. They were to be infused with pure self-giving love.[28] His own life was so saturated with love that one of His closest followers, sensing Jesus' unity with God, affirmed that God Himself is love.[29]

Once more a word brings problems. Love may simply mean desire or want. 'Making love' is equated with sexual intercourse. But the word has other important meanings. In relationships between parent and child, or between lovers, there develops something more than mutual affection and admiration. Feelings move towards delight and even adoration, with a subtle awareness that both people are caught up in some inexplicable wonder. The emotion remains deeply seated in the self, but at the same time it leads to a desire centred beyond the self, that the loved one may have the best of everything, and be protected from all unhappiness. Love which is warm and active opens up deeper awareness of love. Challenges and crises faced together bring out new personal qualities, with the discovery of fresh resources which had previously lain hidden. Older men and women often look back with particular gratitude to times of difficulty as periods when their love for each other has grown. The difficulties themselves have caused fresh riches of personality to be discovered, resulting in deepened admiration and affection.

Where love continues through times of selfishness and waywardness in the beloved, even to degradation and betrayal, it has clear restorative powers. It redeems the loved one from despair or from the grip of evil. Such love is literally life-giving, bringing new hope and new spirit. It has been seen throughout human experience in all manner of circumstances. It goes on quietly in countless homes between parent and child as the rebellious teenager is constantly forgiven. It continues in innumerable adult personal and communal relationships. Such love removes bitterness from human divisions -

between races and nations, cultural and religious groups, and cuts through distinctions of status and wealth. Those caught up in love with its forgiving and recreative powers know that it is supremely important, more so than anything else.

All these experiences are to be found within the Christian understanding and use of the word love. Jesus was clearly concerned with the physical health and well-being of people.(30) But with Him the disciples became aware of qualities and powers in His redeeming and restoring love of a kind they had hardly known or experienced before.(31) His life showed a deep and pure affection for all, with a desire that evil and guilt be removed from their lives so that the fullness of God's love could flow through each person.(32) He was deeply concerned to remove all barriers to full and warm relationships between individuals and communities, and between mankind and God.(33)

Jesus' love continued creatively to the point of His death, as he sought forgiveness for His persecutors, made practical provision for His mother and welcomed the penitent thief into paradise.(34) The manner of Jesus dying on the cross showed qualities of love which were to overcome the worst of all human evils. So the Cross of Christ was to stand for love in action, the heart of Christ's reality and power.(35)

Jesus' concern with the removal of barriers was dramatically emphasised by what happened soon after His death. As the disciples continued to meet together, they wavered between love and loyalty to Jesus and perplexed human fear.(36) For they must have expected to have to live with the memory of their cowardly betrayal of Jesus at His trial and death. Yet not only did they become aware that Jesus was alive, but He repeatedly calmed their fears with simple healing words - 'Peace be with you.'(37)

Shortly after Jesus' resurrection he challenged the disciples to go out and make known what they had experienced.(38) These instructions were coupled with an assurance that they would still be aware of Jesus' presence and guidance in all circumstances. The disciples had slowly come to believe that Jesus was God in human form. So if Jesus could forgive their appalling denial of Himself, this meant that God could forgive them, and forgive anything. So they could still be used for God's purposes.

As Jesus' life and teaching gave new understanding of God's nature and love, so also through Him came a new understanding of sin. The essence of the meaning of the word lies in human repudiation of the supremacy of God, shown in his goodness, wisdom, justice and love. Jesus' own character and personality had made the disciples more aware of their own shortcomings. Nevertheless He had stressed that the root of this lay not merely in wrong actions, but in the depth of human personality.(39) Paul, not many years later, gave a simple analysis of this universal human flaw -(40)

> 'I do not understand my own actions,
> For I do not do what I want,
>   but I do the very thing that I hate ...
> So then it is no longer I that do it,
>   but sin that dwells within me.'

He had put the matter in divine perspective earlier in the same letter-

'All have sinned and fall short of the glory of God.'(41)

Jesus' words and work highlighted both the reality and the consequences of sin. But He made clear that divine love, shown in His life and at His death and resurrection, was more powerful and effective than any, and all, sin.(42) The disciples' experience of the love and the forgiveness of Jesus convinced them that these powers knew no bounds of distance or time.

SALVATION; ETERNAL LIFE

The disciples' awareness that they continued to experience the love and forgiveness of Jesus after His resurrection gave them new perceptions about salvation. This word, expressing both rescue and security, conveyed something of the Jewish understanding of God's total care for His people.(43) With the disciples' realisation of Jesus' forgiveness and continuing love they sensed a security which was more all-embracing than any other they had known. 'Salvation' came to be one of their key words, indicating a central conviction in their new found faith.(44)

Coupled with new insight into salvation came fresh understanding of the meaning of eternal life. God's love and His life were shown by Jesus both before and after His physical death.(45) Here was a new appreciation of life itself. Life was not bounded by time, as measured by the rotation of the earth and by its movement round the sun. A new quality of life was sensed. This quality could be experienced here,(46) but would be felt even more fully after death, when the transformed body would be free from material restrictions and free from sin.(47)

The normality of the partnership between God and man was one of the key emphases to come through Jesus.(48) Within the Old Testament there were various accounts of men and women responding to divine promptings which led to radical changes in the direction of their lives. This happened in a variety of ways, as one and another was led, willingly or unwillingly, into paths they felt to be laid out by God.(49) Alongside this sense of partnership with a loving and caring God, there developed the belief that the key issue was that men and women had to be obedient to laws laid out by God.(50) These laws were greatly developed by Jewish teachers. By the time of Jesus the sense of a warm partnership between God and man was somewhat masked by the requirements of obedience to the laws.(51) Jesus vehemently underlined the importance of divine law,(52) as given in the Old Testament. But He set out a totally fresh understanding of the heart of human life. Fellowship with God was to provide its direction, its power and its delight.(53)

Clearly a partnership between imperfect man and a perfect and righteous God could not exist if man went his own way and sought God's goodwill afterwards. Partnership could exist meaningfully only if men and women sought God's purposes first and were constantly ready to admit their own shortcomings as they tried to work out these purposes. Only then could they fully accept God's forgiving love. Moreover this approach opens up the possibility of sharing in the life of God, as expressed in Paul's extraordinary words about Christian truth and life - 'Christ in you, the hope of glory.'[54]

Holy Spirit

The scope of all the fresh truths which came through Jesus was such that they could not wholly be understood by any one mind. Nor could they be fully absorbed by the initially small community of those whose hearts and minds had been gripped by Jesus.[55] Jesus had foreseen the problem and had indicated that His followers, as they maintained their loyalty to Him and to each other, would be led into further truth by His Spirit.[56] So indeed they came to know more about Him and what it meant to be His disciples. Following the spectacular events which took place at Jerusalem at the Jewish feast of Pentecost,[57] a few weeks after Jesus' resurrection, the disciples became more and more ready to respond to the Spirit of God.[58] However, the consequent enthusiasm of the disciples and the growth in their numbers produced a backlash from the Jewish authorities. This resulted in the first Christian martyrdom, and a persecution against the Jerusalem Christians. This in turn led to some Christians moving from Jerusalem to other parts of Palestine and to Syria.[59]

Rather than hampering the cause of Christ, the dispersal of the disciples resulted in new converts being made, and fresh Christian groups being established.[60] Soon the Spirit of Jesus was driving and leading disciples on journeys to countries bordering the eastern and northern Mediterranean in order to share their beliefs with both Jews and non-Jews.[61] They made clear, by proclamation, debate, sustained teaching and later by correspondence, how their new awareness of God related to their everyday lives as well as to the crises they encountered.[62] They spoke of God's truth with authority and conviction. As converts opened themselves to receive God's Spirit, abilities were kindled within them and new developments were initiated through them. Their new beliefs produced marked changes in character.[63] As a result, renewal and change came to be regarded as normal among Christians.[64]

Throughout the Old Testament, individuals had been powerfully affected by the Spirit of God.[65] Following the transformation of the disciples after Jesus' resurrection all were enabled to experience God's Spirit. The occurrence was so compelling that the disciples sensed that the Spirit was equivalent to the continuing presence of Jesus.[66] This Spirit was spoken about in quite personal terms - 'he' rather than 'it.'[67] The disciples recalled what Jesus had said about His continuing life[56] and found His words fulfilled in what they experienced, even describing this as being 'filled with the Holy Spirit.' [68]

The effect of these new insights and experiences was revolutionary.[69] Paul wrote of the Christian as being a 'new creation,'[64] echoing the startling words of Jesus recorded in John's gospel, 'You must be born again.'[70] Christians were said to be 'the body of Christ.'[71] The gifts of the Holy Spirit were . . 'for the building up of the body of Christ, until we all attain to the unity of the faith and of the knowledge of the Son of God, to mature manhood, to the measure of the stature of the fullness of Christ.'[72] The New Testament records tell of some lapses among Christians but it is clear that their impact around the Eastern Mediterranean was positive and extensive.

Christian belief today

By the end of the first century, Christian churches were to be found in present day Italy, Greece, Turkey, Syria, Lebanon, Jordan, Israel, Egypt and Libya. During the next two centuries the Christian faith spread to large parts of the Roman Empire. Since then Christianity has spread to many parts of the world. Great numbers of people have been affected by it for good. Countless individuals have lived lives of clear consecration, commending their Lord by their words and by their actions. This Faith continues to be demonstrated across the world today. There remains a conviction that, not least because of the grand simplicity of its central beliefs, it must prevail over all other faiths.

We have begun to take a huge leap from the first to the twentieth century. How can a divine revelation, through one man in a Middle Eastern country, relate to people in totally different circumstances nearly two thousand years later? Part of the answer to such a question lies in the nature of the core of Christian belief.

Christian faith centres upon the reality of God, His creation of the universe and in particular His creation of human beings. This belief focuses upon God's work through Jesus for the salvation of mankind, together with the working of the Holy Spirit. These beliefs are grounded in the Christian scriptures and have been demonstrated through the lives of Christians, through nineteen centuries.

While the Bible is primarily concerned with God, His revelation through Christ and the continuing power of the Spirit, it also contains much counsel on practical matters. This covers a very wide range, from personal and domestic questions to national and international issues.[73] But these writings do not claim to lay out detailed guidance for every possible occurrence. A key comment about the relation between Christian belief and daily life was made by Paul when he wrote 'Work out your own salvation with fear and trembling; for God is at work in you both to will and to work for His good pleasure.'[74] So it has been that in every age, Christians have worked out patterns of living appropriate for their own particular situation, under the guidance of Christ's Spirit.

In the first chapter we explored how men and women exercise faith in everyday affairs. The Christian asserts that answers to the fundamental questions about life and its purposes are found as we put our trust in God. God as revealed through Jesus is the centre of our faith; we live by His Spirit. Christian faith gives ground for complete trust in God in relation to our future within this life, and beyond. In daily life also we look to Him to guide and sustain us concerning practical problems and dilemmas. This guidance relates to human involvement with the material world as well as to issues of personal life and relationships. The forgiving love of Christ and His regenerating Spirit provide the means for coping with failure and crises.

So today we can have a faith which provides a strong base for all aspects of life. It has continuously to be worked out within the fellowship of Christians. We have to bear in mind the wisdom and experience of past generations. We need to be aware of what the Spirit is saying to people of different cultures and to those who live in other parts of the world. Such faith provides the ground for individual and communal moral and ethical decisions and for a creative appreciation of human life in all its immense variety. From this faith we have a means for understanding the past and a base for practical vision for the future.

Lives which demonstrate such faith can be seen today in our local communities. But obvious truths need to be emphasised. The faith of the Christian is shown in a number of ways, some personal and inward, some public and outward. Unless Christians show a quality of life clearly more significant than that shown by people professing no such faith, the spread of Christian belief will be inhibited. The man in the street rightly questions the point and even the truth of a belief which makes little difference to its adherents.

God's Spirit surrounds us. The Holy Spirit speaks to the human spirit. We may 'hear' and respond to this Spirit. This awareness may happen in ways we clearly recognise, as when God's truth is brought to us through the Scriptures and Sacraments[(75)] and when we see lives of clear Christian consecration. Awareness may also come through groups of Christians, and as we 'see' God in the beauty and power of nature. Coming alive to God may happen quite unconsciously.

Spiritual experiences are so various that a yardstick is needed by which it discriminate between promptings which are right and good, and others. The test for Christians is whether an experience accords with what has been made known through Jesus.[(76)] So the Christian is to live in co-operation with God's Spirit, responding to Him in the innermost being, in the mind and by word and action.

The qualities which were sketched out in the first chapter find their fulfilment in the Spirit of Christ. Nevertheless it is important to keep in mind features which are apparent in everyday spirituality. For example, joining with others in Christian spiritual experiences normally results in an enlargement of vision of the nature and power of the Spirit. Again, as in everyday spirituality, the Holy Spirit can appear gentle and powerful at the same time in the same company, calling out different spiritual qualities in different people. But a crucial difference remains; the Holy Spirit enables men and women today to experience all the benefits known by those who met Jesus Christ in the flesh two thousand years ago.

As a person may be affected for good (or ill) by everyday spiritual experiences, so the human spirit can be transformed and redeveloped as it is caught up by the influence and power of the Holy Spirit. The Spirit can then work through natural gifts and abilities, and can bring out new qualities, directing them for God's purposes, and infusing them with fresh energies. Also, just as a person is affected by the atmosphere present among a group of people, so the Spirit within the company of Christians can transform that group. It can become, in the words already quoted, the body of Christ,(72) with all the possibilities which this description implies.

As with Christian faith, so with Holy Spirit, the obvious needs to be underlined. Men and women who clearly show Christ's Spirit are to be found today in almost all communities. But unless normal Christian living shows a spiritual vitality which is more significant and attractive than everyday secular spirit, Christian belief and worship by themselves are unlikely to persuade the nonbeliever.

Here, then, is a sketch of Christian belief. The Christian's life and involvement with people and the world are to be shaped by this belief. Accepting these truths requires a revolution in outlook, which then results in a revolution in the pattern of life. The earliest Christians were taunted with the accusation that they had turned the world upside down.(69) There is a good sense in which that accusation should continue to be true. Christian truth needs constantly to be brought to bear upon commonly held assumptions and life patterns.

It is a simple truism to acknowledge that what is wrong with the Christian body today is that it is not sufficiently Christlike.

In all considerations of Christianity there lies the danger of Christian faith being seen as an experience initiated by men and women. So, for example, salvation, the great word which stands for the total security to be found within the love of God, is commonly regarded as being a natural privilege for those who have lived uprightly, or who have done good things. But salvation cannot be 'earned' in this way. It is a free gift from God to those who confess their sin, receive Christ's forgiveness, and live by His power and direction. The Cross of Christ remains crucial.

Those who have been brought up surrounded by Christian understanding still need to take the Faith to themselves as a matter of personal belief. For those who have not been nurtured in this way it is necessary to accept the simple but profound revolution which Christian belief requires.(77) Disturbing this may be, but it results in a peace which goes beyond understanding, coupled with a fresh and joyous awareness of what full-blooded life is meant to be. The Christian does have to respond to the love and power of God, using all human powers to the full. But Christian faith is fundamentally a matter of yielding to the measureless passion and tenderness of Christ's Spirit.

CHAPTER 3

FOUNDATIONS

The Bible; New Testament; Old Testament

Throughout the last chapter the Bible has been used as the authority underlying Christian belief. For the Christian this is natural, for the Bible is the foundation book of his faith. Yet the Biblical books do not make up an ordered text-book such as would be used in engineering or medicine. Rather, looking for example at the New Testament, it seems almost haphazard. After four lives of Jesus comes a brief history, the Acts of the Apostles, covering only some 30 years following the resurrection. Then come 21 letters and the Revelation of John, with its triumphant concluding vision.

However, the gospels of Luke and John deliberately make clear that they were written so that readers might have the essential facts of the life and teaching of Jesus.(1) Matthew and Mark's gospels plainly meet the same need. Of the letters, some were written to answer questions posed by Christian converts.(2) All were written so that new Christians could have a right understanding of the Faith as it related to their own circumstances. All these 'books' deal with matters and question which were being raised by those enjoying faith in Christ for the first time. So these books have provided generations of Christians with the truths they have needed in their own quest for the basics of Christian belief.

Jesus was a Jew and in His early life he was nurtured in the Jewish scriptures. He shared in Jewish customs and worship. Clearly He was very familiar with the bulk of what is called the Old Testament. Jesus found personal strength from its words.(3) He used it as a body of truth he knew to be revered by His fellow Jews.(4)

Some of Jesus' key assertions were taken straight from the Old Testament.(5) As already indicated, within the prophetic books there were passages which looked forward to the coming of a unique servant of God.(6) Jesus applied some of these directly to Himself.(7) He made clear that He would not whittle anything away from the 'Law and the Prophets.' (8) (a contemporary term which included much of the Old Testament). Indeed He deliberately expounded, with deepened insight, some of the Old Testament commandments, making clear, for example, that 'everyone who looks at a woman lustfully, has already committed adultery with her in his heart.'[9] Yet He chided some Jewish scribes for failing to see that these writings pointed to Himself and found their fulfilment in Him.[10] Paul put the same truth in a homely sentence - 'All the promises of God find their 'Yes' in Jesus.'[11] Other New Testament writers make the same point.[12] Clearly Christians must honour deeply this first great part of the Bible.

The whole Bible to be read with Christian insight

For nearly two thousand years the whole Bible has been seen as providing the foundations of Christian belief, but the two great sections - Old and New Testaments - need to be understood as distinct yet complementary to each other. It is obvious that the New Testament provides the historical information concerning Jesus. But both His Jewish heritage and His use of the Old Testament point to the importance of giving proper weight to the whole Bible. Nevertheless care is needed so as not to allow the Old Testament to overwhelm the fact that the heart of the Christian faith lies with Jesus Christ. Three major issues are briefly looked at to illustrate the need for the guiding wisdom of the Holy Spirit in reading the Bible. The first is an example of the timeless strength and significance of the Old Testament. The other two underline the need to see the Old Testament in the light of the New.

CONCERNING JUSTICE AND RIGHTEOUSNESS

The theme of God's justice runs through the whole Bible. But the fact that justice also requires a right ordering of human affairs is particularly evident in the Old Testament. The first five books, commonly referred to as 'The Law,' are full of practical codes for personal conduct and communal living, as well as for religious observances. It is made clear that these requirements reflect the righteousness of a holy God.[13] Land, money and materials are to be handled aright; the young, the old, the weak and the handicapped are to be protected. The Old Testament history books are full of observations about God's requirements and the obedience, or failure, of people and rulers.[14]

The prophets are as much concerned with human behaviour in their own times as they are with visionary declarations - 'cease to do evil, learn to do good; seek justice, correct oppression; defend the fatherless; plead for the widow' says Isaiah.[15] So with the Psalms - 'maintain the right of the afflicted and the destitute. Rescue the weak and the needy; deliver them from the hand of the wicked.' [16] In a simple sweeping phrase the prophet Amos sums up much of this great theme: 'Let justice roll down like waters and righteousness like an overflowing stream.'[17] Amongst the Proverbs the declaration that it is righteousness that exalts a nation[18] stands as a rock-like affirmation for the ordering of human endeavour and human society. Righteousness is of fundamental significance in national life, to be more highly regarded than material wealth, military power or cultural achievements.

As Jesus mixed with the Jews of His time, individually or in crowds, He could assume that they would be aware of the fundamentals of their faith, as written in the 'Law and the Prophets.' Because He emphasised the importance of these writings their truths[19] have entered into Christian belief. The breadth of the Old Testament understanding of God's justice and righteousness with the need for these qualities to be seen in all human life is one of the great strengths of Christian truth.

CONCERNING PEACE AND CONFLICT

God loves all people. He desires the best for all people, and that they should live in harmony with each other, following His will. The more firmly these truths are held, the more it is realised that God is supreme, that He has no rivals and that His will must prevail, completely.

There is inevitably a tension between following God's will and imposing that will, though the two actions are only differing aspects of understanding God, who is both supreme, and supremely loving. The Old Testament writers, as they saw God in action, record

Him leading His people in victory over those who oppose Him. This is shown in the account, in the books of Exodus through to Joshua,[20] of the release of the Jews from slavery in Egypt to their establishment in Palestine. It is also seen in the subsequent precarious hold that the Jews retained on this territory. Opponents were to be conquered or destroyed. The theme continues in the Psalms. Within these poems there are clear notes concerning God's grace, compassion and forgiveness. But over a quarter of them mention war and destruction in relation to those who oppose God.

The other side of the tension is strikingly shown in an extraordinary Old Testament book - Hosea. The prophet is torn between his love for a prostitute and his recognition of her wrong-doing, with the punishment due to her. Hosea sees the prostitute's life as a picture of Israel's immoral life, far gone from the standards of God's people. He sees his own love as a pointer to God's far greater and deeper love for His people: 'How can I give you up ... How can I hand you over ... My compassion grows warm and tender ... I will not execute my fierce anger.'[21]

In the New Testament there is little reference to physical conflict or destruction initiated by Christians.[22] At the heart of all that Jesus taught and achieved in His suffering and crucifixion, it is the power of God's love which is supreme. The divine overcoming of evil is more a matter of redemptive love, as in Hosea, rather than conflict and destruction. In the last book of the Bible there are clear intimations of God's final conflict with evil.[23] But the human disciple's approach is to be one of drawing upon all the many-sided resources of Christ's liberating power, rather than that of physical strife.[24] Yet the language of confrontation has continued strongly in Christian thought and some popular hymns and so into the shaping of present day attitudes and actions.[25]

In such ways the cause of Christ has been hindered. The temptation to see physical force as more effective than the work of long-term spiritual development persists.

During the early years of the development of the Israelite nation it was natural that liberation from slavery and privation in Egypt was associated with comfort and prosperity.[26] While there are Old Testament cautions concerning wealth,[27] there are also passages where God's blessing appears directly linked with material riches.[28] Poverty and affliction are not God's will, but there is a noticeably different perspective concerning wealth in the New Testament. The accumulation of personal riches is rarely commended; rather it is seen as an obstacle to fellowship with God. It is something which detracts from Christian growth and service.[29] Christians are to be ready to share their goods with those in need, well beyond those with whom they may be in normal contact.[30] However, the pre-Christian affirmations remain. They inhibit present-day Christians from a thorough evaluation as to what should rightly be done with material wealth.

The heart of the Biblical presentation of divine truth lies in the New Testament. The whole Bible is essential for a full understanding of Christian belief, but it has always to be read by the light of the Spirit of Jesus Christ.

The Spirit's guidance, into all truth

It is clear that those closest to Jesus, the disciples themselves, did not always find it easy to grasp what He was telling them.[31] This was partly because Jesus was chiefly concerned with truth about God, which cannot always be simply expressed through words. The disciples' perplexity also arose because Jesus presented them with insights which were totally new to them.[32]

Jesus made clear that the disciples would need more of God's truth than they had been able to absorb while He was with them. He promised that God's Spirit would lead them into all truth, but He stressed that fresh understandings which they discovered or discerned should always accord with what He had already revealed.[33] The early Christians were soon faced with a crucial test of this guidance. Did non-Jews who wanted to become Christians have, in effect, to become Jews first? The question was natural enough as all the early Christians were Jews, yet non-Jews were soon responding to the preaching of the apostles in considerable numbers. The issue was thrashed out in a special Christian council in Jerusalem, recorded in Acts chapter 15. The Holy Spirit led the company to make clear that non-Jews were fully welcome into the Christian body with only a few basic requirements which all could accept. Such guidance by the Spirit is evident throughout the Acts,[34] and in the New Testament letters, written to educate and encourage individuals and congregations.

But what did Jesus mean when he told His disciples that the Spirit would guide them into all truth? [35] Is the Spirit as much concerned with scientific and historical truth as with truth concerning God? Clearly as the word is used in the Bible, it is generally concerned with truth about spiritual matters. But it is nowhere restricted to this sort of meaning. In practice it is hardly possible to divide 'Christian' truth from other truth, for God is concerned with the whole of life.

The Christian uses all means available for the discernment of truth concerning God, supremely through Biblical revelation. The fullness of this truth is beyond total human comprehension, as Paul exclaimed in an outburst of wonder - 'O the depths of the riches and wisdom and knowledge of God! How unsearchable are His judgements and how inscrutable His ways!'[36] But truth about the natural and physical world and about people is also to be explored as a matter of fundamental importance. Investigation and research are to be pursued; learning and wisdom are to be sought. It follows that the person who has stopped enquiring, or the person unwilling to accept established truth has, in part, stopped living.

The pursuit of truth will rarely be totally academic, isolated from daily life. There will, in the end, be only two or three reactions to the making of discoveries, whether these be the grasping of existing knowledge, or the finding of completely new truth. All should marvel. Some will give praise and honour to God the Creator.

Others will simply want to put the discoveries to good use, sharing them with others and helping others to benefit by them.

Words are our chief agents in the discovery of truth, but truth cannot be confined within words, and some of the most important matters or experiences sidestep words almost completely. At times of great emotional crisis, whether of celebration or of pain, the warm physical contact of a hug speaks more powerfully than any number of words; indeed at such times words can be useless. Nevertheless, words are supremely precious. In the hands of those skilled in their use, they can convey much more than their face value. Parable and allegory, exaggeration and humour, poetry as well as prose, are all found in the Bible.(37) Yet words are not to be trifled with. Jesus made clear that swearing, in the sense of adding deliberate weight to words, should not be needed. 'Let what you say be simply 'Yes' or 'No;' anything more than this comes from evil.'(38)

A full appreciation of belief and experience goes beyond ordinary understanding.(39) There is much more to truth than that which can be weighed, measured and stated in purely material or physical terms. Reason and logic are not the only ways of developing understanding of truth. When Jesus spoke of Himself as being the truth,(40) He was using a concept which had centuries of usage behind it. Truth, in the Old Testament, is closely associated with righteousness, judgement and faithfulness; it is part of the nature of God Himself. The word includes factual accuracy, but concerns much more than the sum total of information to be found in a textbook or encyclopaedia.

Christians will always be ready to search out truth using their powers to the fullest extent possible. They recognise the limitations of intellectual enquiry and reasoning. They realise that the Holy Spirit of truth will lead them into fresh insights concerning both God, and His creation. Personal involvement with God is a matter of rationality and supra-rationality.(41)

As truth is so vast in its range, and while the human mind is so small in comparison, there is a constant need to compare and contrast differing understandings. It is vital to reason, to criticise and to debate, so that a greater appreciation of truth may emerge. The free flow of facts, information, experience and wisdom is paramount, not least in matters concerning religious belief and Christian understanding. Censorship and secrecy must be at the lowest possible level, to protect the tender growing mind, but for little else.

Research into nature, and enquiry into the human condition across the world, have developed enormously with the speed and range of today's communication systems. Yet with all the advances in the conveying of information the ability to read remains crucial. Enabling each person to read and write, wherever they may live, is one of the single most important 'tools' for the development of human personality.

Truth is precious, but truth is not all on a par. It is possible to fill one's mind with truth concerning wrongdoing, destruction, degradation, perversions, failure, ugliness, breakdown and the like. Some of this is necessary for a full understanding of the range and diversity of human behaviour. But it is a distortion of human abilities for these matters to be pursued to the point that the abnormal is seen as acceptable or even normal, or to the point that bad news appears to outweigh good. It is obviously destructive of positive values to do so. There is much plain sense in the counsel of the apostle Paul -[42]

> 'Whatever is true, whatever is honourable,
> whatever is just, whatever is pure,
> whatever is lovely, whatever is gracious,
> if there is any excellence,
> if there is anything worthy of praise,
> think about these things.'

CHAPTER 4

CHRISTIAN SPIRITUALITY - ETERNAL LIFE IN THE PRESENT

A new outlook on time

Central to the Christian understanding of life is a new outlook on time. We experience time through material change. We see changes over time in people, plants and animals, and in materials. We measure time by reference to the rotation of the earth, giving day and night, and by the earth's movement round the sun, giving seasons and years. God is not a material being. His life is different from ours. Time, as we understand it, does not apply directly to God.[1] Then how do those traditional words of Christianity - 'everlasting life,' 'eternal life,' 'for ever and ever,' relate to everyday matters?

The person who has an active faith in God shares in the life of God, for Christ has broken the barriers, both of ignorance[2] and sin,[3] between man and God. This life is shared, in new ways, after death. Because of the glory and perfection of God, the delights of this eternal life far outstrip anything that can possibly be imagined in this present time scale.[4] In this life we are frustrated by failure, and restricted by bodily limitations. Here, time is a limiting factor in all we do; for there's never enough of it. These constraints will be altered or removed in life with God beyond the grave.[5]

The problem of finding words to explain spiritual truths has already been seen. Words like 'everlasting' and 'for ever and ever' do not give the best understanding of the Biblical words which speak of eternal life. Eternal life points to a different quality of life, associated with a different sphere of life, where God is totally supreme. Paul approached the same truth from a different angle when he wrote 'our citizenship is in heaven.'[6] He was indicating that Christians have an additional framework of relationships within which a different sort of life is experienced. It is dominated by the reality and love of God, and can be experienced now. This eternal life will be a far greater experience after death.

We have to saturate ourselves in the Biblical ideas of time to taste the full flavour of these truths. Some appreciation of Christian eternity can be gained as we recall occasions when we have been taken totally out of ourselves. We use phrases like 'Time stood still,' 'I lost all count of time,' or 'The day went by in a flash.' Clocks and calculators are not the only pointers to thinking about time. They are essential in today's world, but they are not always the best.

The promise of eternal life beyond death is a powerfully attractive feature of Christian belief. This hope of a far better future has sustained great numbers of individuals and whole communities through times of grinding poverty and hard work. Looking forward to life in heaven resulted in the evocative 'spirituals' of the West Indian and American plantation workers, together with many yearning traditional hymns. The belief has helped to produce lives of great strength and beauty of character. The power of this conviction has been shown, for example, by Kenyan Christians facing Mau Mau hostility or Ugandans suffering under Amin's tyranny. Christians have been enabled to face martyrdom not only with courage, but with a grace that has won converts to faith in Christ.

Nevertheless the way in which eternal life is understood can result in weakness of practical faith.[7] Just because Christian faith is so strongly linked with life after death some people have been tempted to take little care about obedience to God in the present. The occasional caustic comment 'He's so heavenly minded that he's no earthly use' may sometimes be near the truth.

The Christian hope for life after death remains an essential part of Christian belief. But it is a gross distortion if this hope should push vision, planning and work in the material world into a secondary position. The glories of heaven are not a prize for regular worship and private devotion with little other than lip service towards following Christ in working life. Faith in Christ must be demonstrated with integrity in this world within the present time-scale.[8] Eternal life stands for a God-centred pattern and quality of life to be lived now. If this is not done, the faith will be found to be less than completely satisfying. Its full significance will also be misunderstood by those outside its orbit. Christian faith and life have to be worked out in this world, but within an overall time-scale which has its framework and goal beyond physical life.

Timeless qualities and daily life

Working out life within a God-centred perspective means that clear significance is given to spiritual matters in daily life. The physical senses - sight, smell, sound, taste and touch - with all the varieties of their combinations, make a more or less instant impact. But there are other experiences, which also come largely through the senses. Their impact is less immediate, yet very important.

Consider integrity and its associated qualities such as honour and incorruptibility. Each quality relates to the assumption that what a person says, writes or does today, ties up with the words and actions of that person in the past and in the future. These qualities point to the expectations that actions and words hold together, whatever the circumstances. Clearly, from their nature, time is needed to appreciate these qualities. Equally, time is needed for these qualities to be developed.

Similar considerations apply to faithfulness. The word is inescapably involved with the passage of time. So it is with love. Love which has any depth of quality cannot be just an instant matter. It has to be shown over time. It has to be seen and sustained through all circumstances. Its quality is judged in part by the way in which difficulties and setbacks are surmounted by those within a loving relationship. Similarly, forgiveness can be declared in an instant, but its significance has to be shown over time.

Faithfulness, love and forgiveness have powerful healing qualities. The love of God, shown in the life, death and resurrection of Jesus, is the source of these qualities and has timeless power.

SPIRITUAL QUALITIES - THE HEART OF HUMAN NATURE

The qualities just mentioned cannot be separated from the physical world. People are aware of them, in considerable measure, through the natural senses. But it is qualities such as these, which come from the nature of God, which lie closest to the heart of what it is to be human. These are qualities which are primary in human nature and central in human activity.[9]

Consider Paul's list of the fruit of Christ's Spirit - love, joy, peace, patience, kindness, goodness, faithfulness, gentleness and self-control. Paul adds[10] 'If we live by the Spirit, let us also walk by the Spirit' implying that these 'fruits' are to be valued and used. In another letter, Paul, writing about spiritual qualities, says 'covet earnestly the best gifts,' (quoting the words of the Authorised Version). The British character shies away from pursuing goodness. Self-righteousness is understandably scorned. It is the opposite of Christian holiness. Yet Jesus was uncompromising - 'You must be perfect ...'[11] There is a very important sense in which the best qualities are to be coveted and pursued. Yet they are best seen as qualities which follow naturally as Christ's Spirit is allowed to take over the Christian and produce His fruit in the personality.

One of the dramatic concepts concerning the love of God, first used by Jewish, then, sparingly, by Christian writers, is that of redemption. The word today speaks of the freeing of an object or, in the case of slavery, a person. That freedom is often obtained by a payment, seen in New Testament terms as the cost to Jesus of the love and pain of His life-giving work, culminating in the actual giving of His life on the Cross. What is at first sight a curious use of the word crops up once or twice in the New Testament, when Paul urges his readers to redeem the time.[12] Modern versions tend to translate the original word by 'making the best use of ' the time. But this weakens the force of Paul's expression. Time is to be emancipated, to be freed for use in God's purposes.

The person who knows the love of Christ knows also that the forgiving love of God removes the power of nagging memories from the past, such as 'I'll never forget what he did to me.' The person without an understanding of forgiveness can carry resentment through the whole of his life. It may simply result in a grudging character typified in the phrase - 'He's got a chip on his shoulder.' It may result in a bitterness which distorts a whole life. When harboured by a community, past injuries, grievances and quarrels can issue in sustained hostility which may erupt in violence, as can be seen all over the world today.

The Christian's redeeming of past time is, in part, a transforming of past bad experiences into memories which can deepen love for God and for one's neighbour. The experience of forgiveness enables a person to enter sympathetically into the problems of others. So the timeless love of God is both redeeming and creative, releasing fresh powers for the present and future.

One of the clearest results of the technological revolution of recent decades is that tasks can be carried out much more quickly than was possible only a few years ago. Whether in communication, in transportation, or in getting work done, actions can be completed far more speedily than could have been imagined a generation back. The time needed for the basic work of living is much reduced. There is, for vast numbers of people in the West, more time available than is needed for activities which are essential for a basic rounded life. This is seen in the general reduction in the standard hours of work for many in the West. But how is the excess time to be used? Clearly there is the possibility for giving more time in care and concern for others than was possible a generation or two ago. The potential for living a Christ-centred life more richly than ever before is obvious. The Christian's use of time has to be rescued and reshaped so that time, resources and energies are used for matters which come first in Christian priority.

Christian Spirituality

The word spirituality itself points to the fundamental challenge which faces each Christian - that of bringing Christian spiritual insight to bear upon everyday life. Much of what any person does is shaped by everyday needs and customary practice. Nevertheless Christian belief requires a distinctive response, in both attitudes and actions.

The principle underlying Christian spirituality is shown more than once in Paul's writings. In his letter to the Christians at Philippi he sees the broad sweep of Jesus' whole life and work as demonstrating the crucial significance of consecrated service. He writes of Jesus emptying Himself of divine privilege in a life which climaxed in a seemingly premature death.(13) Then Paul writes simply, '*therefore* God has highly exalted Him.' There could not be a more powerful pointer to the Christian understanding of life as lying in Christ-like service. Paul goes on to encourage his readers to work out their own salvation with this in mind, knowing that God would be working in them and through them.

Paul makes a similar point in his letter to the Christians at Rome. Two thirds of the way through, as he deals with practical matters, he writes: 'Do not be conformed to this world, but be transformed by the renewal of your mind, that you may prove what is the will of God, what is good and acceptable and perfect.'(14) But how is this transformation to be tackled in practice?

There are clear problems over any command that one should love. But Jesus' particular attention to the two great commandments is important in setting a broad field of practical vision for Christian action(15) -

'You shall love the Lord your God with all your heart, and with all your soul, and with all your mind, and with all your strength' and 'You shall love your neighbour as yourself.'(16)

The imperatives 'You shall love ...' can helpfully be seen as pointers to the way in which the human has been designed to function. Life can either be run along these lines - with the grain. Or it can be run while ignoring these principles - across the grain. The consequences of the first will be an enlarging and development of personal character and achievements. The consequences of the second will be the limiting of vision and actions.

The first commandment is supreme in itself. But it also points to the source and quality of the love upon which we are to draw in our obedience to the second. By His teaching and His actions Jesus made clear that concern for our neighbours is to extend to any person whatsoever of whom we may be aware[17] and to those of whom we may have no present knowledge. The quality of this love is to be that of Jesus, shown through His whole life.

Jesus further emphasised the significance of the two laws by adding 'On these two commandments depend all the law and the prophets.'[18] By these words He made clear that the life and history of the Jewish people related intimately to these fundamental principles. Jesus also added 'There is no other commandment greater than these.'[19] Clearly there is good ground for using these commandments as a base from which to develop guidelines for life today.[20] First, though, it is necessary to underline the importance of the physical and material elements of a contemporary spirituality.

CHAPTER 5

PRACTICAL PERSPECTIVES

Spiritual qualities, as seen with Christian insight, lie at the heart of human nature. Within these qualities God's love, shown by Jesus Christ in His whole life and teaching and by His death and resurrection, stands supreme. That love is to be kept strong, pure and active in life. But it is not just a glorious experience, with personal security for the believer. This love is to be shared, in practical ways, with all others. But it has to be recognised that times and places of present day Christian vitality are surrounded by Christianity which is pedestrian and compromised.

Christian belief developed out of the Jewish faith. Throughout the centuries before Christ there were men and women of great faith in God whose lives portrayed in the Old Testament remain timeless inspirations. But there were also periods of sad failure. The prophet Isaiah found himself driven by God to declare to the people of Judah and Jerusalem[1] -

> 'The Lord enters into judgement with the elders and
> princes of His people:
> It is you who have devoured the vineyard,
> the spoil of the poor is in your houses.
> What do you mean by crushing my people,
> by grinding the face of the poor?'

Isaiah goes on to speak of the coming judgement of God:[2]

> 'Instead of perfume there will be rottenness, and
> instead of a girdle, a rope;
> and instead of well-set hair, baldness;
> and instead of a rich robe, a girding of sackcloth;
> instead of beauty, shame.
> Your men shall fall by the sword
> and your mighty men in battle.
> And her gates shall lament and mourn;
> ravaged, she shall sit upon the ground.'

Such failures and warnings (and there are many other similar declarations within the Old Testament) were the result of the widespread failure of the Jewish people to live up to their own laws and instructions. The requirement 'You shall love your neighbour as yourself,' which Christians think of as the second great commandment, was intimately related to the demand that God be honoured above all else. It is taken from an Old Testament passage (Leviticus chapter 19) which focuses on the need for holiness in all people. But this holiness is to be worked in social and material matters as much as in spiritual ways and worship ritual. Concern is expressed about foreigners and travellers as well as about the poor and elderly of the Jewish people. Right handling of wages is counselled alongside sexual matters. Generosity at harvest-time and just dealing in everyday affairs are all seen as essential in holiness.

Such instructions and warnings would have been well known in Jesus' day. But Jesus could still see evidence of the failure of some of the spiritual leaders of His own time. In Matthew's gospel (chapter 23) His cutting words are brought together as a sustained tirade against the narrow and at times petty religiousness which He saw[3] -

> 'The scribes and pharisees sit on Moses' seat; so practise and observe what they tell you, but not what they do; for they preach, but they do not practise.'

He goes on to say that they do all their deeds for show. They don't fully embrace their faith and don't work it out in integrity. By their examples they prevent others from enjoying fully the benefits of faith. They may tithe mint, dill and cummin in accordance with Moses' laws, but they forget the weightier matter of the same Law, justice, mercy and faith. The whole passage needs to be read to sense the power of Jesus' denunciation. It ends with His yearning cry[4] - 'O Jerusalem, Jerusalem, how often would I have gathered your children together as a hen gathers her brood, but you would not.'

Towards a significant spirituality

How can a vibrant faith lapse into weakness and travesty? Some of the saddest words of the Bible are to be found in a passage where Timothy, Paul's young colleague, is warned about probable developments among religious people. After a catalogue of human failures he is cautioned about people 'holding the form of religion, but denying the power of it.'(5) A glance over the new Testament letters suggests that within only a short time after the resurrection of Christ it was clear that such warnings were needed. How can Christian faith, with its promise of spiritual power and with, from earliest days, demonstrations of that creative power, wither into a shadow of what it should be? We may find one clue to a re-vitalising of faith in a re-reading of the two great commandments.

'You shall love the Lord your God with all your heart, and with all your soul, and with all your strength and with all your mind.' (6) Between the Old Testament verse and its quotation in the first three gospels there are some verbal variations. But the thrust is clear. The whole of human personality, with all its abilities, is to be brought into the service of God.(7) Mind and strength are included in their own right, not simply to indicate totality of commitment, as if underlining the need for whole-hearted devotion with heart and soul.

Physical and mental powers are to be used as integral parts of the human response to God. Two to three thousand years ago technology was, by present day standards, primitive. But craft work, finance, commerce, property and business management all came under the divine direction or judgement in the Old Testament records.(8) In the New Testament Luke's gospel, especially, shows a similar concern with financial and business matters.(9)

It is fair to infer that Jesus Himself, in the years before He started on the period of ministry recorded in the gospels, was closely involved in all aspects of everyday life. He did not marry or have children, but He knew what it was to live in a large household. Matthew's gospel suggests that this numbered at least eight people. He worked as a carpenter,(10) doubtless being involved in the purchase of timber, in matters of design, and the maintenance of His tools. He would have been involved in commercial matters as His products or skills were sought. There are few references to Joseph after Jesus was twelve years old. So it may be that He had to be the chief breadwinner and supporter of the family, perhaps for as many as 15 years.

In the years of Jesus' public ministry He was seen to be steeped in knowledge of the Jewish Scriptures, and regular in His public and private worship.(11) He also carried with Him a great breadth of practical experience and vision concerning human work, social affairs, and the material world. These two parts of His life were totally and perfectly integrated in all He did and taught.

The way in which the Christian's involvement with the material world is worked out today varies enormously. Men and women still respond to a call for a virtual separation from everyday affairs. This may, in some monastic orders, result in an austere simplicity of life, so that there may be continuous engagement in divine worship and in prayer. Other monks and nuns are deeply involved in practical service. If little is heard of the first group, the name of Mother Theresa remains a byword for the second. Church leadership is clearly regarded as an avenue for dedicated service, supposedly separate from worldly problems and compromises. A feeling persists that certain sorts of work, such as medicine, education and the caring professions, provide natural spheres into which Christians should be drawn.

But where do other occupations come in this list? Agriculture does have a distinct significance. Here workers obviously co-operate with the Creator in their labour. But without the men and women who are engaged in engineering and manufacture, commerce and banking, government and administration, few of the other spheres of work could be sustained. These are basic and essential. They must be key elements in any Christian appraisal of life as a whole.

The seemingly impersonal spheres of technology, manufacture, finance and commerce may not, at first sight, appear to be areas where spiritual issues should predominate. Yet without good faith, the development of warm relationships and a creative spirit, such work cannot operate to its best effect. There are hard ethical issues to be faced in the commercial and industrial world upon which Christian insights must be brought to bear, and these must be tackled. Otherwise financial and material concerns are left open to self-interest and blatant market forces. Certain major manufacturing and commercial firms have been well-known for their positive attitudes to employees. But financial self-interest, coupled with the interest of those who have provided the firm's capital, remain dominant factors in large areas of commercial activity.

Because of the huge financial power of contemporary industry and commerce, the community at large is over-influenced by a market outlook. The effect can seem overpowering. Because such secular matters are not normally subjected to the searching light of Christ, it becomes easy to feel that commerce is propelled by impersonal and uncontrollable forces. Christians are then tempted to restrict the working out of the faith to areas of personal morality and church life. So Christian faith appears to be relevant to certain parts of life only. Christianity seems, in effect, to give up over matters which are at the heart of daily life. Faith appears weak, and becomes weak.

THE NEED FOR WORLD-WIDE VISION

It is necessary to go, time and again, to the fundamentals of Christian belief. The Bible starts with creation, not merely of the world, but of the universe. It ends with a vision of a world transformed. God is concerned with the material and physical world as much as with the spiritual nature of men and women.

Consider an important verse from John's gospel (chapter three and verse 16) widely regarded as putting God's whole purpose in a nutshell:[(12)]

'God so loved the world that He gave His only son, that whoever believes in Him should not perish but have eternal life.'

The starting point is crucial. God loves the world, a word which takes in the whole material world, as well as its people. The material world reflects the power, beauty and glory of its Creator. It sustains the physical life of mankind. God's purposes are spiritual and personal. Equally they are material and world-wide.

In short, in our evaluation of Christian spirituality we shall have two specific matters before our minds. Spirituality must start from a comprehensive world-view, of people and nature. Also, while not detracting at all from the central significance of the forgiving and re-creating work of Christ, crucified and risen, we need to consider what it means to co-operate fully with God in His materially creative work.

CHAPTER 6

WORSHIP

'You shall worship the Lord your God ...' We are to love and honour God as our foremost delight, with our whole being and with all our abilities. We give Him supreme worth. Here is William Temple's fine description of what Christian worship is to embrace(1) -

> 'Worship is the submission of all our nature to God.
> It is the quickening of the conscience by His holiness;
> the nourishment of the mind by His truth;
> the purifying of the imagination by His beauty;
> the opening of the heart to His love;
> the surrender of the will to His purpose;
> and all of this gathered up in adoration, the most selfless emotion of which our nature is capable, and therefore the chief remedy of that self-righteousness which is our original sin, and the source of all actual sin.'

One of the great by-products of worship is the enlarging of vision and awareness of God, of human nature and the natural world, and the part each has to play in God's purposes. The greater the awareness of the glory of God and the greater the integrity of worship, the more each worshipper may be a channel for God's work in the world.

In his description Temple makes no reference to the size of the company gathered for worship, or to its accompanying activities. Worship in private, normally based upon the reading of the Scriptures, remains of crucial importance. The Christian is nourished personally, and enjoys his own communion with God. Solitary it is, but there is a vast wealth of experience of personal private devotion upon which to draw. There are plenty of contemporary aids to help in this bedrock of disciplineship.(2)

For many people, exploring faith and sharing understanding of the Bible in a small informal group is a liberating experience. In this setting, doubts and questions, as well as insights and strengths, can be shared and explored. There has been a tremendous growth in such groups over the last few years. In many, their value is reinforced by membership being drawn from a variety of Christian churches.

Worship at a local church continues to be part of the Christian's staple diet. This is the natural setting for corporate sacramental [3] worship which has had an honoured central place through all the Christian centuries. Gone are the days when worship was led exclusively by professional clergy. As more people are actively engaged in the conduct of services so the significance of worship is sensed in fresh ways. The occasional large gathering for Christian celebration or affirmation is an enriching experience; its value remains long after the particular occasion has passed.

Challenges and tensions

In the course of an extraordinary conversation recorded in John's gospel, Jesus comments that God is Spirit and those who worship must worship in spirit and truth.[4] Spirit cannot be marshalled and truth cannot be contained, so worship is bound to have some untidiness and to bring with it challenges and problems. In worship we are caught up in an experience which has otherworldly dimensions. Those who have tried to express this in words are driven to the limits of language. The worshipper is uplifted, transported, beside himself, caught up to heaven ... We need the twofold gifts of poets, their insight into the experience, and their ability with words, to help us. The whole realm of art can provide means for expressing praise and adoration. Drama, dance and visual presentations, as well as the great variety of vocal and instrumental sounds, may all be brought into the worship of God. But silence is also important. It provides space during which the Holy Spirit can speak to the human spirit.

In Christian worship we may be taken beyond the bounds of rational understanding, for limited and imperfect minds cannot take in the whole of divine reality. But in all such experiences we shall not expect to leave aside our rational selves. There can be problems if this happens, for life must normally be under the control of our minds. Minds are to be transformed,[5] to be infused with divine truth, not left without guidance.

But care is needed, for example, in sharing in statements of Christian belief or in affirmations about forwarding Christ's rule on earth. It smacks of dishonesty to use exalted phrases of adoration and intention in worship, and then to forget God's purposes as soon as worship is left behind. On such grounds Christians can understandably be accused of hypocrisy. The Bible contains a number of cautions about basic honesty in speech as, for example, in the pungent words of the Preacher:[6] 'When you vow a vow to God, do not delay paying; for He has no pleasure in fools. Pay what you owe. It is better that you should not vow than that you should vow and not pay. Let not your mouth lead you into sin.'

Worship is crucially important, but this importance brings particular problems. Because the key revelation of God in Jesus occurred nearly two thousand years ago, it is inevitable that Christians look back to the Biblical era and the years immediately following, when matters of belief were being established. This is important, for during this period the bedrock in matters of Christian faith was being hammered out. But constantly looking back can breed a conservatism which inhibits a forward looking and adventurous outlook through which the Holy Spirit may have full play. God is honoured as one who is unchanging in His nature. Yet part of this nature is seen in His forgiving love and transforming Spirit. Part is seen in His continuous work of renewing His creation. Permanence and change are each to be seen in the nature of God. Some, especially older people, may be drawn in worship to timeless and traditional forms; others to the new and contemporary. Both aspects need to be experienced so that the rich variety of ways in which God shows Himself may be appreciated.

The Christian's experience of worship must have the sort of breadth sketched out for it to be effective as the springboard for Christian life and action. Yet it continues to remain too closely identified with public worship at a local church. A standard service, in the mainstream Christian churches, does contain most of the ingredients which experience has shown to be central in spirituality. But the normal church service does not provide the best means for full benefit to be gained from all its basic ingredients.

Acknowledgement before God of sin and failure, with the acceptance of God's forgiveness and redirecting power, is essential in Christian maturity. But in public worship there is simply not enough time to do these things thoroughly. On the other hand, while confession is a very personal matter, it is easy to delude ourselves in solitary personal reflection. It is easy, too, to forget the crucial necessity of obedience to a forgiving, but fundamentally righteous God. Confession and absolution need the help of a wise guide, at least on occasions, for God's cleansing power to reach to the roots of self-will.

Likewise worship lacks integrity if Christian declarations are not clearly related to daily work. While preaching and the public reading of the Scriptures are essential ways of declaring Christ's truth, the application of these truths to daily work cannot be tackled with any thoroughness in public worship.

In some professions and occupations groups meet regularly, with members drawn from a variety of Christian churches. Such gatherings need to be developed. They should not simply be forums where particular problems can be aired, and mutual support given. They should tackle basic issues such as the aims, policies and effects of the work, together with its administrative, financial and organisational practices. Every aspect should be examined in the light of Christ's truth and purposes.

In moving to the practical consequences of belief, one important matter needs to be faced - the relationship of worship to daily life. God is the source of life and the goal for the whole of life. But not many people can be thinking about Him all the time. Some have largely routine work; some work may be monotonous. People in such occupations may have opportunities for quiet thought and worship. But many find daily work absorbing every moment of their time. God cannot be given any attention during their working hours.

The problem occurs in many areas of life. The parent kisses the child leaving for school, or going to bed, demonstrating that the parent's love will surround the child all through the day and the night. Presents at birthdays and Christmas, for adults and children alike help to make clear the giver's continuing attention and care.

So in Christian life, morning and evening prayers make clear the framework of honour to God in which the whole of life goes on. At particular times, for example in giving thanks at meal times, we may move towards God in specific prayer. Over certain matters or at times of crisis we may deliberately seek God's forgiveness, or His wisdom. But the regular daily and weekly times given in worship are acts which signify that the whole of life is given over to God, to be infused with His Spirit. The practice of Christian spirituality is little more, in essence, than the centering of our entire selves upon God, as He has been made known through Jesus Christ.

CHAPTER 7

LOVING THE NEIGHBOUR - SOME PRACTICAL MATTERS

Our primary aim - the sharing of belief

'You shall love your neighbour as yourself.' We are to be active in honouring and meeting the needs of our neighbours in the same measure as we honour and meet our own needs. The neighbour, as Jesus' parable of the good Samaritan [1] made clear, is any and every person with whom we may be involved, or of whom we may be aware.

This second great commandment is a natural consequence of the first. For the practical results of honouring, loving and serving God are shown in large measure as we love, honour and serve our neighbours. This honouring of others is shown not least through material means, for we show what we are and what we believe through the actions of our physical bodies.

Nevertheless, 'Man shall not live by bread alone.'[2] We honour others primarily as we share with them what is of supreme importance to ourselves, enabling them to be aware of God as the source and goal of life, and His Spirit as guide and enabler. So the fruit of Christ's Spirit, His love, joy and peace, with all else that comes from His goodwill, are able to infuse the whole of each other's life.

We have already affirmed[3] that qualities such as love, honour and forgiveness, concepts which may sound sentimental or pious, lie at the heart of daily life. Their absence is clearly central to many personal and social problems, from domestic matters to international disputes. Homelessness among young people, for example, stems largely from a lack of practical understanding and forgiveness in the home. The same factors contribute to marriage tension and breakdown. Racial tension stems, to a significant degree, from a lack of ability amongst people, Christians included, to honour those from different cultures and races. International unease is fuelled by reluctance to forgive past wrong actions, or even an inability to appreciate the way of life of other people. By contrast, the practice of commerce at its best starts with assumptions of goodwill and good faith, with honour and integrity in business dealing.

In short, the practical honour, care, forgiveness and support which come from the Christian understanding of love are essential in all human relationships. They are needed not only in the restoring of life for the poor and broken, but also for fullness of life for the physically fit and mentally satisfied.

The truths of Christ, with their searching and disturbing power, as well as their comforting assurances, should be made known to all, both by word of mouth and by quality of life. They need to be directed to those of high intellect as well as to those of humbler understanding. They must be made clear to those who live in palaces and plenty, as well as to those in poverty and penury, and to those of all philosophies and political persuasions, the world over. Enabling others to have faith in Christ, commonly called evangelism, is crucially important. There will, however, be little further direct reference to it in this book, for a very simple reason.

Unless the lives of Christians as individuals, and the life of the Christian community as a whole, bears a clear relationship to the character of Jesus Christ, then the task of evangelism is drastically impeded. Both from within and from outside the churches come constant reminders that a credibility gap exists between what Christians affirm and what they do. The main thrust of what follows is a fresh look at what Christian living means today. We shall be largely concerned with the visible actions of people. But the Christian's relationship with God, from whom strength and direction come, remains fundamental.

This book is written with Christians, or those with some sympathy with Christian belief, chiefly in mind. But the practical principles laid out here apply not just to Christians, but to all people. We have already contended that our understanding of what it means to be human comes from our belief in God. In order to underline this we need to go back to some basic Biblical declarations.

There has been much debate as to the precise meaning of the declaration that 'God created man in His own image...'[4] Whatever its literal meaning, this statement clearly implies that all humans possess something of God's nature, and are therefore able to know and to respond to God. Because Jesus Christ is acknowledged to be one with God, and because Jesus showed, in His life, perfection for all humanity, His ethical counsels are God's principles, and are therefore significant for all people. Equally, all people may have an awareness of God's truth and love. All may share in the divine work of creation and redemption, and in the gifts and graces shown through Jesus. All may be enriched to the full by the Holy Spirit.

Throughout history and across the world, people have shown aspects of their character which are far removed from any human ideal, let alone a divine standard of perfection. When Paul asserted that 'all have sinned and fall short of the glory of God,'[5] he was describing a universal reality which remains true. But it should not be inferred that humans are depraved throughout the whole of their being. Christian understanding of sin asserts that every aspect of human life is tainted with self-centredness and imperfection.[6] The divine image has been seriously marred, but it has not been totally erased. Otherwise people would not be aware of their own failings, and they could not be appealed to on grounds of Christian moral standards.

Because all humans have been created in God's image it is not surprising to find non-Christians whose lives and ethical standards put many Christians to shame. So it is that some who do not share a Christian belief are ready to join in upholding and working for high standards in personal and communal life. They may well, and sometimes do, provoke and stimulate Christians to greater dedication in their faith and work.

Honouring others - a primary factor in shaping human life

Because Christians worship God, whose nature may be summed up in the word 'love,' it ought to be obvious and natural that love and honour is shown to all people. Jesus Himself lifted the concept of love to a new level when, in a conversation with His close disciples, He said 'Love one another as I have loved you.'[7] Though He was speaking to a small and special group of men, He nevertheless set out a standard which could not simply be restricted to those He was addressing. This love and honouring of others is to be a chief factor in the shaping of all human life.[8]

The ideal of love and honour to all remains paramount. But this raises immediate problems, two of which must be tackled as practical matters are approached. How can self-fulfilment be fully developed if there is an over-riding concern with other people? And how can world-wide needs be realistically faced at the same time as a person has to take proper care for himself, and immediate dependants? To deal with such questions we need to go to the heart of Christian belief.

Clearly there is much more to Christian belief than seeing Jesus as the ideal for human personality. But this belief is distorted if Jesus' life is not recognised as an immensely important pointer to the way all are meant to live.

It is evident that Jesus was a compellingly attractive figure. He won the loyalty (with Judas Iscariot as the one later notable exception) of a group of young men in their prime.[9] Women were drawn to Him.[10] Crowds followed Him.[11] It is possible to give so much attention to His crucifixion and resurrection that insufficient attention is given to the whole character of His daily life. The attractiveness of Jesus was surely not just because of what He said and did as a teacher and leader. The quality of His life stemmed from total self-giving, to God and to other people. This characteristic developed in the early years of His life, within the family and community, in His daily work, and in His deep faith in God. Selflessness, with purpose and joy,[12] as He drew on the Father's love, was central to Jesus. It should be a natural part of human life.

Amongst ordinary people it is clear that self-fulfilment is found time and again as a person pursues goals which are not primarily self-centred. Not only do personal needs get set aside, but the enthusiast appears able to draw upon exceptional resources of physical and mental energy. These characteristics and qualities are seen as innumerable men and women give of their time as magistrates, in trade and professional unions, in local and county councils and in charitable work. They are seen when the artist, or scientist, consumed by the discovery of new beauty or new truth, leaves aside all concerns for personal needs. Handel's composition of the 'Messiah' in three weeks is only an outstanding example of a common experience. Those in business are often regarded as working solely for money. Clearly they have to make their business financially viable. Nevertheless selfless concern is found within all sorts of business activity, especially where the quality of the product and the need of the customer overtake narrowly personal considerations.

Viewed by those who have never entered into self-giving activity, the amount of time and energy spent by those who do may seem absurd and is often ridiculed. There are paradoxical aspects in such patterns of life. Something of this was expressed by an unknown writer two and a half thousand years ago. The circumstances of the time must have been basic, yet he wrote, 'One man gives freely, yet grows the richer; another withholds what he should give, and only suffers want.'(13) The words may have been written with material matters in mind, but they are equally true of the generous-hearted person, in contrast to the one who neither develops, nor shares, his own gifts. That self-fulfilment through selflessness should be thought odd is an indication of how far people have moved from a spiritual understanding of life. It is also a matter of how wealth is viewed, a matter to be tackled further in later chapters.

The more money or material goods which are kept for one's narrowly personal use, the less is available for others, whether this is in direct provision, or capital for enterprise and development. But this material argument leads to a more significant spiritual factor. The more that wealth is accumulated and retained beyond what is needed for rounded personal and family requirements, the more the actual possession of material wealth is shown to be of greater importance than any response to the needs of others. The argument can obviously be extended to include the amount of time spent on one's self beyond that taken up with daily work, because time is strictly limited. One's attitude to others, in short, is made clear by the way in which personal wealth and resources are used, whether these be of money, possessions, energy or time.

There is a constant temptation, once one is clearly past the level of meeting basic needs, for energy to be directed towards one's own interests, and those of the family. Clearly it is difficult to define the line between adequate concern for ourselves, and self-indulgence. Self-concern must make room for leisure in one form or another; it is essential for rounded health and well-being. But recreation can easily develop so that it dominates spare time, with the diversion of resources from more important matters.

To all parents, the nurture and development of their children is of prime importance. It obviously involves financial and material resources. But proper care for the young can easily move towards indulgent spoiling. It may not be possible to give too much care to one's children. It is certainly possible to spend too much money on them. If there is little creative time spent by parents and children together, this is not compensated for by the provision, for example, of toys, electronic entertainment, or spending money, on however lavish a scale. The fundamental concern for the honouring of others must also be kept clear. For young people to see practical generosity extending outside the family is an important feature in their nurture.

A positive and creative respect towards all others remains fundamental. Here is the framework within which all aspects of personal development and fulfilment, creative and competitive instincts, and material rewards, are to be seen. We may recall with shame the way in which the poor were exploited, and their situations largely ignored, by wealthy landowners in centuries past. Equally we may be appalled to realise the ways in which sub-human urban conditions have developed during the last two centuries. It should be a matter of simple basic common sense that we prevent similar deprivations developing today amongst those with whom we have any trading and commercial links, wherever they live.

Honouring others - practical matters

Virtually every part of daily life involves manufacture and commerce. Enterprise is constantly needed, on the smallest and largest of scales, so that new opportunities coming from the discovery of new resources and new technologies can be seized. New initiatives are also required as the needs of others become apparent. Any consideration of the work of the creator God must involve commercial life. God provides resources which are turned to practical use through this vast area of human work. The fact that Jesus was a carpenter underlines the conviction that manufacture and commerce can clearly be part of a holy life.

Practical respect and concern for others, on a world-wide scale under the guidance of God needs to be recovered as the overriding and dominant vision for everyday life. This ties up with basic human nature and purpose; it provides the possibility for the fulfilment of personal potential, both spiritual and material, for all, in developed and less developed areas. Commerce needs to be freed from a seeming bondage to serving human short term material and sensual appetites and fancies.

The many New Testament cautions about the handling of material wealth should not obscure the fact that holding money is not, in itself, condemned. The young Timothy was indeed warned that the love of money underlies all evil.(14) Its use can be abused. But money is an essential part of contemporary life, not just a necessary evil.

Capital provides a vital springboard for development. It is essential for the launch of any enterprise, from the provision of a ladder for a window-cleaner, to the vast sums needed for education and health care, or the building of a space station. Capitalism has its shortcomings, but the need for money as capital cannot be sidestepped. All philosophies across the whole political and economic spectrum embrace capitalism, from its use in free enterprise on the one hand to state capitalism on the other, with all sorts of combinations in between. What is best under any government or in any particular situation has to be debated and worked out from both underlying convictions and practical experience. There are rarely clear answers to economic problems, as debates in national parliaments and in all sections of the media constantly show.(15)

Similar factors are evident over the way in which businesses are run. There is a huge variety of business methods and organisation in both small- and large- scale systems and practices. Their evaluation is not simply a matter of cold logic or mathematical calculation. Any opinion about economic or commercial matters implies a view of human nature and the whole physical order. Are people and things to be used, or to be respected, even to be honoured? If they are to be honoured, why? And in what ways? Christian belief provides pointers to answers to such basic questions. The questions, together with the answers given, are crucially significant in dealing with everyday practical matters of finance and commerce.

In honouring others there will be concern with education in its widest sense, enabling young people to develop their own physical, mental and spiritual potential to the full. Respecting others means enabling them to work, for worthwhile purposes in good conditions, with a concern also for those who are unemployed. It involves health care, both personal and public. It embraces housing, law and order. The list can obviously be extended. Within most countries, part of this care is carried out, and is stimulated, within the interactions of family life, within local groups of people, and in local government. It is vital that Christian insights concerning human nature, human potential and human relationships are brought to bear upon the continuing debates in all these matters. But no consideration of communal matters can ignore the overall framework of national government.

In recent generations, government has developed enormously to affect every area of life. No-one is outside its influence. The variety and complexity of social and commercial relationships, and interactions within society have contributed to widely differing outlooks, which are often presented as if they are fundamental. But they are not, and they leave aside vital areas of life.

Uncontrolled individualism, within a free market, can leave the weak crushed and the poor neglected. It can also set free a whole host of unhealthy excesses. Centralised governments, whether of the political left or right, can distort, constrict and damage individual lives and the whole life of a nation. It is far too simple to divide political outlooks into neat camps. But the twentieth century has shown the weaknesses, and some strengths, of situations where one political philosophy has been over-dominant. The working of democracy itself needs to be watched with constant alertness. Its establishment is an important step towards healthy government. But democracy is not an end in itself. Even where there is no corruption it can leave the wishes and needs of minorities unsatisfied. In the words of Judge Curran 'The condition upon which God has given liberty to man is eternal vigilance...'[(16)]

Human abilities result in a huge variety of actions; material resources can be used in almost limitless diversity. The manner in which abilities are used and the ways in which others are involved are not ethically all on a par. They need to be evaluated with rigour from Christian assertions regarding human nature, the purpose of human life, and the primary importance of spiritual qualities such as love, forgiveness and justice.

Christian belief about human nature and relationships should permeate all political and governmental debate and action as well as the whole gamut of commercial and professional life. Clearly care is needed by those who comment on technical aspects and details of such matters. Yet it is essential for the overall health of society that Christian insights are brought to bear upon all aspects of the nation's life, especially concerning the assumptions underlying debate and actions. It is correspondingly essential that Christians show the reality of the beliefs they profess, in personal, family and community life. The Christian church must also be evident as the ever-present alternative society, a society open to all, and concerned with all.

Once the crucial significance of honouring and serving all others has been accepted there should be a powerful force to bring the intention into effect. This should be transparently clear among Christians, for it is constantly declared and agreed to in Christian worship. But the reality is different. Much of the rest of this book looks at some of the matters underlying the fact that we fail to live up to what we profess.

CHAPTER 8

LOVING THE NEIGHBOUR - SOME PROBLEMS AND CHALLENGES

Fair Dealing - no discriminations

Early in the life of the church, Paul had to make clear that there were no distinctions in God's attitude to people and that this belief must be reflected in society. He pointed to three particular areas(1) - race, between Jew and non-Jew; class, between slave and free; and gender - where problems over discrimination were continuing. Present-day attitudes need to reflect the same impartial concern.

Gender is clear at birth; racial distinctions come at birth, but are often sharply reinforced through lack of mutual respect; slavery is an oppressive practice, imposed by people upon people. Each of these factors can provide the ground for hurtful actions and traditions. Other matters needs constant watchfulness. Positive concern for the elderly is deeply embedded in Biblical counsels, but their care can easily be sidetracked, not least by their own families. Similarly, without constant concern, it is easy for the disabled, whether the disability is mental or physical, to be given a low priority in society's care.

Cautions like these are reminders that it is one thing to profess love and care for our neighbour, but it is another matter to carry out the intention. We should not wait until problems are brought to our notice by headline-making crises before moving to action. Slavery may have been outlawed, but it remains very much alive.(2) Child labour may also have been eliminated in Britain, but its evil side remains a reality in other parts of the world,(3) as also is child prostitution. All these corruptions are practised in countries with which we have commercial links. The Christian should be constantly alert to share the outgoing love of God in the most earthy and practical of matters, and on the most extensive of scales.

The materially poor

Vast numbers of people across the world live in poverty, working, where they can, to provide food and some form of shelter.[4] Within these groups there are those for whom these necessities do not exist. They starve; they fall prey to illness and disease; they die.[5] The statistics are known, and descriptions of the circumstances are readily available.[6] The key issue is the perennial one of our failure to respond realistically to the information we have.

Here is one figure to highlight the scale of world need today. Over the world, some 30,000 children die each day.[7] There are many reasons for these deaths. They include poor diet, lack of food and clean water, inadequate pre- and post-natal care, infections and disease, even deliberate parental abandonment due to extreme poverty. Deaths also occur as a result of paedophilic excesses, communal violence and direct murder, as with some street children.[8]

Many in the West, Christians included, effectively ignore such facts. Considerable numbers will respond in times of crisis. Certain groups of people work towards finding medium and long-term solutions to problems connected with poverty.[9] Most western governments give money for development work, though the ways in which this may be spent are often restricted by being linked to the interests of the donor countries. But none of these current approaches, nor all of them taken together, are adequate for meeting the challenge. Certainly none of the world's poor are excluded from the concern that all should be able to share abundant life.

The countries of the West have trading relationships with most, if not all, of the countries where the materially poor live. Some provide primary resources, such as tea and coffee, cereals and meat, timber and minerals. Some provide locally produced goods such as textiles, which bear the stamp of imaginative creative abilities. Other articles are manufactured to Western designs to take advantage of the relatively low local wages. If we mean to carry out business with honour and respect for all people, then this has to be expressed practically. We ought generally to pay substantially more than at present for what we obtain from developing countries, in order to encourage and enable more people to have the means for their own personal development.

Certain organisations in Britain have combined, within the Fairtrade Foundation, to ensure that particular commodities are produced by workers under fair conditions with above average pay and confidence that the better wages reach the actual workers.[10] Campaigning pressures slowly increase this development.[11] The readiness to pay local employees realistically is fundamental. This provides the possibility of improvement. Not to do so perpetuates evil.

The crippling burden of loan debt on many poorer countries remains, in spite of some steps towards improving the situation. The fact remains that what is given to certain countries in financial aid for development is less than the interest which has to be paid by those countries on loans they have been granted. The terms on which loans have been made have also hit the poorest people hardest.[12] Money is obviously needed to deal with these problems. It can be found; the challenge is tackled in later chapters. But the alteration of attitudes is needed first, and is crucial.

The alleviation of poverty and the development of human potential are not merely matters of the transfer of money and materials. EF Schumacher's familiar comment that a fish will feed a man for a short while, whereas to teach him the art of fishing can help him all his life, is simply an illustration of his pungent opening words of the paragraph in which it occurs.[13] 'The best aid to give is intellectual aid, a gift of useful knowledge. A gift of knowledge is infinitely preferable to a gift of material things.' There needs to be a great increase in technical education and basic provision for development. Such training and enabling requires a shift of emphasis with a provision of resources which may seem huge. But the amount is not large compared with what is spent in the West on matters marginal to full life.

In all matters of relationship with poorer countries, and with impoverished people generally, the transfer of resources is less significant than the spiritual attitudes which these transfers betray. A key question lies in understanding of the word 'development.' Does this primarily concern the earth's reserves, or human potential? As applied to an 'under-developed' country does the word relate primarily to materials, or to human and personal abilities? Are underdeveloped material resources seen chiefly in terms of what will be of clear importance to the development needs of the local people, or for trading purposes outside the country? Human potential and material development are intimately related, for we are material beings in a material world. But it is central to the Christian understanding of humanity that the spiritual issues are of primary importance. There is a slowly growing awareness that economic 'realities' must not obscure the fundamental spiritual issue that respect and care should be extended to all. Unless Christians are in the forefront of this movement their professions concerning the love of God, and their claims to show this, will ring increasingly hollow.

Concepts such as world development and the use of resources are constantly used as shorthand terms for material issues. Yet the development of materials must come hand in hand with the development of personal potential. The calling out of the potential of the human spirit is fundamental. As the West continues to measure its own development largely in material and financial terms, so its outlook over world development has moved in the same direction. Further, this development is seen to a significant degree in terms of what will benefit the West's need of resources for its own requirements, rather than for what benefits the local people. So a warped outlook in the West spreads its infection.

Even in material considerations, mean arrangements indicate mean hearts with small vision. They reveal little practical care for those who help sustain our inflated standard of life. They indicate that we have little understanding of the personal human abilities locked up in millions of lives which are limited by impoverished circumstances. Mean arrangements imply that we have no imagination to see that the release of such abilities will benefit humanity all over the world, ourselves included. They show that, whatever professions may be made about spiritual values within the western way of life, we are largely self-centred materialists at heart. Those who look at us take note.

Within the mass of the world's poor there is a vast and growing number of people who are indeed materially poor, yet physically close to those who are relatively wealthy. The actual situations of these urban poor vary greatly. Those in Britain are in a totally different position from those of the expanding cities of Africa, Asia and South America. Relatively few in this country may be actually starving, though thousands do 'sleep rough' night after night. A far greater number eke out an existence with few personal resources. Life in such conditions is limited and frustrating.

Urban poverty is bad enough in the West. In poorer countries the situation is far worse.[14] Some people survive next to rubbish dumps, living off discarded garbage. Some live in vast unregulated shanty-towns with negligible facilities for water and sanitation. Others live in urban slums with festering social problems, which become breeding grounds for the headline-making problems of violence, drug-peddling and murder. It is estimated that half the world's people will be living in cities by the year 2000. As a result, whatever the precise time-scale, we have the possibility of a vast time-bomb waiting to explode.

We have addressed the challenge of loving our neighbour, on a world scale, in a few paragraphs only. The task is huge and complex. But much trumpeted failures over matters of personal morality within Britain are all of a piece with failures over world underdevelopment. Equally, loving, honouring and respecting the neighbour requires an integrated response across the whole spectrum of relationships, from those between individuals in Britain, to links with people who may be thousands of miles away. The perspective of our love for others, reflecting that of Christ, should be limitless and comprehensive.

In spite of the size of the problems, large scale issues cannot be left to governments, international organisations and commercial bodies. Yet many people, while accepting that the persistence of gross material inequalities is wrong, whether these are within one country, or on a world scale, nevertheless feel powerless. The first step away from such despair is to recognise that the challenges are being tackled and that the individual can be effectively involved.

'He never made a greater mistake than he who failed to act because he could only do a little.' Burke's saying relates to many areas of possible action. It is all too easy to point to situations where aid has gone astray, or where development has been misconceived or misdirected, whether within the West, or in other parts of the world. It is also clear that there are countries where there are limited possibilities for assistance from outside because of internal communal, political or organisational factors. But Christians in the West should not continue to accept uncritically their huge advantages in educational and material standards compared with those in so many other countries. Most look back with horror at the appalling conditions in which large numbers lived in Britain in the past. Yet we close our minds to a similar situation, on a world scale today.

Impediments to action

It is a truism to say that the basic reason for Christian ineffectiveness is a lack of Christian love. Some problems, particularly those of a personal nature, can be relieved directly by the transforming love of Christ. But humans are complex beings, and relationships within and between nations have many intricate and interlocking strands. In many areas of life, difficulties cannot be solved by a simple application of a spiritual remedy. Certainly it is a fallacy to suggest that problems, whether personal, communal or worldwide, would disappear if everybody became Christian.

In today's imperfect world there are many problems where solutions cannot even begin to be effectively applied until underlying attitudes have been changed. With some issues a radical shift of attitude is needed before a problem is recognised, let alone alleviated. Too often Christians allow sub-Christian views to persist within their own outlooks. Jesus' words[15] 'You are the salt of the earth, but if salt has lost its taste, how shall its saltness be restored?'

have a sad contemporary ring about them. We look briefly at five common attitudes which should not be part of the Christian's outlook. The comments apply as much to concern with the person next door as with those who live thousands of miles away.

IGNORANCE

One of the commonest appreciations heard about a person goes something like this: 'He would always do a good turn for someone if he could.' The notion is a fairly basic one. Most of us would like to feel that we would always respond when faced with need. But the actual degree of response varies widely. In practice, even when we are aware of distress, we can all make excuses to avoid taking action, as the story of the Good Samaritan makes clear.(16) The parable certainly highlights practical generosity, but it also shows how easily indifference and hypocrisy can affect the attitudes of people who profess high standards.

But what of need of which we are not directly aware? Enormous problems and deprivations remain outside our knowledge, except in the most general of ways. This is in part due to the sheer amount of information available about privation and distress. Editors of newspapers and radio and television programmes have obvious problems in selection and presentation from the mass of information they receive. But in a very real measure there is a widespread reluctance to know of matters which would disturb our pattern of life. It seems easier to settle for shutting minds and ears.

Ignorance regarding poverty, for example, easily leads to a position where we find it difficult to accept that particular instances of need are genuine, whether in our own country, or outside. The situation may be dismissed as being 'their own fault.' We may excuse ourselves on the grounds that little can be done, as the problems are so big. Yet simple creative opportunities abound for extending aid, care and development in the fullest senses of these words.(17) Ignorance can dress itself up in a great variety of ways. We can easily become inoculated against accepting, or responding to, unpalatable truth.

It is sad that we remain ignorant of people's needs. It is even sadder that we ignore people's achievements, not only in material ways, but also in matters of art and intellect, and in generosity of spirit. It is a source of inspiration to know of achievements, whether small or large in scale, particularly those accomplished by people in relatively unsophisticated circumstances.

PREJUDICE

Prejudice exists in so many forms that it appears all-pervasive. Few people, if any, are free from it. Its cause is an attitude to another which is decided before meeting that person. It comes from a mind which has been made up on an issue before any real move has been made towards understanding it. It shows narrow-mindedness and self-centredness which refuse to accept new information, or to change present patterns of life. Paul's caution about social distinctions has already been quoted. He clearly saw their potential for evil.

Prejudice easily results in active bias and discrimination. It exists on the large international scales of colour and race. Yet hurtful unfairness can exist on these grounds in a school playground or in a social club. It is still widespread concerning gender. Women are discriminated against in almost all societies at all levels.[18] In many parts of the world they are treated as a distinct sub-group within society. Prejudice is reinforced by ignorance, but it is so deceptive that the stubborn person may stick to his views in the face of clear contrary truth. Prejudice involving national pride has a powerful momentum. It is right to be grateful for good inherited qualities and traditions. It is wrong to allow national pride to inhibit the sharing of privileges with others.

HURT FEELINGS

Generous action is inhibited by the persistence of hurt feelings. They exist between individuals. Where friendship and intimate trust has broken down, hurt feelings can smoulder on almost indefinitely. Hurts may be material or financial, through theft, dishonesty or fraud. They may be physical as a result of personal, communal or international strife. The resulting feelings feed on ignorance and prejudice and may be actively fostered over generations.

It is nevertheless striking that moves towards the healing of some deep hurts on an international level have come about as the result of natural impulses towards the re-establishment of trading and cultural links. This has happened all over Europe in the aftermath of the last world war. Healing within nations can also be seen in some countries after years of civil war, such as in South Africa, where a determination to work together has helped to overcome bitterness and suspicion. Problems and tensions remain, but reconciliation and healing have developed. Yet in spite of human incentives, hurts can continue to hinder mutual care and respect, as is still evident in many parts of the world.

FEAR

Throughout history, many of those possessing power, education and wealth have feared the development and rise of the powerless, the ignorant and the poor. Clearly, a considerable majority of western people are reluctant today to see significant steps being taken towards a realistic and creative world-wide sharing of resources. It is necessary to learn again and again from the history of the developed countries. As poorer people have been enabled to share comprehensively in the material, cultural and spiritual wealth of nations, so there has been enrichment for all.

The more that people across the world are able to bring their minds to bear upon the problems which affect mankind as a whole, the more possible it will be for creative solutions to be found, to the mutual benefit of all. We need to have the faith and confidence to see that it is only by going along this path that the world community can tackle seemingly insuperable challenges such as the growth in world population, and the need for feeding greatly increased numbers of people. It smacks of condescension that the industrially developed nations should seek to impose upon less developed nations the conditions under which the development of their own resources may take place.[19]

Fears cripple human action. The greater the number of people who are enabled to share the world's wealth, the more all will be able to share the immense diversity of insights and beauties with which humanity is endowed. It is good to be able to enjoy marvellous sights and scenes, with the tremendous variety of plant and animal life, as easy travel enables us to see more of the world. But as we take time to enter into the cultural and spiritual experiences of people, there are new dimensions to life to be savoured which are liberating and enriching.

For those with eyes to see, one of the greatest delights of recent decades has been the fresh revelations of human creativity and achievement, not least those in the less developed parts of the world. Some of these discoveries have come from stores of human history and culture which have been hidden for centuries. Other revelations have come from awareness of great resources of vision, talent and creativity of all sorts.[20] These are to be seen in the whole range of art, music and literature; in all manner of individual achievements, athletic not least; in discovery and national development, and in Christian discernment and experience. Human wealth is crucially to be seen in great resources of practical forgiveness. To close our eyes to such refreshing revelations is to shut ourselves in our own spiritual poverty.

COVETOUSNESS

The word indicates a strong desire for anything, especially that which belongs to someone else. It is forbidden by the last of the ten commandments. In the New Testament the meaning broadens and becomes equivalent to greed, the active desire for money and wealth in general. The pursuit of wealth easily displaces God as the primary object of our lives and worship. Wealth itself becomes an idol.[21]

Covetousness starts from a very simple base. Everyone wants to have a good home and adequate food, with all that makes for a reasonable way of life, and a bit over as well. But these desires easily grow beyond basic needs, and fulfilling them becomes a goal in itself. Advertisers work on covetousness; it is a common ingredient of everyday conversation. It is virtually ingrained in western culture, and Christians are easily caught up in it. Coveting fuels jealousy. So human personality is distorted. Certainly the desire for material possessions quickly obscures the primary human objective of honouring and caring for our neighbours, wherever they may be.

In the race to keep up with the visible standard of living of others, resources are used unnecessarily and depleted, in some cases to the point of elimination. Coveting is an ingredient in many social evils, being an obvious cause of theft and even, in places, murder. The covetousness of the developed nations as a whole underlines the poverty of vast numbers across the world, as it blinds people to the needs of others.

Paul wrote tersely that the love of money is the root of all evils.[22] Today this particular variety of coveting is as significant as the desire for material possessions. The acceptance of money as a commodity in its own right has been around for centuries. But the stock, bond, and foreign exchange markets have grown enormously in size and importance in recent generations. This growth has been aided by a loosening of regulation, together with the almost incredible speed and ease of global communications.

Focusing on money deflects attention from the fact that all financial transactions affect people. Financiers, investors, and the managers of large organisations may have little or no direct awareness of those who are affected by organisational decisions and paper or electronic transactions. Financial 'rewards' can be huge while concern for human beings can virtually disappear. Greed of this sort is increasingly being seen as immoral, evident in growing concern over six and seven figure payments to financial operators.

Dealing with impediments

Ignorance, prejudice, hurts and fears, covetousness. One ought to be able to declare simply that the person who looks to God through Christ has a power to overcome these and all other impediments to effective action in obedience to God. It is easy to point to individuals and to communities, who bear the name Christian, who have shown attitudes which fall far short of that ideal. But there has also been a stream of people who have shown that pure sustained love does overcome all hindrances to its flow, even where these obstacles have taken the most bitter and violent of forms. So it is necessary to return again and again to the heart of the Christian's faith, to the crucifixion and resurrection of Christ, to find a powerful redeeming and recreative love. It is constantly available and should be seen as normal.

Dealing with impediments to the flow of love, respect and care to all others requires professional and technical knowledge together with personal, organisational and commercial experience. But the fundamental and crucial need is for radical change at the heart of daily living.

As we go again and again to the worship of God we can find strength to deal with the roots of all obstacles to working out a comprehensive love and practical care for our neighbours. Then energies can be redirected, with fresh powers being released for God's purposes. But that worship has constantly to go to the fundamental truths of God's revelation and work through Christ. It has to be carried into daily life with total integrity, drawing upon the wisdom of those who have known and lived out these truths in their own experience.

All the matters considered in this and the last chapter need to be worked out in a material and physical world. We need to face the fact that one of the biggest, if not the biggest practical hindrance to loving our neighbour as ourselves is covetousness, coupled with reluctance to part with 'our' material wealth. We therefore need to look directly at our surroundings. How is the material world to be regarded? What do we understand by the term 'wealth?' We must look for answers to these questions in order to have a thorough-going basis for Christian discipleship and spirituality in today's world.

CHAPTER 9

PURPOSE IN LIFE.
MATERIALS; WEALTH; REWARDS

The fact that mutual care is carried out in large measure through material means may suggest a purely practical outlook towards the natural order. The Christian view is larger and more positive. The material and physical order is, in origin, good.[1] It is infused with glories which point to a generous creator.

But we are dealing with an immense, almost inconceivable range, which includes the whole extent of the animal world; the extraordinary interaction between earth and seed, producing an incredible variety of vegetation; the mineral world with its recently discovered huge quantities of oil and gas; the resources of the oceans in plant and animal life, and energy; the atmosphere with its delicate balance of gases, and immense aerodynamic power. Is it not glib to speak of it all as good?

The animal world shows itself all too often as 'red in tooth and claw;'[2] the sea has claimed far too many lives through its storms and calms, its ice and its currents; the earth produces devastation through its earthquakes and volcanoes. So it is with the atmosphere, as it produces both flood and drought, and winds of great destructive power. There is plenty of evidence to support a view of nature as user-unfriendly, even hostile. It is not surprising to find that the Christian perspective includes an outlook which sees nature as being riddled with imperfection.[3]

Yet few withhold respect and wonder for the natural environment, showing as it does an infinite variety of beauties and glories. Those who have most to do with nature's seeming fickleness, seamen and farmers, have been among the first to accord it a respect which has often moved towards reverence. There is, too, a large body of literature, both prose and poetry, which sees glory in nature. This has flowed from people through the ages, most of whom have known little or no luxury in their everyday life, commonly experiencing poverty and hardship.

In all attention to the world of nature the truth expressed centuries ago by the Psalmist provides an important starting point:(4) 'The earth is the Lord's, and the fullness thereof, the world, and those who dwell therein.' The whole created order should therefore have respect in its own right. This is a concern different from simply seeing that the world's resources are properly used. The notion is obviously complex. But there is a growing awareness that all parts of the earth's order are interdependent.

Great care is therefore needed before one part or another of the natural order is used for human requirements. We may not simply take from nature what we want and use it in the way we choose. Clearly wise stewardship has to be exercised over the material world. But people do not have a simple right to do as they wish with natural resources.

The Psalmist's declaration clearly implies that material objects can never be possessed in an absolute sense. Paul, quoting from the book of Job, underlines the same point(5) - 'We brought nothing into this world, and we cannot take anything out of the world.' The amount that anyone can possess, in the sense of carrying it with him all the time, is clearly very small. Whether we speak of land, buildings, money, or artefacts, things can be owned, whether by individuals or by companies, only by general consent, or by enforced regulation, expressed through the laws of the country. Where consent does not exist, or is questioned or grudged, unease grows. This unease can be seen on all scales today - personal, communal and international.

Human nature is endowed with wide-ranging creative powers, evident in substantial constructions and works of art, originating thousands of years ago. The Old Testament gives clear prominence to the importance of manual work and to the significance of craftsmanship.(6) Jesus worked as a carpenter,(7) no doubt to share in provision for His family. His teaching is, at times, quite uncompromising on the need for people to use their abilities for developing and producing material wealth.(8) Paul took the principle to the extreme - 'If a man will not work, let him not eat.'(9)

But Jesus is equally uncompromising on the wrong, and the dangers, of the continued acquisition of personal wealth.[10] This blinds the owner to God; it deflects him from awareness of the importance of his spiritual nature, and so distorts his personality. It distracts him from care for his neighbour.

Wealth creation is very important, but it is not to be dominant, or to get out of hand. A key assertion of Jesus puts human privileges and human responsibilities very close together: 'Everyone to whom much is given, of him much will be required.'[11] While this statement was made about material possessions, it obviously relates to every area of life. Some have been able to develop personal potential to a greater degree than others. Some are set in circumstances which are much more congenial than those of others. The principle is clear. The greater one's abilities and resources, the greater the responsibility that these gifts are used on the widest of scales for the benefit of others.

In a previous chapter the Christian insight that there should be no limit to the extent of our concern in loving our neighbour was underlined. The assertion needs to be worked out in practical terms. The development of new forms of fuel - gas, oil and nuclear, in addition to coal, enables them to be used for the easing of all manner of physical labour in all parts of the world. Power can also be used for purposes undreamed of in the past, as is shown by the scope of modern industry. These developments extend enormously the field of responsibility of those in the developed nations.

With the privileges of scientific and technical knowledge and material wealth come the crucial obligation to use these powers for the benefit of mankind on the largest of scales. These privileges are not merely for the benefit of those who possess them. At the very lowest estimate, to assume this means the acceleration of inequalities between people across the world. At the same time the increasing ease of communication means that material disparities are recognised more quickly than before, leading to increasing strains in relationships. In short, privilege may initially be personal and local;

it must be coupled with public and widespread responsibility, with no global limits.

The purpose of life

Jesus' statement that a person's life[12] 'does not consist in the abundance of his possessions' develops naturally from the truth that the earth belongs to God. The affirmation is, in fact, self-evident from the large numbers of ordinary people with no great material wealth whose lives show integrity and purpose. Even from the materially prosperous, the wistful comment can be heard, particularly at times of personal crisis, that wealth is not the most important matter in life.

Nevertheless, many older people in the West can remember times when daily work was physically hard and domestic conditions were grim. Austerity, weariness and shortages were usual and the average family had little, if anything, to spare. This way of life had been accepted as normal for centuries.

Life is different now. Increasing numbers of people in the West have enough, and something over. Hours of work have been reduced, so that huge numbers now experience a practical freedom unknown by past generations. Partly because of the newness of this experience, it is not surprising that concern with material wealth still looms large in the outlook of many. But this has produced very questionable results. Life, it is widely assumed, *does* relate to the abundance of possessions. Success *is* seen by the possession of a larger house, a newer and more powerful car, and by the opulence of the life-style. Personal significance *is* seen in a greater ability to have and to use material possessions.

Nowadays, as well as 'standard of living,' a good deal is heard about 'quality of living.' But this is still closely related to material and financial standards. As the term is commonly used, quality of life suggests increased facilities and opportunities for recreation and pleasure rather than for service to others. Yet many a humble home is a centre of infectious joy, with solid strength for family, friends and neighbours alike. In such homes, as in the past, there may be little money to spare, but there is a stream of generosity in time, action and goods. Neither standard of living, nor quality of life can simply be related to personal income, quantity of possessions or opportunities for leisure or recreation. To do so shows a lack of understanding of the purposes of living.

If we are counselled(13) 'not to lay up treasure for ourselves on earth,' if we are told that(14) 'it is better to give than to receive,' some will naturally ask what life is for. When asked by a Jewish lawyer how he could inherit eternal life, Jesus told him to look at his own scriptures. The lawyer's recitation of the two great commandments was met by Jesus' simple commendation:(15) 'Do this and you will live.' The words which Jesus used, and the whole setting of the saying make clear that in the working of these commandments lies a key to purpose and fullness of life.

To live is to honour, love and serve God, and to love and serve other people. So to be rich is to understand these declarations and to put them into everyday practice. Whether faith in God through Christ is comprehensively affirmed, or whether attempts are made to follow a Christian ethic only, the direct teaching of Christ cannot be avoided. In this way avenues are opened for the full flow of the warm generous Spirit of God, in all its forms, and activities. Life then lies in this flow of Spirit, between God and humans, and between one person and another. In this lies its essence.

Then what of rewards in life? These are chiefly to be found as people get on with life as God intends it, and share creatively in the flow of God-given spirit, coveting and using, the 'best gifts.' Rewards will come through mutual encouragement as men and women join in meeting all kinds of everyday needs, sharing in enterprise and struggle, and in support through crises. They will be found in the hilarity and heartaches of the nurture of the young, and in the quieter pleasures of sensing the wisdom and experience of older people. Rewards come as the immense varieties of human qualities in different people are discovered and shared. They will be found in the enjoyment of art in all its forms; in fun and laughter, recreation and rest. Rewards come in the sharing of celebration, especially when the worship of God is allowed to embrace all human experience. Ideal? Maybe. Unrealistic? Certainly not. From time to time a person will say - 'The real rewards in my life are...' and words will continue, picking up some of the threads just sketched out.

Jesus, involved as He had been in the craft and commerce of carpentry, didn't hesitate to speak of material benefits and rewards in the course of His teaching.[16] But even the parable of the talents, which gives clear encouragement to the creation of material wealth, gives no support for the wealth gained to be used for personal ends. The reward for the successful entrepreneurs was that they were given greater responsibilities.[8] The over-riding principle is laid out in the Sermon on the Mount[13] - 'Do not lay up for yourselves treasures on earth... but lay up for yourselves treasures in heaven... for where your treasure is, there will your heart be also.'

Material rewards must always be seen within an overall spiritual perspective. With many actions in the home and among friends, material reward is neither asked for nor given. There is simple satisfaction in what is done; an expression of thanks is reward in full. The majority of acts of service or supply outside the home do result in a material reward. But the purpose of the work, and the spirit in which it is done, are still crucially important. If the purpose of the work is marginal to rounded human needs, or if a good spirit is lacking, the level of pay itself may not compensate for a lack of job satisfaction. Material rewards are obviously significant, but by themselves they are less significant than the spiritual rewards of God-inspired living.

Our use of the material and physical world

To find a standpoint from which to gain a broad view of nature we must accept that those in the developed world have been given a good heritage, but it is a heritage which is laced with challenges. The wealth of the world is not evenly spread and its benefits do not simply fall into our hands. We have to co-operate with the world, to see God's glory in it, and to use it for His purposes. This will mean, for example:

- constant sensitive awareness of the circumstances of people in all parts of the world, with a practical concern for their needs.
- enquiry, research and investigation into nature; the pursuit of knowledge and of science.
- technological development - the application of science for material creation and practical purposes. The technology has to be appropriate for the local circumstances. What is appropriate for one climate may not be so for another. What is suitable for a materially sophisticated society may not be so for another.
- the development of commerce - the use of the world's resources as a primary means in serving and caring for our neighbours.
- the recognition that the world's resources are limited;(17) stocks do not automatically keep up with demand; plant and animal species continually disappear.
- that we recognise that the natural world is a primary source for our experience of beauty and recreation.

Nevertheless, apart from obvious inequalities in the distribution of material resources across the world, what of the 'natural' disasters, and the illnesses, which affect people? Surely the natural world, and therefore God, as nature's creator, has a lot to answer for? However, there is a growing awareness that it is wrong simply to blame nature for the misery and loss of life arising from its seeming extremes, on the one hand, and from the way it is misused, on the other.

People do not have to be left in circumstances where they will be open, almost certainly, to life-threatening occurrences. We do not have to ignore the plight of people who have to scratch a living from the margins of the world's habitable areas, where a weather variation produces calamity. We do not have to dismiss from our minds people living only a few feet above water level, where floods may bring disaster in a flash, or those in earthquake zones where serious problems are almost certain to occur. We do not have to leave people undernourished and open to weakening or killing diseases.

But helping people to cope with major problems does not usually require mass resettlement. Support for those in areas at risk is better tackled by means of education, technical innovation and pump-priming capital for people where they are.(18) It is said that three-quarters of the people now suffering from disease are curable now, with the knowledge and resources that are currently available. In some cases this can be done by very simple means.(19) There are also clear possibilities for avoiding some of the consequences of natural disasters. At present an earthquake in parts of Asia may kill far more people than a comparable one in North America simply because of the way houses and other buildings are constructed.(20)

Similarly, within the developed world there are huge numbers of people suffering illnesses with identified causes which can, given the will, be tackled and removed. The clear link, for example, between tobacco smoking and lung cancer is proved. But the habit is not easily eradicated. So with a considerable amount of heart disease. Causes, linked to the excesses of accepted life-styles such as over-eating, and alcohol abuse, are well known. But the will to tackle them is lacking.

Knowing that progress on some major world and domestic problems can be made much more speedily than at present, it is vital to take up such challenges. It is far more significant and rewarding to seize present opportunities for remedial and development work than to use the West's resources for questionable improvements to our 'standard of living.' Our reluctance to move in the facc of clear creative opportunities at home and abroad indicates that we need to re-consider the way we take material wealth to ourselves.

CHAPTER 10

Pay; the market. Materialism and consumerism; critical comments. A radical Christian response

How often, when a person is faced with misfortune, do we hear the cry 'What have I done to deserve this?' Frequently, though not always, the answer is - nothing, at least directly. But how rarely, when a person has achieved material success, is the same question asked, with the same answer in mind? When proper regard has been given to the personal qualities and individual effort put in by the 'successful' person, the ancient comment must be made over and again: 'What do I have that I have not received?'[(1)]

If we have brains, vision and flair, and if we have been able to develop these gifts, that is only partly our own achievement. Success generally relates considerably to inherited attributes and early surroundings, not least as an enterprise develops. Many commercial successes have come about as a result of circumstances having been right for one person, whereas another, equally gifted, hard-working and visionary, has not been as fortunate. Hundreds of millions of people across the world have hopes and energy, insofar as these are not undermined by malnutrition. Lacking modern power resources, and in many cases lacking mineral reserves or agricultural potential, there is little present possibility of turning these hopes into reality. What have so many of us in the West done to deserve such great advantages?

Life is a gift from God, to be offered to Him and to be lived in service to others. To begin to accept this view is to embark on a revolutionary way of looking at rewards, pay and the holding of material wealth. We have to query sharply the twin assumptions that it is right for some people to receive pay at a markedly greater rate than others, and that families may retain excessive material wealth through generations.

While a predominantly materialistic and self-centred view is maintained, it is easy to understand some of the reasons why, within any particular country, certain rates of pay are significantly greater than others. The professional may assert that he should receive material rewards for years of study and training with no income, for long hours of work, and for accepting large responsibilities. In practice, another factor has been significant. When a person is in great pain, or is in difficult personal circumstances, he cries: 'I'd give anything to be rid of this problem.' Medical and legal fees for the help given may be almost unquestioned and the temptation to present large accounts is great. On the other hand, it should be acknowledged, some professionals waive fees totally for those in particular need.

Men and women of commerce may assume that it is their skill and determination, or their company's organisation and drive, which enables others to enjoy their products. Surely, they claim, the providers of these benefits can keep a realistic proportion of their considerable turnover for themselves, to enable them to take risks, seize further opportunities and to cover periods of downturn or failure?

For vast numbers of working people, pay remains a matter of personal or collective bargaining. In many situations bargaining is hardly practicable. Employees have to take what is offered. As in all human involvement, there are possibilities for insensitivity and ruthlessness to grow. On a world scale, little regard is paid to the needs and hopes of great numbers of manual workers. The result is that wages and conditions in many places, even in parts of the developed world, are unacceptably low and, in places, appalling. Yet pay differentials across the whole field of commerce and industry continue to widen, and basic pay in developed countries is princely compared with that received by most of the world's workers.(2)

In short, in large parts of the world, the market provides the guiding principle over pay. Workers' wages are pitched at levels where any protest causes little disruption. Similarly, the charge for a commodity or service is put at a level which it is expected the customer or client will pay. That level may be well above the realistic costs.

The market is important. It can stimulate enterprise, efficiency, healthy competition, speedy work, cheapness, and variety of products. It can offer a spur to perfection in craftsmanship. Nevertheless, the market may also encourage the production of shoddy goods and poor professional services; it provides a temptation for cutting corners over honest financial dealing. It focuses power in the hands of the materially wealthy and can lead to indifference towards the materially poor.

The basic flaw in seeing market forces as primary in the provision of goods and services lies in their preoccupation with financial matters. Important as these are, they are not as important as matters of the human spirit, and practical love to others. So the value of countless people can be sidelined or ignored. To leave customary approaches to pay as they are reinforces a materialistic outlook and consumerist practice. It is important to look critically at what happens as these views continue to predominate.

Materialism and consumerism; some consequences and comments

Materialism and consumerism both stand in clear contrast to the Christian view of the material world, and the way it is to be used. Materialism is an outlook which sees materials and artefacts as of primary importance, and material possessions as one of the chief means by which a person is to be evaluated. Concern with material assets does not only result in their accumulation. The latest, and whatever is supposed to be better, is to be desired and obtained. The good article may readily be discarded in favour of the new. So materialism, in its preoccupation with the material world, breeds consumerism.

Consumerism is the continuing cycle of the manufacture, purchase and use of items for periods well short of their likely life. Their disposal may be for further use, shown by the increasing number of high street shops dealing in second hand clothes and other goods. But often discarded articles are simply recycled or destroyed.

Consumerism is obvious over clothes, where changes in fashion keep the process moving. But it now involves many articles which used to be regarded as having a life of a century or more, such as furniture and furnishings. Almost any item of domestic, professional or commercial equipment may now be viewed in this way, designed to be used for a limited period only, and then to be changed. At the same time a profusion of articles, with a brief life-span only, floods the market. So manufacture for the short term becomes increasingly important and the problems related to the accelerating turnover of goods are intensified.

DISTORTION OF NATIONAL ACTIVITY

For many in the West, when full account has been taken of a comprehensive breadth of provision for their needs, there remains a considerable amount of financial wealth. The total of this excess wealth is huge. It can be used for the primary purposes to which we are directed by our faith, and spiritual nature, or it can be used in other ways. Any list of these alternatives will be selective, but it may include -

Luxury - such as the larger house, the second house, the second car, more, and more lavish holidays, the sophisticated facilities for the hobby or leisure activity. Rooms may be little used; the second home may be empty more than it is used; the cars encourage laziness; enthusiasm for the hobby or recreation may wane. 'Never mind,' the owner says. 'I have these things, I can do what I want, people can see I'm successful.'

Fashion - Changes are part of life. They are inevitable as technology develops, as needs alter and creative insights flourish. Variety coupled with choice enables personality to be expressed. But change for change's sake is another matter. Parts of the clothing and cosmetics industries are dominated by fashion. But it invades all areas of domestic furnishing and is a factor in almost every aspect of merchandise.

Reshaping of industry and commerce The years since the last world war have seen huge changes in Britain's industries and commerce.

Some heavy industries, such as coal and steel, have been greatly slimmed down. Others, as those concerned with communications, transport and domestic appliances have developed enormously. With the increased spending powers of great numbers of people, other industries have grown markedly. These include advertising, packaging, insurance, cosmetics, pet food, security, money markets, leisure and amusement provision, and many more. None is irrelevant to modern life. But each has developed to a degree unimaginable a generation or two ago.

Such businesses have developed their own powerful forces. Associations of companies with similar interests promote the importance of their concerns. The enterprises have developed considerable economic power and have helped to alter the whole make-up of national enterprise and commerce.

THE NATIONAL OUTLOOK RESHAPED

Developments such as have been sketched out have both risen from and contributed to a subtle reshaping of the national outlook over the last generation or two. The trivial, as with the gambling industry, becomes mainstream. The potentially lethal, as with the arms trade, is glamorised. All sorts of secondary matters come to be regarded as essential. As a result ironies abound. Efforts are sidetracked into dealing with problems of over-eating and slimming, while millions go hungry. Many own holiday homes while practical indifference remains over the poor and homeless. The advertising, packaging, fashion and promotion industries expend huge energies in attempts to improve market shares for inessential commodities, while provision for the basic requirements of national life is grudged and lacks resources. Just because we have allowed our perspectives on life to be altered, the boundaries are blurred between right and wrong in, for example, the handling of money and securities. Governments raise funds from gambling while at the same time they are faced with large-scale financial fraud.

Because of the way in which secondary developments have moved ahead, the general thrust of western commerce has become seriously warped. Nations are deflected from the pursuit of excellence in some primary tasks such as the comprehensive provision of adequate housing, thoroughgoing education, purposeful work, and rounded health care for all. There has been a serious shift in the way in which national life is viewed.

Coveting thrives. For some it results in blatant greed. For many, Christians included, it just happens as contemporary outlooks take over. Money becomes available, and is spent on ourselves.

It has now become more important to live well than to care about others. The fundamental truth that it is righteousness - right and generous dealing - that exalts a nation,[3] is submerged. As a result, Western society, with all its vast material wealth, exhibits an inability to respond creatively to basic needs, whether at home or abroad. Sadly, developing countries, as they look to wealthy developed nations, are given a false vision of the aims of a mature state.

MISUSE OF NATURAL RESOURCES

Misuse at source

It is becoming increasingly clear that the rate of consumption of many natural resources is markedly greater than the rate of their replacement. In places, forests are still disappearing more rapidly than they are being renewed. So it is with the world of living creatures, notably, for example over fish stocks around Britain. It is not only large scale problems which are significant; certain plants used in medicine are under threat. In parts of the world, the affluent West included, water itself is becoming a scarce commodity;[4] in places river water supplies lead to international tension. Serious concern is being aired about the adequacy of water stocks for the world's demands in the future.

Problems at disposal

At the other end of the chain lies the problem of disposing of what has been discarded, either in the course of production, or as what has been consumed is cast off. The problem grows as more and more material per person is needed to satisfy the demands of individuals and of society as a whole. It shows itself in difficulties which range from getting rid of domestic rubbish to the disposal of toxic and nuclear waste.

Misuse of materials in consumption

Shortages develop at one end of the production and consumer chain; disposal problems appear at the other. But in between are the growing problems of damage being done to the natural order of the whole terrestrial and atmospheric system. This shows in obvious ways such as industrial accidents and oil tanker spillages, or in water pollution, whether of rivers, inland lakes, or of large areas of the oceans. Other huge and many-sided problems already face us as, for example, over transport. More and more people want the personal independence which is brought by owning a car; more and more goods have to be transported to meet material demands. Shortages in road and air space are producing increasing dilemmas. Some problems over the atmosphere, such as city air pollution, are obvious; others, such as acid rain, ozone depletion and global warming(5) are less so. But the list grows relentlessly.

Governments may tackle the latest crisis; they may attempt to co-ordinate action across the world. But as more and more people develop technological skills for the generation of power and the manufacture of goods, it is inevitable that other problems and crises will follow. Environmental difficulties cannot be adequately tackled by trying to deal with the environment by itself. They can be dealt with only by re-evaluating human use of materials and power.

HARMFUL EFFECTS UPON PEOPLE

Physical effects

Accidents at work have always been part of life. They have happened in the simplest of rural societies. But the chase for material goods has meant that industry has often focused more upon output than upon the lives of the workers.

In recent years there have been terrifying examples of avoidable accidents. Bhopal(6) and Chernobyl(7) will forever be associated with great loss of life together with terrible effects upon those surviving, both nearby and further afield. But the headline-making mishaps are only the tip of the iceberg. There are thousands upon thousands of smaller-scale, or less well-known occurrences, such as the continual loss of life in shipping disasters.[8] Along with accidents have been working conditions which have blighted the lives of millions. The effects may have been direct, as with miners and chemical workers. They have also been indirect, as poor living conditions have combined to replace rural poverty with urban deprivation. Social reformers and groups of workers have fought long battles to improve conditions in the West. In other parts of the world, the situation remains grim, not least in places where western concern with low labour costs still leaves the establishment of good working conditions as a low priority.

Personal effects

Young people want, as they leave school and home, to work, and to become self-sufficient. Older people also want work, not least to provide for their families. There is inevitably a strong desire in each person to have work, of almost any sort, which brings in money. However, the personal chase for material wealth is by no means universally accepted as a central purpose in life.

Increasing personal wealth results in more 'spare' wealth being available in the community, with the result that increasing amounts are spent on the marginal and inessential rather that in tackling the challenge of rounded provision for all, especially for those with few privileges. Work dissatisfaction and half-heartedness may be difficult to evaluate, and many have no option but to continue in uncongenial jobs. Nevertheless in Britain, significant numbers of people change to work which is more closely involved with people and their needs, even though it may be less well paid. It is not surprising that a few opt out altogether. Within this ferment there are some ingredients of a social sickness.

Perversions

Materialism and consumerism are distortions of a proper human involvement with the physical world. But for some these distortions pass over to perversion. There are those who peddle drugs for their own gain, to the near or total destruction of others. There are those whose greed involves the distortion of truth and the corruption of justice, even to the extent of violence and murder. The appalling description 'contract killing' is now an accepted term. All these, and other perversions, occur within western society. Some of these travesties occur among professional people, and in areas of society where the outward signs of respectability are easily assumed.

It is easy to be destructive in criticism. Parts of the media, reflecting human fascination with perversity, seem to thrive on abnormality and depravity. The aim of this book is to set out a creative and positive approach to life. Nevertheless it would be naive to ignore the destructive power of the distortions and perversions which exist in contemporary society. Where material goods and financial gain are all-important, the chase for them will over-ride truth, morality, traditional good practice and conventional law.(9) It is inevitable that the grey or black economies will flourish, for these enable the goal of greater material wealth to be reached more quickly, while responsible sharing of financial rewards is avoided.

A Christian reappraisal

There is widespread and continuing comment which points to materialism as a fundamental dilemma which underlies problems such as have been reviewed. Material development brings great benefits. Once past a certain level, however, it easily becomes a goal in itself. As a result certain problems, such as the accelerating use of resources, come directly. Others, to do with the impact of materialism on individuals and society as a whole, follow.

A comprehensive Christian view of life changes attitudes to physical things. As a central part of God's creation, materials are to be respected and used rightly. But human nature is first and foremost spiritual. Materialism and consumerism are put aside. Material and financial rewards occupy an important, but not a dominant place in human attitudes. Pointers to the way in which materials, especially possessions, are to be viewed, and in which pay is given and received, are to be seen throughout the teaching of Jesus and the example of His life.

Biblical counsel on wealth and covetousness has already been touched upon, in chapters 3 (p.26) and 9 (p.72, 75). A recurring theme in Jesus' teaching is that concern with material wealth obscures spiritual vision and distorts human lives. It detracts from maturity and service. He states:(10) 'A man's life does not consist in the abundance of his possessions,' counsels 'Lay not up for yourselves treasure on earth,' and asserts 'You cannot serve God and money.'

Concerning others, men and women are to go further then to love others as they love themselves. They are to love others with the quality of love which Jesus showed for His friends.(11) This is underlined by His laying out of the principle that much is required of those to whom much is given. John, in writing about human love, made clear that this has to be seen in material ways:(12) 'If anyone has the world's goods and sees his brother in need, yet closes his heart against him, how does the love of God dwell in him?... let us not love in word or speech, but in deed and in truth.'

In practical terms, the accumulation of personal wealth indicates a measure of self-centredness, displays a false goal for personal maturity, and develops greed. The greedy person is not only side-tracked from care for others, but is deflected from awareness of fine qualities and achievements to be seen among those in humbler circumstances, both within and beyond his own contacts.

PAY DIFFERENTIALS TO BE RADICALLY CUT

None of the affirmations just made denies the importance of the material world. But they do challenge commonly held assumptions. Differences of income within the developed countries should be far smaller than those currently accepted. Rather than top pay being ten or twenty times the average, rising far above this in some instances, it should be much lower. The differential should be of the order of two or three only, a practice by no means as revolutionary as it might seem, as shown in recent Japanese practice. (13)

The necessity for radical re-direction

For the present, most people in developed countries appear to hope for continued growth in personal wealth. But it is obvious that this cannot continue unchecked, and there are plenty of warning signs on this matter already. Neither can it be assumed that international opinion will allow certain nations or groups of nations to continue to increase their share of the limited resources of the world. The developed nations must not only give more for development of material and personal resources across the world, but they must take far less of the world's wealth to themselves. As with personal incomes in the developed countries, differentials in national incomes across the world have also to be reduced, so releasing huge resources of human riches, for the mutual benefit of all.

Material solutions do not provide complete remedies for disorders which are basically moral and spiritual, such as greed and covetousness. But on material grounds alone, there is a clear moral compulsion to reshape attitude to life around the needs and potential of all others.

For those who profess faith in Jesus Christ there is a simple clear issue. We are commanded not to covet anything which belongs to our neighbour. Positively we are counselled to covet the best gifts. These are to be seen in the love of Christ, resulting in outgoing care, forgiveness and practical love for all others, powered by Christ Himself, through His Spirit. Christians cannot be expected to be taken seriously in their concern to commend faith in Christ if their own way of life bears little relation, in priorities and practice, to that of Jesus.

In a world where publicity seems obsessed with material wealth it is important to make clear that radically different approaches to pay, wealth and life in general are pursued by considerable numbers of men and women. From America there has come an account of the ways in which a variety of people have given away substantial fortunes.[(14)] In most cases they have retained no control over the money released, and have adopted a relatively simple pattern of life. In London's Bromley by Bow, Kingsley

Hall[15] remains as an active memorial to two sisters who, earlier this century gave away the bulk of their inherited fortune in order to establish this community centre.

Many people continue to show an attitude to reward for work which is quite different from the market and materialist approaches. Thousands of young people deliberately choose extended periods of work with low rates of pay, or none at all, in conditions of material simplicity.[16] There is a considerable stream of people, some with family responsibilities, who change to work they find rewarding, at lower rates of pay. There are some viable businesses where staff pay does not reflect traditional market practices.[17] Some men and women in public positions radically reduce the pay they accept. There are a number of communities following centuries of tradition and experience, where there is no sense of personal ownership of property and no pay in the normal sense of the term.[18]

The practice of stipendiary pay, widely accepted by Christian ministers, also stands as a working alternative to common assumptions over income. The minister is provided with accommodation, with an income which is adequate for the rounded maintenance of the household, enabling the work of ministry to be carried on without charge. Differentials may hardly exist over a wide variety of clergy occupations.

Apart from matters of pay for everyday work, it is important also to recognise that family life has at its heart a spirit of generosity and practical love which is not exercised for what can be gained in return. The family unit is under much pressure. Within western domestic relationships, many question, and some reject, the traditional concept. It is drastically affected by failures. But the family is constantly seen as the basic and most important grouping in the whole of society. However distorted any individual family has become, by breakdown, strife or poverty, somewhere in almost all of them there can still be found a spirit of love and practical generosity. For the majority of people, a significant part of their life is spent in a sphere where love, care and generosity are more important than material reward.

Those who accept the ancient Jewish principle of tithing, widely accepted by Christians, would not regard this as a radical practice. Tithing, the giving of a tenth of income, is one expression of the great principle set out in the record of David's declaration on the completion of the Jerusalem Temple.(19) 'Our' possessions are only on loan; at no stage are they our property. As with the whole direction of our lives, material possessions are to be used for God's purposes, for His glory.

Tithing continues to be used by people in the humblest of circumstances, where the tenth is given in kind from the cereal harvest. For those in the developed world, the practice makes clear that they can happily manage at a financial level markedly below what custom, or the market, suggests. It can be the first step towards personal liberation from the dominance of money in one's perspective on life.

Radical changes in matters affecting lifestyles are not achieved overnight, except in times of war, or revolution. But as hearts and minds are invigorated by fresh understanding and fresh vision a movement develops so that what originally seems impracticable becomes possible and achievable, with enthusiasm.(20)

Among the sayings which have circulated over material problems, Ghandi's comment may be heard: 'There is sufficiency for the world's need, but not for its greed.' In this pithy sentence can be seen the direct association between spiritual values and earthy necessities. Human spiritual integrity requires that a clear practical shift is made away from understanding reward primarily in material terms. Christians have not always been prime movers in the reshaping of national life, but their involvement has often been important, as is shown by the history of social reform in Britain. Sometimes it has been crucial, as over the abolition of slavery. On the whole range of matters concerning material wealth Christians need to be galvanised afresh. The issue is crucial both in relation to future life on the planet, and as a matter of fundamental spiritual integrity.

CHAPTER 11

PERSONAL MATTERS

What of the human person and the body with which the person is inextricably entwined? Clearly it has immense physical, mental and spiritual capabilities. The body needs to be tended with great care, yet it can cope with brutal treatment, and has inbuilt powers of restoration which are continually at work. Instinctive promptings to ensure that the body gets adequate air, food and drink and to make sure that the human race continues, are also inbuilt. The human person has the ability to communicate, directly and indirectly with other people and with the world of nature.

Each of the senses, and all the abilities, can be enhanced by training. As the body grows, the mind can develop its own skills. With the rapid development of information technology, the ability to obtain and manipulate knowledge opens up almost unlimited possibilities. To a considerable degree, each person can observe and control his thoughts as well as actions. We can dream dreams, we can shape our purposes; to some extent, we can shape our lives.

Nevertheless, in all considerations of human personality it is vital to underline the conviction that the spiritual nature is primary. Continuously involved as we are in the material world, we need constantly to allow God to shape and reshape us according to His pattern and purposes.(1) The process involves our wills, but the direction and power belong to God. In Christ's forgiveness of our sins lies the ground for our righteousness. We should be free from the power of inner sins and bondages which inhibit the flowering of personality. We are called to practical holiness, to be made like Christ Himself. Along this path lies the way to the liberation and development of human potential.

The realisation of human potential

Something of the scope of human potential is shown when an individual is faced with new creative opportunities. The challenge can galvanise a modest talent to show energies and ingenuities which can reshape the personality. Such transformations happen daily as young people are excited by human love, as younger and older men and women are gripped by a new enthusiasm, and as new businesses are launched, or fresh openings are exploited.

Not only does human personality have enormous scope. It has also great depths of resources, seen when a crisis has to be faced. For example if a person is hurt, a loved one is injured, or a relationship has been soured, it is not only mental and physical abilities which are brought into play. Resources of willpower, together with practical love and concern, may show creative qualities previously unknown. Such experiences have been almost commonplace in times of war, or when major catastrophes such as natural disasters and travel or industrial accidents have occurred.

The extraordinary abilities of ordinary people, when taken hostage or prisoner, for coping with physical deprivation and torture, have become known through a number of recent memoirs.(2) These abilities have been paralleled by equally remarkably capacities for coping with the spiritual aspects of affliction. Hope has been maintained, superb qualities of fortitude, generosity and care have emerged, together, sometimes, with an absence of bitterness and a readiness to understand and forgive their tormentors.

In seizing an opportunity or meeting a crisis there has to be a response from within the individual concerned. Every parent, teacher, factory manager or office supervisor knows the problem of kindling enthusiasm. But equally the drawing out of enthusiasm also needs an objective appropriate to human potential and gifts. Because human nature is fundamentally spiritual, aims which are only material or economic cannot bring out the best and the fullest of human responses. Yet given an engrossing vision, human potential is almost unlimited, as a prophet knew, writing some 2500 years ago.(3)

> 'They who wait upon the Lord shall renew their strength,
> they shall mount up with wings like eagles,
> they shall run and not be weary,
> they shall walk and not faint.'

Western society, which has had the priceless privilege of freedom to nurture and share Christian truth and faith, shows only a pale reflection of the prophet's vision. With all the spiritual potential, intellectual abilities and economic wealth of the developed world, prosperous nations appear largely impotent in the face of obvious opportunities for meeting the clear needs of people on a global scale. Within the wealthy nations, no less than in the underdeveloped world, large numbers of people have spiritual and mental resources which continue to lie dormant. Ambition which aims primarily at self-fulfilment and self-satisfaction is, by its aims, limited. Ambition should be centred on the limitless goal of the glory of God, with the resulting drawing out and deployment of personal abilities for the service of others on a world-wide scale.

Personal fulfilment to be found within divine love and purposes

Paradox it may be, but the fullest of human possibilities are realised as a person yields himself to the love of God. With the security and the spur of the love of God come both motive and power for the full and free flowering of human personality. Freedom, however, needs to be associated with purpose. Human abilities are so great that without purpose the individual is open to varieties of stimuli which may have no connection with each other. Freedom can then easily turn back to the mere satisfying of the self. The Christian's purpose is evident in a seemingly contradictory truth, expressed in an old prayer which addresses God, adding(4) ' .. whom to serve is perfect freedom.' The Christian is totally given over to serving God within the framework of His moral law, and so to serve all others. Here is the key to the blossoming of the personality.

The spiritual security which the Christian has within the love of God soon weakens and becomes eroded if it is not used for its primary objects. Jesus made clear that the pursuit of personal security was incompatible with whole-hearted Christian living. 'Whoever would save his life will lose it; whoever loses his life for My sake, he will find it. For what does it profit a man if he gains the whole world, and loses or forfeits himself?'(5)

While the Christian seeks to allow God's Spirit to direct his life, he may well find that he is physically fit and mentally fulfilled, with some measure of success, as it is understood in everyday usage. But Christian salvation brings no guarantee of physical well-being or material security. In today's world Jesus' counsel should not be taken as an invitation to dispense with insurance, but the Christian will be much less concerned than others to try to cover himself against every possible eventuality. God's assurances are ultimately more significant than any material safeguards.

Freedom is a fundamental and crucially important experience. Yet hundreds of millions of people across the world do not share to any realistic extent in its privileges and the opportunities which it should provide. Even so, freedom is not an end in itself. Freedom opens up possibilities for personal development. But if it is not used for the service of others under divine direction, those who are free may fall back into lethargy, self-centredness, or indulgence, any of which can deaden the personality.(6)

There are similar paradoxes over other experiences, such as peace. A sense of peace is needed in personal relationships, and within each person. Peace is vital within and between nations. But peace is not to be equated with inactivity. If peace is not used as a springboard for developing abilities and serving others, unease grows, not least as one becomes aware of the needs of others, and of ongoing conflicts. Frustration and perplexity grow. So we have no peace.

Timothy, as has already been quoted, was told that(7) 'the love of money is the root of all evils,' for such love can easily deflect a person from the honouring of God. Equally, the pursuit of sensory experiences lies at the root of much that is wrong. The neutral word sensory is deliberately used here to include all those experiences directly recognised through the senses.

Sensory experiences are obviously of immense importance, but seeking them as means for personal gratification can easily displace the honouring of God. The physical pleasures available to people are so rich and attractive that, both for one's own sake, and for all others, they need to be savoured rightly. They are not to become jaded through surfeit, or squandered through misuse. They are to be used in ways that allow positive values of the spirit to remain paramount.

Personal economic freedom has developed so much in recent years that the pursuit of sensory experiences can be followed to a far greater extent than was possible even a generation ago. Drinking has obvious value for refreshment as well as being essential for bodily maintenance. It is appreciated the more in company; a pleasure shared is generally a pleasure increased. Having a drink together is both a sign of friendship and an occasion for developing friendship. Nevertheless, excessive alcoholic drinking is wasteful, has harmful personal effects and increases problems on a communal scale.

These consequences, wastage, with harmful results on both individual and social scales, may be present in all indulgences. They are obvious in smoking. They can be seen in over-eating, with its variety of effects, and in continuous over-loud music, particularly when this is combined with disorientating visual projections.

The quest for sensory experience finds its most intense expression in sexual intercourse, in which all the senses may be brought into play together. The act of intercourse is widely recognised as a crucial stage in mutual experience between a man and a woman in which their knowledge of each other passes a unique and irreversible threshold. Leaving aside for the moment any consideration of procreation, the tradition which restricts intercourse to hetero-sexual marriage, deeply rooted in Christian and some other religious beliefs, contains much practical wisdom. Within the marriage bond, fears are removed, and the experience can become the culmination of a creative fusion of the two personalities. Christians should not let libertarians get away with the assumption that they alone have the fullest of sexual delights.

Sensory experiences bring much delight. They are means by which life can be lifted above the purely practical, to be touched by the glory of God. Each is to be used in appropriate measure; none is to dominate.

Marriage - the basic social unit

Variations in understanding the relationship between the sensory and spiritual aspects of life can clearly be seen in the current variety of approaches to a sustained relationship between a man and a woman. Not everyone is married, or even enters into a long-term association with someone of the opposite sex. But everyone has come from an involvement of some sort between people of opposite sexes. The great majority have been influenced by the care and nurture of a parent. Everyone, whether parent or not, has a concern in parenting.

The traditional understanding of life-long marriage needs constant reaffirmation. The assumption that marriage should be based upon total love and commitment between one man and one woman, for the life-time of either, is today widely questioned, or simply ignored. It is challenged by other patterns of relationship now adopted by large numbers of couples. Yet there remain huge numbers of people, not merely within the western world with its background of Judea-Christian morality, who regard monogamy as basic, and who find it the most significant relationship which is entered into by choice.

Simply and supremely, life-long marriage provides a setting where God-given spiritual qualities may flower to the full through the contrasting and complementary natures of the two sexes. This approach requires trust between the partners, developed out of knowledge and understanding gained in the courtship beforehand. Within this period, enough ground for trust can be found as the personalities are shared and explored. This trust is then carried on into marriage by mutual faith. Love and trust which are sustained and developed provide a strong setting in which children may be conceived and nurtured to maturity.

Where spiritual values have been shared and love and trust have been developed and are sustained, virtually any problem in the relationship can be overcome. Other compatibilities such as those of physical attraction, recreation, ambition or culture provide inadequate grounds, on their own, for the development of a full and creative partnership. Shared spiritual values are fundamental. Marriage not only continues to be entered into by very large numbers, but time and again after failure, couples start afresh to work for the ideal. It remains realistic, and needs constant support.

The physical body to serve the whole person

A constant challenge which has to be faced throughout life is that the physical body is to serve the person as a whole. God-given human powers are so great that, without control, physical abilities can be used in ways that are harmful, even destructive. As put by Paul:[8] 'God did not give us a spirit of timidity, but a spirit of power and love and self-control.' That control is crucial to the direction and experience of all life.

Paul used an extraordinary phrase to highlight understanding of the function of the body.[9] 'Do you not know that your body is a temple of the Holy Spirit within you?' He was expressing a truth which he also stated in other places - that God invites each person to be an instrument for His purposes in the world. The language may seem high-flown, but it comes in a passage where Paul was writing of the basic appetites of food and sex. Self-control will nevertheless allow for times of spiritual release, total celebration, and physical, mental and emotional delight. Each person is to be developed and trained for God's purposes. The living Spirit of God is to infuse and transform the human spirit so that men and women may increasingly be given over the fullness of divine will and glory.

CHAPTER 12

GLORY

This brief survey of Christian belief and life is an attempt to work out what it means to honour Christ as God in service and care to others, on a comprehensive scale, today. Inevitably much of this review has been at the level of workaday matters. Then are the tasks of daily life, those activities without which all else would fall apart, to be left at the level of routine and custom? Is life only to be seen as a duty - 'You shall love the Lord your God...' and 'You shall love your neighbour....?'

We may find clues to the answers to such questions as we look at an experience in which millions are caught up in Britain each winter week-end - watching football. It makes no difference whether the spectator is at a local amateur game, at a premiership match, or is only watching on television. A player weaves his way through the opposition with uncanny skill, and scores a goal. 'Marvellous, super, fantastic, amazing...' The words pour out. The watcher struggles to express admiration for something which may be expected, yet which is carried through in an extraordinary way. But our spectator is showing something more than mere admiration. The skill *is* to be marvelled at; it *is* brilliant and beyond his understanding.

This sense of wonder may be found in daily experience and is surely meant to be part of everyday life. It can occur as one sees the first smile of a baby, or when a child takes his first faltering steps. It will be sensed on countless occasions in the development of a young person as initiatives are shown and skills of body and mind are developed. It is to be found in the kitchen as the cake, perfect in shape, colour, texture, taste and smell, is brought out of the oven.

Wonder is to be experienced in the perfection of all sorts of craftsmanship as mental and physical skills combine to produce a creation which has about it qualities of beauty. It can be felt as members of a team work together in science or technology, bringing their inventiveness and resources to their work. It may be sensed as vision is enlarged when customs and actions, insights and creations, of people from traditions and cultures other than our own are seen.

Wonder stems in part from the fact that we cannot understand everything that we see around us. Even when we can describe what is happening in more or less precise scientific terms, as with the perfectly baked cake, there remains a sense of wonder at the way in which it all happens.

Glory is a curious word which defies clearcut definition. It has been used in relation to light, particularly that unusual light associated with the sun, when thin cloud, or mist near the ground, seems to add lustre to an object. The word points to an additional quality, beyond that which is expected, which enhances, or even transforms, what is seen.

There are a number of words, some of which have already been mentioned, which express something of the same elusive meaning, such as radiance, splendour, magnificence, or sublimity. Each in its different way suggests an extraordinary manifestation pointing to some quality beyond that which the senses recognise directly. The occurrence has been formalised in the halo of religious art. The experience is far more dynamic, as seen, for example, in the excitement of a child, or on the face of bride and bridegroom on their wedding day. It is to be seen on the face of the triumphant athlete, or as anyone makes a fresh discovery, or fulfils an achievement. It can be seen in the quiet serenity of an older person.

Elusive as these experiences of wonder and glory may be, beauty and art are two of their close companions. Beauty comes in the almost infinite variations of colour, smell, taste, sound, movement, shape and texture in the natural world, and as we observe and interact with people and their creations. Such experiences may be immediate. But there are other perceptions of beauty. The mathematician sees it in the elegance of what may appear to be an abstruse argument or demonstration, presented entirely in symbols. The scientist sees it as he is enabled to peer further and further into the composition and construction of the natural world, and as he is given new insights into how it all works. The engineer, too, will use words of delight and wonder at the performance of his machine or apparatus when everything works together in a perfection which borders on the exquisite.

There are still other perceptions of beauty. These may be less immediate and have less direct impact. Yet they have no less significance, as the quality becomes evident and is savoured over time. We may find, in almost any experience of beauty, a pleasure which grows as it is enjoyed, as fresh revelations come from the same material.

There is, too, a different kind of beauty, to be seen in a person's character. There may be little that is remarkable in the physical appearance; indeed it may be deformed by wear and tear over years, or by accidents. There may be no great material or intellectual abilities or attainments. Yet fine qualities of the human spirit seem to radiate as one comes to appreciate the whole personality.

Awareness of beauty is only one of our privileges. We also have the ability to use and re-order the beauty which exists, as can be seen in the gardens of countless homes. We may also create art, in seemingly infinite variety, in poetry, literature and drama; in drawing, painting and sculpture; in music and dance, in dress. Some art has been with us for so long that no-one knows its precise origins. Some is the work of genius, which can yet be performed or reproduced. Art still comes out in a stream of creations which may require little sophistication for their production and appreciation.

The act of creating a work of art, however humble, is itself an enriching experience. So it is as one reads, looks at, listens to, or performs an existing work. When this is a shared experience, it can provide even greater delight. One of the pleasures of the present time lies in the number and variety of new or rediscovered artistic techniques which are now available. Simple musical instruments, and methods used in visual arts, are being used to enable children to enjoy artistic experiences in which all may share.

Wonder may be kindled as we experience dark or negative passions, visions or encounters. Art is sometimes used to express some of these insights and occurrences. But in much of our awareness of wonder, glory, beauty and art one significant ingredient is the sense of well-being which they can impart. However simple such experiences may be they can kindle hope and fresh vision, as we are temporarily taken out of a perhaps humdrum daily round. The reaction of some to these potentially heart-warming experiences may be indifference or cynicism. But others will see such happenings as coming from God, providing further grounds for thanksgiving and worship. They will naturally associate glory with the divine nature. 'For from God, and through God, and to God are all things'(1) wrote Paul. When he continued: 'To God be glory for ever' he was affirming that only to God should glory be ultimately ascribed.

GLORY IN DAILY LIFE

Clearly glory is not to be confined to times away from the earthy realities of everyday life. It must be possible, and it should be natural, for glory to be found in the provision of food and drink, of clothing and housing, and in all those occupations which make up the inter-related patterns of daily life. There is an old 'spiritual' which says: 'You've got to get a glory in the work you do,' expressing the feeling that without a touch of glory, the daily round is a deadening routine. George Herbert put this conviction simply and positively in his poem:(2)

> Teach me, my God and King
> in all things Thee to see;
> and what I do in anything
> to do it as to Thee.
>
> A man may look on glass
> on it may stay his eye;
> or, if he pleaseth, through it pass
> and then the heaven espy.

All may of Thee partake;
nothing can be so mean
that with this tincture 'For thy sake,'
will not grow bright and clean.

A servant with this clause
makes drudgery divine;
who sweeps a room, as for Thy laws
makes that, and the action, fine.

This is the famous stone
that turneth all to gold;
for that which God doth touch and own
cannot for less be told.

The poet saw the possibility of transforming the humblest of tasks into a means of glory, and clearly felt that every action could come within such a compass. But does every occupation today have the potential for bringing glory into the workaday world - a glory which comes from God and which may be offered back to Him?

There is a glory in work which provides for the necessities of life. There can be glory in agriculture, in mining, in the harvest of the sea, in transport, in technology and manufacture, commerce and administration, in government and law. It may not be an instantaneous experience, but it can be discerned.

There can, nevertheless, be little glory in the overproduction of things which pander only to comfort and self-indulgence. There can be little glory in the production or provision of inessentials for the already wealthy, as is commonplace in the West. When this also means that we relegate the needs of the poor to a place below the supposed needs of the wealthy it is doubly inglorious.

There can be little glory in the manufacture of, and trade in, weapons which are designed to destroy life as well as constructions; an assertion powerfully underlined by the General Secretary of the Church Mission Society:(3) 'At the end of the twentieth century the commodities that are most sought after on the world market are arms and addictive drugs - those things that work to destroy humanity. Indeed the arms-related industry is the largest in the world today. What corporate madness has seized humanity that this should be the case?'

There can be little glory in the futile distortions and excesses of national life such as those upon which we have already touched. As with glory so it is with inglory. It may not be sensed immediately, but it becomes evident in the heart, both of the individual and of society.

Without touches of glory life is drab, and can be soul-destroying. Nevertheless, the quest for glory is a chase after something which changes as it is pursued. The pursuit of personal beauty, whether by cosmetics applied, or clothing worn, is a chase after a delusion, unless it is matched by an inner beauty of personality. Otherwise it remains incomplete and almost literally skin-deep. So it is in the workplace. Where work relates to the rounded needs of the community, or where there is a clear pursuit of excellence, there can be a satisfaction, with glimpses of glory, which may be sensed by all.

Glory as a human experience is not to be sought, calculated or compared. It is a wonderful bonus above the stuff of living. We can be caught up in it when life itself is seen as a gift from God, to be lived by His power and for His glory, to be offered back to Him in praise and thanksgiving.

CHAPTER 13

AND IF NOT?

Any picture of human life and human relationships can be only a sketch. However, examples of everything that has been sketched here can be seen around us. These patterns derive from convictions which have been tried and tested through all the Christian centuries. This book is an attempt at what is constantly needed, a re-working of the application of timeless Christian truth for the contemporary scene.

Nevertheless, if this sketch gives an outline for the right ordering of human life and relationships, then departures from these guidelines must bring difficulties. For a realistic evaluation of Christian life it is important to look further at the consequences of ignoring God's ways.

The person who has committed himself to God sees his primary aim as the honouring of God. In daily life he has, to a real degree, his instincts and abilities under control. He seeks opportunities for developing his potential in co-operation with God, working this out in care and service to others. He rejoices in the prospect of a life-time of rich experience. He still sins and makes mistakes, and is affected by the sins and mistakes of others. This happens, in the words of a well-known prayer(1) 'in thought, word and deed; through negligence, through weakness and through our own deliberate fault.'

Man's inner conflict is dealt with by the Christian's continual yielding of himself to the forgiving and re-creating power of God, shown through the whole life and work of Jesus, culminating in His death and resurrection. Though he knows that sin affects every area of life, he is not downcast, for he knows that God's forgiveness and love are limitless. He knows that this love will sustain him on either side of physical death. As he takes this love to himself he develops a greater love for God, with increasing personal integrity, and a continually renewed concern and love for others.

In effect, there is one fundamental choice to be faced, consciously, or unconsciously, by each person. We may exercise honour, love and goodwill for God and for each other and seek to work this out in everyday life. Or we may exercise love and goodwill primarily for ourselves.

God's judgement is perfect and impartial. This conviction, as has already been indicated, is deeply embedded in the Old Testament.[(2)] Yet this judgement is tempered with mercy.[(3)] In the New Testament these concepts are built upon and developed, towards standards of divine perfection which may seem impossibly exalted, as in Jesus' words:[(4)] 'You therefore must be perfect, as your heavenly Father is perfect.' At the same time the teaching and actions of Jesus show God as deeply merciful[(5)] as well as perfectly just.[(6)] Nevertheless, we should not ignore the need to alter our ways when we have received God's forgiveness.[(7)]

During Jesus' earthly life His presence made people aware of their own imperfections and inadequacies.[(8)] Those who respected Him and responded to His love and direction found themselves infused with new life and power. Others listened, but drifted away, unwilling to change. Others still were so incensed by what they saw as a challenge to their traditional religious wisdom and their way of life that they plotted against Him.[(9)] By their attitude to Jesus, people showed what they were.

Beyond this life the divine judgement will face men and women inescapably with the reality of their motives and actions, their achievements and failures.[(10)] Those who have come to live by the forgiving and re-creating power of God will welcome the searching light of God's perfect judgement. That light will bring before them their sin and failures. It will also show the way they have, at times, been misunderstood and wrongly judged in their earthly life.[(11)]

In the light of the divine glory all failures concerning truth and righteousness will be revealed. We shall be enabled to see that we have failed ourselves as we have set aside the love and trust which God has given to us. Light will be thrown on our petty and gross selfishness and on our failure to love and forgive. There will come the realisation that we have missed opportunities and inhibited our own development, apart from having failed and hurt others.(12) Excuses and pretences will be stripped away.(13) Perfect judgement will have many other concerns, but failure in matters of wrong worship, of truth and integrity and of personal and social righteousness will be made inescapably clear.(14)

The person who is not inclined to accept the perfect judgement of God will not escape that judgement. The purity and righteousness of God will be made clear and all personal evasions will be shown up. In one sense judgement is a matter of a person facing up to past events (... 'I just didn't realise my failures and wrong actions ... now I do'); in another sense God brings judgement to bear upon each one. Once again, it is the fact of a meeting between a person and God which results in judgement. When Jesus stood in chains before Pilate, who was free and surrounded by all the power of the Roman empire, it was nevertheless Pilate who was being judged and found wanting, not Jesus.(15)

God's love, peace and joy can be experienced within this earthly life and its time-scale.(16) Moments lived in near perfect harmony with God, infused with His Spirit, can be savoured now. We can be lifted out of ourselves and our earth-bound vision to glimpse something of the glory of God. In short, we can have glimpses of heaven now. For heaven is where God is supreme over all things and where His creatures rejoice in that supremacy.

Beyond this life we believe that, for those who have lived in response to the love and truth of Christ, life will open out into new experiences of God's glory,(17) and the glories of His creation, spiritual and material. There will also be fresh awareness of other people, with relationships rediscovered and renewed. For human personality will be freed from the bodily restrictions of space and time, and people will no longer live with sin and failure. Eternal life, beyond physical life, indicates a type and quality of existence which is quite different from present experience, within a material setting and conventional time scale.(18)

The lack of a warm living relationship with God is the basis for all that is included in the meaning of hell. The root of this separation lies in man's ignoring or even scorning God, with a setting aside of His moral law. God's love is ever-present and outgoing, but if that love is not welcomed, it will not be forced. Yet without a warm relationship with God, with its continuous possibilities for forgiveness and re-creation, there is no ultimate security. There is a real sense in which a person with no relationship with God is anchorless and lost.

Just as a person may carry the seeds of physical illness for years with no unpleasant symptoms showing, so it may be in life without God. But sooner or later problems are likely to become apparent, as when a person is desperate for understanding or love at a major personal crisis, accident or illness. Another simply longs for purpose or direction in life, especially when there appears to be little prospect of employment. When normal standards of truth, integrity and moral living have been set aside, acute unease may result in a lonely sense of division and conflict within the self. Hellish experiences are obvious when failure in love, or actual ill-will has drained a relationship of any warmth. Some of the worst occur within the closest of relationships when a bond of deep trust is broken. Hells are all too evident when enmity is assumed between social, ethnic or national groups.

Separation from God remains the key element in Biblical vision concerning hell beyond this life. But in all thought on the matter two factors must be kept in mind. In a non-material life, words referring to material and physical matters have to be seen as parables of spiritual reality. Heaven being described in terms of jewels and gold, or judgement being accompanied by 'fire and sulphur' are graphic images continuing the way in which Jesus used everyday terms and stories to illustrate spiritual truth.[19]

So also, the experience of time will be different from that of the present. Words indicating the passage of time, such as days or years, or words indicating sequences, such as before and after, may have little meaning in a totally different spiritual world.

Nevertheless, two convictions in particular undergird Christian belief concerning the separation from God, for some, beyond this life. Firstly, beyond present life God's glory, perfection and holiness will be supreme, and obvious.[20] Secondly, no untruth will be able to stand or prevail.[21]

A clue to the joy of heaven lies in the worshipper's prospect of a far greater awareness of the glory and love of God than has been experienced on earth. So the person who has no pleasure in God, or who has ignored or mocked God, would not find heaven comfortable. The person who has side-stepped truth and integrity and who has scoffed at purity, unselfishness and righteousness will be nonplussed by the dominance of all such values. For heaven will be full of qualities and occurrences of which he has had little understanding.

Hell can be seen as awareness of the consequences of failure to honour God, His righteousness and perfection, as the worship of God has been replaced by the inward looking worship of one's own personality. The fires of hell will come, in some measure, through knowing the whole truth about one's self. Coupled with this will be the experience of living with those self-centred attitudes which have stifled personal development, with the greed and lusts that survive after the power for finding pleasure in them has gone. Hell will be, in part, awareness of failure to love one's neighbour, with a realisation that concern on both spiritual and practical levels would have saved lives.

It is important that matters of judgement, heaven and hell are kept in proportion within the breadth of Christian truth. It has been affirmed[22] that too much concern with life after death may weaken the practice of faith in everyday life. Verses from a seventeenth century Spanish poem, common in older hymn books, set some of these matters in fine perspective:[23]

My God, I love Thee, not because
I hope for heaven thereby,
Nor yet because who love Thee not
Are lost eternally.

Thou, O my Jesus, Thou didst me
Upon the Cross embrace,
For me didst bear the nails and spear
And manifold disgrace.

Then why, O blessed Jesu Christ,
Should I not love Thee well,
Not for the sake of winning heaven,
Or of escaping hell;

Not with the hope of gaining aught,
Not seeking a reward;
But as Thyself hast loved me,
O ever-loving Lord.

The fact of a perfect judgement to come remains one of the great strengths and assurances of the Christian Faith. God is not mocked.(24) Both his righteousness and His mercy stand eternally, with His glory. This ultimate judgement nevertheless provides further stimulus to the shaping of life towards God's standards. In particular, the Christian's failure to shape his life according to the perfection of Jesus Christ is as significant before God as the committing of particular wrong actions.

The well-known words of the general confession of the Book of Common Prayer lay as much stress on sins of omission as on those of actions actually committed: 'We have left undone those things we ought to have done and we have done those things we ought not to have done.' But there is little doubt that the weight of concern has tended to focus on wrong actions, rather than on failure to act in accordance with what is right.

Jesus made clear that lazy selfishness, or a failure to use personal abilities to the full, were to be roundly condemned.(25) Equally, failure to act in the face of need provided grounds for condemnation. The great assurances which follow from faith in Christ - forgiveness of sins, and eternal life, amongst others - stand. But the New Testament is peppered with reminders that the Christian's response to the love of Christ is to be one of constant alertness, and readiness to follow Jesus' leading.[26] To honour and to love a person is a dynamic and ongoing adventure. So it must be in love towards God. Paul cautions the Corinthian Christians: "Let anyone who thinks that he stands take heed lest he falls.'[27] Jesus Himself made clear that verbal confessions of faith were by themselves inadequate, and warned that judgement might well find people of faith unprepared.[28]

Spiritual integrity and practical righteousness

In this book particular attention has been given to the two great commandments. Taken from the Old Testament and given particular significance by Jesus, they provide concise starting points for Christian living. They are nevertheless only a summary of a wealth of practical instructions and counsel which runs through the Old Testament.

The linking of divine worship, personal morality and neighbourly responsibility is closely made, as has already been mentioned, in a great early chapter of the Bible.[29] The writer records the Lord saying to Moses: 'Tell the people of Israel - You shall be holy, for I the Lord your God am holy.' There follow counsels on worship and fair dealing, all tempered with mercy, over a variety of personal social and agricultural matters. Throughout the chapter, the linkage between the divine nature and practical obedience is stressed. A holy God demands a holy and righteous people. The theme continues through the Old Testament. Worship, words and actions should be all of a piece.

In the New Testament the word righteousness is often used as almost equivalent to salvation; for one who trusts in the forgiveness of Christ is accounted righteous before God. But this quality has to be worked out in daily life. Paul brings this matter of righteous integrity in worship and daily life into sharp focus as he writes about the Lord's Supper, already, only a decade or two after Jesus' death, an important Christian observance. He mentions people coming to the meal with greed and drunkenness in their lives, and with unresolved personal divisions in the church.[30] He goes on to assert that people who lack integrity bring judgement upon themselves. 'That is why many of you are weak and ill, and some have died.'[31] The word translated 'have died' literally refers to sleep, though it is also used of death.[32] It seems so strong that some have taken the standard to be concerned only with spiritual piety; such people have fallen right away from God; their faith has died. That is important enough, but the truth has other implications, a point to which we return.

The Christian understanding of righteousness[33] is inextricably tied up with the Christian understanding of human failure and divine forgiveness. Righteousness is a gift from God, as Christ's forgiveness is accepted.[34] It is a living experience rather than a status to be achieved. It is part of a movement towards Christian maturity. Properly appreciated it should be invisible.

The Christian is constantly aware of the godly ideal of holy perfection. At the same time he is aware of his sin and shortcomings, whether in wrongdoing, or in failure to do right. He has little or no righteousness in himself,[35] and acknowledges this before God, continually accepting God's forgiveness, and taking His redirecting power into his life. Only by God's gift does he develop the will and experience the power for his movement towards the 'measure of the fullness of the stature of Christ'.[36]

The whole process is a precious privilege within Christian discipleship. Yet it can easily degenerate into a formal self-righteousness. This is quickly seen by others to be a travesty of faith, resulting in lives which give little honour to Christ. The remedy is simple, a constant taking to one's self of the love and mercy of Christ, with a continuous readiness to reshape and redirect life by the Spirit's leading and power.

James, in his letter, throws in a sharp comment as he writes of the double-minded person, adding that he is unstable in all his ways.[37] The comment may sound extreme, but common experience suggests that it contains considerable truth. Some would suggest that licentious sexual behaviour is irrelevant to a person's working life. Nevertheless, dishonesty to spouse or lover (and it is usually both) damages integrity; it damages the person and the relationship; each person involved is demeaned. There are similar attempts to draw distinctions between financial misconduct involving business or public accounts, and that concerning personal affairs. But the tradition which expects moral standards in private life to be consistent with those shown in public persists, tying up with the Christian view.

Today there is a widespread lack of ethical integrity, more commonly referred to as a credibility gap. Each term points to serious inconsistency. Teachers have to deal with a child or young person who denies responsibility for an action seen to have been done at the same moment. Professional negotiators have to master the art of concealing the full truth; politicians evade answering direct questions. It comes to be accepted that there is a level of dishonesty which is tolerated in some seemingly reputable commercial organisations, and amongst members of the professions.

Whatever the circumstances, one truth ignored, or one lie told, make other lapses easier. One unjust or greedy action makes the next less of a problem. So integrity is weakened. The ground for trust between one person and another is impaired. The foundations of personal, social, professional and commercial morality are eaten away and human nature is debased. Paul's stark assertion about moral and spiritual dishonesty leading to death may sound extreme, but it has a contemporary ring. Illness, breakdown, even suicide and murder, continue to occur amongst those who tamper with truth or integrity.

God's perfect judgement will include a reckoning on all matters of spiritual integrity and practical righteousness by the standards of Jesus Christ. That judgement should be a spur to a lively radical discipleship in Christian life, contrasting with the powerless and passionless spirituality which is widespread today.

The poor, and wealthy unconcern

If one acid test of Christian discipleship relates to personal integrity in daily living, an equally crucial test is concern for the poor. A majority of the world's inhabitants live in poverty, material obviously, but in other ways as well. Ours is a globally unjust world. The facts are evident for those with eyes and ears to see and understand.

The poor are human. They should have the opportunity of developing their lives under the two great commandments which lie at the heart of the way in which all are to live. Many materially poor people have embraced the faith of Jesus Christ. There are qualities in the practice of their faith which are both heart-warming and challenging to those who have far greater privileges. But for large numbers of people living near or below subsistence level, there is much injustice and little personal scope for the development of their abilities.

This book has focused, after laying out spiritual foundations, on material matters. It is obvious that meeting material need is fundamental, for we are material as well as spiritual creatures, living in a material world. But other serious deprivations persist. Often they are linked, as where political freedom is restricted, where there is little or no freedom of speech, where there is no freedom for religious expression and where personal movement is restricted. But material poverty remains crucial. While poverty persists, little progress can be made in getting rid of other deprivations.[38]

Poverty in itself may not be a ground for wrongdoing. Throughout history, and across the world today, unsophisticated groups of people, with little material wealth, have held to high standards in communal life. Nevertheless poverty, when ignored by those with wealth, is a fertile ground in which the perplexity of the poor about the rich can grow into resentment towards the rich. It is the awareness by the poor of the wealth of others with, in large cities, their physical closeness, which is significant.

Communications continue to develop rapidly. As more and more of the world's poor sense how their situation might be improved, while their hopes are frustrated, resentment cannot indefinitely be contained. In one place and another it will continue to erupt, in individual or communal disturbance and violence. All are sinners and wrongdoers. But when sinning 'haves' point condemning fingers at sinning 'have-nots,' the wrong of the former is compounded by the sin of their blind insensitivity.

Which is the greater evil, the hard-heartedness of the wealthy, or the frustration and anger of the poor? Those of us who count ourselves as Christians in the privileged parts of the world need to take stock of such a question, both in eternal and contemporary terms. For the way in which we respond bears immediately upon our ability to share the supreme wealth of the gospel of Jesus Christ. The heart of the 'problem of world underdevelopment' does not lie chiefly with the poor. For most of them the poverty of their material circumstances has remained unchanged for centuries. Rather, it is a problem of how the spiritual, intellectual and material wealth of the world is shared, or not, by the wealthy. Whether we consider the wealth and poverty within a nation, or between nations and blocks of nations, it is the continuation of indifference by the wealthy which is crucial.

Contemporary judgement; a continuing ferment

In this book the word potential has been used in its everyday sense, as it is applied, for example, to the young person on the threshold of adult life. But as used in electrical practice it has a clear technical meaning. In thundery conditions, differences of electrical potential develop between parts of a cloud, and between clouds and the earth. There will generally be a slow leakage of current, with no violent effect, as the clouds build up. But when the potential difference reaches a certain level, a flash occurs, always with violence and sometimes, when it strikes the ground, with material damage.

The picture is similar in human affairs. Material inequalities between people of a country can exist side by side for a considerable time. If there is mutual respect and understanding, as may be found in all parts of a nation's life, there may be no major problems. But if there is no such respect, discontent will grow. Just as there may be a considerable period of atmospheric calm before a storm breaks out, so it is in human affairs. Life may continue with outward calm, while a ferment grows. There is nevertheless an inevitability about this lessening of differences in the material circumstances of people. Large differences cannot be sustained without stresses; these may lead to acute problems, which can in turn lead to crises.

It is obvious that material deprivation and material imbalances are not the only causes of wrongdoing. It is equally obvious that, where there is a lack of material fairness and material care, grievances or frustrations due to other causes will fester, and may result in wrongdoing and crime. Without mutual fair sharing, minor social problems will occur. Financial and commercial short cuts will be taken. Irregular and illegal malpractices will increasingly take place in all areas of society. The ground for communal conflict and violence is made more fertile.

It should be obvious that the parable has a similar application on a global scale. Across much of the developed world there is an unspoken assumption that personal financial and material wealth is to increase steadily. At the same time only limited practical steps are taken to deal with large scale problems of poverty and under-development in the rest of the world. Leaving Christian insights aside, ordinary understandings of right and wrong, and of fairness and justice, will not allow this imbalance to continue indefinitely.

On grounds of expediency alone, it is insufficient that those in the affluent parts of the world should be generous with 'their' wealth. The way in which the world's resources are taken and used by the already wealthy has to be re-evaluated, towards a fairer and more just sharing of global assets. Otherwise, viewing the challenges at a simple selfish level, we of the presently privileged minority simply perpetuate problems, and bring judgement upon ourselves.

All over the world a ferment continues. As the developed nations continue to seek sustained growth in wealth, resources will be depleted and in places the resulting problems will be acute, producing further environmental crises. There will be, on small and large scales, proximities of wealth and poverty which will not be sustainable. As communications become more effective, disturbances and conflicts are likely to grow from which people, even in the wealthiest parts of the world, will not be able to shield themselves.

In so much consideration of resources there is a widespread blindness to the importance of by far the most important world resource - human personality, liberated and directed by divine love and will. It is possible to view history in terms of the slow, but ultimately irresistible, movement of the poor and dispossessed towards a fairer share of the world's plenty - spiritual, artistic and intellectual plenty, as well as physical and material plenty. There will surely come a time when people will look back with astonishment at this present period of the developed world's blind and deaf affluence. Judgement on our privileged lives may well come in physical and material ways more quickly, and in ways less predictable, than can presently be imagined.

POSTCRIPT

The writing of this short book arose out of a long-term disquiet. Amongst Christians, particularly in the developed countries, considerable numbers appear to pay, in practice, little attention to the blindingly obvious. So, as we Christians have, in effect, set aside certain practical applications of our belief, growth in faith has been inhibited. So, too, we have prevented ourselves from sharing in the thorough-going, full-blooded life for which we have been created; and we inhibit the flow of the inexhaustible riches of spiritual gifts and graces with which life, on a world-wide scale, is meant to be infused.

It has therefore been essential to go back to Christian fundamentals, and to take as large a view as possible of the whole of life and nature. Before we begin to look at Jesus' life, work and teaching in any detail, one cardinal fact should strike us, powerfully expressed by Paul:(1) 'Have this mind among yourselves, which is yours in Christ Jesus, who, though He was in the form of God, did not count equality with God a thing to be grasped, but emptied Himself, taking the form of a servant, being born in the likeness of men. And being found in human form He humbled Himself and became obedient unto death, even death on a cross. Therefore God has highly exalted Him...' Jesus set aside all the privileges which were rightly His, to enable all to 'confess that Jesus Christ is Lord, to the glory of God the Father.' Paul goes on to encourage those to whom He was writing to 'work out your salvation in fear and trembling; for God is at work in you both to will and to work for His good pleasure.'

Christian belief has its centre in the crucifixion and resurrection of Jesus, coupled with the release of the Holy Spirit, enabling all to share in divine grace and power. However these events are perceived, one key result must be that the pattern of out-going consecrated practical love of Jesus' life must, as Paul emphasises, be fully taken into the lives of Christians today. The body of Christians, especially in the West, has to show much more of the consecrated love which it praises in its worship.

Christians are to covet the best of spiritual gifts and qualities, supremely sharing in, and then sharing with others, the forgiving and re-creative love of Christ, on the largest of scales. We should use the material world rightly as a clear part of our godly discipleship. We should not continue to be caught up in the coveting of goods and money, after the fashion which seems to drive the wealthier nations.

Within this reappraisal of Christian spirituality one outcome has emerged as crucial. A radical shift has to be made in the way in which rewards, particularly material rewards, are understood, given and received. 'No-one can serve two masters.' 'You cannot serve God and money.'(2) Christians have to be clear as to where their primary allegiance lies. Serving God wholly necessarily involves dealing with financial and material matters, with comprehensive integrity. Serving money, on the other hand, easily becomes an over-arching concern which relegates other vital matters to second place. Those two ancient declarations have a very contemporary ring. There is, in practice today, an effective conflict between preoccupation with personal wealth, and realistic concern for God and His priorities.

Materially privileged individuals, and nations as a whole, have to take markedly less of the world's resources than at present. Personal pay for those markedly above the average must be decisively reduced. Likewise the level of national wealth of the poorer countries has to be brought closer to that of the wealthier countries. Then people, the world over, can be stimulated more effectively towards the realisation of their full potential.

For Christians, unless changes of this nature are made,(3) our profession of Christian belief will continue to lack credibility; we weaken our ability to commend faith in Christ, with all its privileges and delights; we shall continue to give an ineffective lead in tackling issues which face society; so we share in the coming of further crises, social, environmental, political and international.

And finally ... it has to be reiterated that at the root of all social evils lies human sin. Unless this is dealt with, a fairer distribution of wealth will leave the fundamental problems of materialism untouched. Christ's victory over sin, on the Cross, is crucial. In this lies the power, not only for individuals, but also for society, from the smallest to the largest of scales, to be changed.

It is easily to caricature the Christendom of today in the so-called civilised parts of the world. Some of our behaviour invites ridicule, even scorn. It is, as it always has been, tainted by worldliness and sin. Yet, through the ages, the Christian body has not only shown remarkable powers of regeneration, but it has also shown ability and strength to challenge the most powerful of national institutions, and some seemingly established philosophical views. If we go back to the roots of our Faith, and if we use eyes and ears to be aware of what is going on around the world, we may see the body of Christ, free from impediments of the past and materialism of the present, continuing to show the truth and life of its Master.(4)

'For from Him, and through Him, and to Him,
are all things.
To Him be glory for ever.'

END

NOTES AND REFERENCES

Foreword

Note

1 Mark 4 v.19.

2 Exodus 20 v.17; Deuteronomy 6 v.21;
Mark 7 v.21,22; Luke 12 v.15; Romans 13 v.9.

1 Introduction

Note

1 John 10 v.11.

2 Psalm 119 v.71 (BCP)

2 Christian belief and Christian life

Note

1 For example, I and II Samuel, I and II Kings,
I and II Chronicles.

2 For example, Isaiah chaps. 40,43,49.

3 Genesis chap. 1; Psalms 19,24.

4 Jeremiah 9 v.24, 22 v.3.

5 Jeremiah 22 v.6-12.

6 Exodus 34 v.6; Hosea, especially chap. 11.

7 Personally, as in Job 19 v.25; corporately, as in the release from slavery in Egypt, Exodus chap. 1 on; and in the return from exile in Babylon, Isaiah 40 v.1-11.

8 Leviticus 11 v.44,45; 19 v.2; Psalm 22 v.3;
Isaiah 6 v.3.

9 Psalms 145-150.

10 Jeremiah 31 v.31-34; Ezekiel chap. 37.

11 Isaiah 9 v.2-7, 11 v.1-5, 42 v.1-4, 49 v.1-7,
50 v.4-9, 52 v.13 to 53 v.12.

12 Mark 6 v.3.

13 Matthew 12 v.38, 16 v.21.

14 Matthew 5 v.1; Matthew 14 v.14,15 = Mark 6 v.34 = Luke 9 v.11, 12.

15 Matthew 4 v.18-22 = Mark 1 v.16-20; Matthew 10 v.2-4 = Mark 3 v.16-19 = Luke 6 v.14-16.

16 As in Matthew chap. 27, Mark chap. 15, Luke chap 23, John chap. 18; see also Luke 13 v.32.

17 Luke 19 v.1-10; John 4 v.1-30, 7 v.53 to 8 v.11.

18 Luke 8 v.1-3; Matthew 27 v.55,56 = Mark 15 v.40,41 = Luke 23 v.49.

19 Matthew 19 v.13, 14 = Mark 10 v.13,14 = Luke 18 v.15,16.

20 Luke 4 v.16,17.

21 Matthew chap. 23.

22 (a) Luke 22 v.42; John 5 v.30, 6 v.38; (b) John 8 v.49; (c) John 10 v.30, 17 v.22,23.

23 For example Isaiah chap. 1, Jeremiah chap. 3, Ezekiel 5 v.5 to 7 v.27.

24 Luke 2 v.41-52, 4 v.16,17.

25 Matthew 7 v.28,29.

26 Matthew 5 v.6.

27 (a) John 4 v.27, (b) Mark 10 v.45; John 13 v. 5-15, (c) Matthew 19 v.14 = Mark 10 v.14 = Luke 18 v.16, (d) Mark 7 v.24-30.

28 John 13 v.34, 15 v.12.

29 I John 4 v.8.

30 Miracles of healing and provision.

31 I John 4 v.10.

32 Matthew 23 v.37-39 = Luke 13 v.34-35.

33 John 17 v.20-26.

34 Luke 23 v. 34,43; John 19 v.26,27.

35 I Corinthians 1 v.22-25; Galatians 6 v.14.

36 Matthew 28 v.8,17; Luke 24 v.13-43; John 21 v.4-14.

37 John 20 v.19,21,26; see also Matthew 28 v.10.

38 Matthew 28 v.19,20; Luke 24 v.47,48; Acts 1 v.8.

39 Matthew 15 v.15-20 = Mark 7 v.18-23.

40 Romans 7 v.15-17.

41 Romans 3 v.23.

42 John 12 v.31,32.

43 For example Exodus 15 v.2; Psalm 62 v.1,2, Psalm 96 v.2.

44 As in Acts 4 v.12, 13 v. 26,47, 16 v.17.

45 By, for example, His words of forgiveness and peace; Luke 23 v.34; John 20 v.19,21,26.

46 John 3 v.16, 3 v.36, 17 v.3.

47 For example Philippians 1 v.21,23.

48 As shown by the use of 'Father' as an address to God. Matthew 6 v.8,9 = Luke 11 v.2.

49 Genesis 12 v.1,2 (Abram), Exodus 3 v.1-12 (Moses), I Samuel 3 v.1-10 (Samuel), Isaiah chap. 6 (Isaiah), Amos 7 v.14,15 (Amos).

50 Expanded from the Ten Commandments as in much of Leviticus, Numbers, Deuteronomy.

51 Matthew 23 v.1-37.

52 Matthew 5 v.17-19.

53 For example John 15 v.1-11.

54 Colossians 1 v.27.

55 Luke 8 v.9; John 10 v.6.

56 John 14 v.16,17, 16 v.12-15.

57 Acts 2 v.1-13.

58 For example Acts 8 v.29, 10 v.19, 11 v.12, 13 v.1-4, 16 v.7.

59 Acts 6 v.8-12, 7 v.54 to 8 v.1.

60 Acts 9 v.31, 11 v.19-26.

61 Acts 13 v.1-4.

62 Acts chap. 13 onwards; generally in the epistles.

63 Romans 12 v.6-8; I Corinthians chap. 12; Ephesians 4 v.11,12.

64 II Corinthians 3 v.18, 5 v.17.

65 For example Numbers 11 v.16,17, 24-29; Judges 3 v.10, 6 v.34, 11 v.29, 13 v.25, I Samuel 16 v.13.

66 As in Romans 8 v.9-11 where God, Jesus, Christ and Spirit are clearly equivalent names.

67 Romans 8 v.16,26.

68 As in Acts 2 v.4, 4 v.8,31, 13 v.9, Ephesians 5 v.18.

69 Acts 17 v.6.
70 John 3 v.3,7.
71 I Corinthians 12 v.27.
72 Ephesians 4 v.11-13.
73 For example, I Corinthians 7 v.1, 8 v.1, 12 v.1, 16 v.1.
74 Philippians 2 v. 12,13.
75 A sacrament is an outward sign, combined with particular words, regarded as conferring Christian grace upon those who receive it. Those associated in the New Testament with Jesus, Baptism and the Lord's Supper, are generally regarded as primary.
76 John 15 v.26, 16 v.14,15.
77 See, for example I Corinthians 1 v.18 to 2 v.16.

3 Foundations

Note

1 Luke 1 v.1-4; John 20 v.30,31.
2 As seen in I Corinthians 7 v.1, 8 v.1, 12 v.1, 16 v.1.
3 Matthew 4 v.1-11 = 4 v.1-13.
4 For example Luke 10 v.26; John 5 v.39.
5 Matthew 22 v.34-40 = Mark 12 v.28-34 = Luke 10 v.25-28 (Quoting from Deuteronomy 6 v.5; Leviticus 19 v.18).
6 See Chapter 2, note 11.
7 Isaiah 61 v.1,2; quoted in Luke 4 v.16-18.
8 Matthew 5 v.17.
9 Matthew 5 v. 22,28,34.
10 John 5 v.39,40.
11 II Corinthians 1 v.20.
12 Hebrews 1 v.1-3, 10 v.1, I John 2 v.7,8.
13 Through the covenant and commandments, Exodus 19 v.4-6, and on to 24 v.1-8; also the Law of Holiness, Leviticus chaps. 19-26.

14 For example David - I Samuel 16 v.11-13, but see II Samuel chapters 11,12. Also Solomon I Kings 3 v.5-10, but see 11 v.1-8.

15 Isaiah 1 v.16,17.

16 Psalm 82 v.1-4.

17 Amos 5 v.24.

18 Proverbs 14 v.34.

19 Matthew 5 v.17-20.

20 Exodus 15 v.3; Deuteronomy 7 v.1,2, chap.20; Joshua 10 v.28-43; also Judges chap.5; II Samuel 8 v.13 etc.

21 Hosea 11 v.8,9.

22 But see Luke 22 v.36,38, and note 24.

23 Revelation chapter 12 onwards.

24 For example Matthew 5 v.38-48 = Luke 6 v.27-36; also Matthew 26 v.51-53 = Luke 22 v.50-51; compare John 18 v.10,11.

25 Historically, in the Crusades, and the use of force in colonising developments. Currently, the widespread acceptance of guns and violence in entertainment, and conflict resolution.

26 Epitomised by the 'milk and honey' picture of Palestine, as in Exodus, Leviticus, Numbers, Deuteronomy and Joshua.

27 For example Deuteronomy 8 v.13, Job 22 v.24, Psalms 49, 62 v.10, Proverbs 23 v.5, 28 v.20, Ecclesiastes 5 v.10-17, Jeremiah 17 v.11, Amos chap.3, 6 v.4-6.

28 Genesis 39 v.2,3; Deuteronomy 28 v.1-14, 30 v.9; I Chronicles 29 v.12; II Chronicles 1 v.12; Job 42 v.10-17.

29 Matthew 6 v.19-24; Matthew 13 v.22 = Mark 4.19 = Luke 8 v.14; Mark 10 v.23-25; Luke 12 v.16-21; 16 v.19-31; 18 v.18-30.

30 I Corinthians 16 v.1-3; II Corinthians 8 v.1-5.

31 Matthew 13 v.36; Matthew 13 v.10 = Mark 4 v.10 = Luke 8 v.9; Mark 7 v.17; Matthew 16 v.7 = Mark 8 v.16; John 6 v.60.

32 Seen in the words 'You have heard... but I say unto you...' repeated through Matthew chap.5.

33 John 16 v.12,13.

34 See chap 2 note 58.

35 John 16 v.17.

36 Romans 11 v.33.

37 Allegory - Matthew 21 v.33-46 = Mark 12 v.1-12 = Luke 20 v.9-19. Exaggeration - Matthew 19 v.24 = Mark 10 v.25 = Luke 18 v.25.
Humour - I Corinthians 12 v.14-17. Poetry - Psalms, Song of Solomon; also short passages in New Testament, as Luke 1 v.46-55; Revelation 15 v.3,4 and 19 v.1,2.

38 Matthew 5 v.37.

39 Colossians 2 v.3; Ephesians 3 v.19.

40 John 14 v.6.

41 See I Corinthians 1 v.18 to 2 v.16.

42 Philippians 4 v.8.

4 Christian Spirituality - Eternal life in the present

Note

1 II Peter 3 v.8, quoting Psalm 90 v.4.

2 John 14 v.6,9.

3 Matthew 9 v.3-6 = Mark 2 v.6-10 = Luke 5 v.22-24; John 1 v.29 etc.

4 I Corinthians 2 v.9.

5 Matthew 22 v.30 = Mark 12 v.25 = Luke 20 v.36; I Corinthians 15 v.42-50; I John 3 v.2.

6 Philippians 3 v.20.

7 See, for example, Philippians 3 v.12-17, James 1 v.22-25.

8 Philippians 2 v.12,13; Colossians 1 v.9,10.

9 Jeremiah 9 v.23,24.
10 Galatians 5 v.22,23.
11 Matthew 5 v.48.
12 Colossians 4 v.5.
13 Philippians 2 v.5-13.
14 Romans 12 v.2.
15 Matthew 22 v.37-39 = Mark 12 v.29-31 = Luke 10 v.27, quoting Deuteronomy 6 v.5, Leviticus 19 v.18.
16 See also Romans 12 v.9,10, 13 v.9,10; Galatians 5 v.14; James 2 v.8.
17 Luke 10 v.29-37; Acts 1 v.8.
18 Matthew 22 v.40.
19 Mark 12 v.31.
20 I John 5 v.3.

5 Practical Perspectives

Note

1 Isaiah 3 v.14,15.
2 Isaiah 3 v.24-26.
3 Matthew 23 v.1-3.
4 Matthew 23 v.37.
5 II Timothy 3 v.5.
6 Deuteronomy 6 v.5, quoted in Matthew 22 v.37, Mark 12 v.30, Luke 10 v.27.
7 See Romans 12 v.1.
8 Exodus 36 v.1, II Chronicles 2 v.7-14, on craftsmanship; Amos 8 v.5,6 on finance; Proverbs 11 v.1 on commerce; Isaiah 5 v.8 on property management.
9 Luke 12 v.13-21, 16 v.1-13, 19 v.11-27 on business management; 12 v.42,43 on responsible service; 19 v.1-10 on financial honesty; 20 v.21-25 on taxes.
10 Matthew 13 v.55,56; Mark 6 v.3.

11 Luke 4 v.16-19.
12 John 3 v.16.

6 Worship

Note

1 Readings in St. John's Gospel p.68;
Macmillan Press Ltd. 1945.
2 Any bookshop specialising in Christian literature will provide starting points. The Bible Reading Fellowship and Scripture Union are two organisations, among several, which specialse in aids to daily Bible reading as a foundation in Christian spirituality.
3 See Chapter 2 note 75. Sacramental worship has several names - Breaking of Bread, Lord's Supper, Holy Communion, Eucharist, (from the Greek word meaning 'Thanksgiving'), Mass.
4 John 4 v.24.
5 Romans 12 v.2.
6 Ecclesiastes 5 v.1-6; see also
Deuteronomy 23 v.21-23, Psalm 50 v.16,17.

7 Loving the neighbour - some practical matters

Note

1 Luke 10 v.25-37.
2 Matthew 4 v.4 = Luke 4 v.4, quoting Deuteronomy 8 v.7.
3 Chap. 4 p.32, 33.
4 Genesis 1 v.27.
5 Romans 3 v.23.
6 See, for example, Romans 3 v.10-18, where Paul brings together a number of Old Testament assertions.
7 John 13 v.34, 15 v.12.
8 See, for example Matthew 20 v.25-28 =
Mark 10 v.42-45, and Luke 22 v.25-27; also

John 13 v.2-5, 12-17.

9 At start of Jesus' ministry, the twelve apostles - Matthew 10 v.2-4 = Mark 3 v.16-19 = Luke 6 v.14-16; At the end, the eleven - Matthew 28 v.16, Mark 16 v.14, Luke 24 v.33, John 20 v.20,24.

10 See Chap 2 note 18, with Luke 10 v.38-42, 23 v.27,55.

11 See Chap 2 note 14.

12 As in John 15 v.11, 16 v.22,24, 17 v.13.

13 Proverbs 11 v.24.

14 I Timothy 6 v.10.

15 As shown in, for example, 'The seven cultures of capitalism' by Charles Hampden-Turner and Fons Trompenaars;Piatkus 1994.

16 Concise Oxford Dictionary of Quotations, OUP 1981 P.81.

8 Loving the neighbour - some problems and challenges

Note

1 Galatians 3 v.28.

2 See for example, 'New Internationalist' June 1996; 'Burma - a cry for Freedom'.

3 See 'New Internationalist' July 1997. Whole issue on 'Child Labour.'

4 See 'New Internationalist' January/February 1997. Whole Issue on 'State of the World.'

5 See 'New Internationalist' May 1995. Whole issue on 'Hunger in a world of Plenty.'

6 See, for example, information given by organisations such as Oxfam, 274, Banbury Road, Oxford OX2 7DZ and Save the Children, 17, Grove Lane, London, SE5 8RD; or Christian Societies, as Christian Aid, P.O. Box 100, London SE1 7RT; CAFOD, Romero Close, Stockwell Road, London SW9 9TY, or Tear Fund, 100, Church Road, Teddington, TW11 8QE.

7 Unicef Facts and Figures.

8 See, for example 'Street Children;' Andy Butcher. Nelson Word Publishing 1996.

9 See organisations given in note 6. There are many others such as the World Development Movement, 25, Beehive Place, London SW9 7QR, and Shared Interest, Newcastle upon Tyne NE1 1BR. Many universities have departments specialising in world development.

10 Christian Aid, CAFOD, New Consumer, Oxfam, World Development Movement and Traidcraft Exchange established the Fairtrade Foundation in July 1992. As a result, Maya Gold chocolate bars, Cafedirect and Percol coffees, and Clipper teas are available in a number of major supermarket stores. These commodities, and certain others, are produced by growers under conditions and trading arrangements, and for pay, markedly more favourable than average.

11 Christian Aid's 'Change the Rules,' for example.

12 The issue is comprehensively tackled by Paul Vallely in 'Bad Samaritans, First world ethics, and third world debt.' Hodder and Stoughton 1990.

13 'Small is Beautiful,' Hutchinson 1974 p.165.

14 See for example, 'New Internationalist' May 1997. 'The City our Stepmother; Ten years in the life of a slum.'

15 Matthew 5 v.13.

16 Luke 10 v.25-37.

17 Health depends greatly on supplies of pure water and the availability of good sanitary disposal systems. Immunisation of children against the six major childhood diseases - diphtheria, measles, polio, tuberculosis, tetanus and whooping cough - is currently widely practicable. Acute diarrhoea can be prevented by an oral rehydration sachet of sugar and salt costing pence ony. A few pounds per month can support a health worker for six months in India, or provide tools for villagers to dig a well

in the Sudan. And how to feed the lives saved? 'The world produces more than enough food to feed its entire population. Yet an estimated 35,000 people die of hunger each day ('New Internationalist' © May 1995 p.19) See also Ghandi's comment (p.90)

18 'New Internationalist' August 1995. Whole issue on 'Women - Still something to shout about.'

19 As seen in the widely resented Structural Adjustment Programmes, virtually imposed upon certain poor countries.

20 It is invidious, and inevitably selective, to point to particular achievements, but from contemporary Africa alone have come Nobel literature prizewinners (Egypt and Nigeria), outstanding athletes (e.g. Ethiopia, Kenya and Morocco), world class sculpture (e.g. Zimbabwe), brilliant woven cloth (West Africa), and innovative dance and music from various countries. It is even more significant to see the emergence of practical forgiveness of a quality lacking in parts of the more 'advanced' West which has issued from a number of countries, amongst which South Africa is the most recent.

21 Exodus 20 v.17; Deuteronomy 5 v.21. See also Ecclesiastes 5 v.10. See chap 3 p.23; also Luke 12 v.15; Ephesians 5 v.5, where covetousness is equated with idolatry; Hebrews 13 v.5.

22 I Timothy 6 v.10.

9 Purpose in life. Materials; wealth; rewards

Note

1 Genesis 1 v.31.

2 Tennyson 'In Memoriam.'

3 Romans 8 v.19-22.

4 Psalm 24 v.1, also 89 v.11; Leviticus 25 v.23; I Chronicles 29 v.14.

5 I Timothy 6 v.7, quoting from Job 1 v.21.

6 Exodus 20 v.9, 31 v.1-6; II Chronicles 2 v.7-14.

7 Mark 6 v.3.

8 Matthew 25 v. 14-30 = Luke 19 v.12-27.

9 II Thessalonians 3 v.10.

10 Matthew 6 v.19-24, also Luke 12 v.33,34; 'Do not lay up for yourselves treasures on earth.' Matthew 13 v.22 = Mark 4 v.19 = Luke 8 v.14; Parable of the sower; concern with wealth inhibits spiritual maturity. Matthew 19 v.23,24 = Mark 10 v.23-25 = Luke 18 v.24,25; Hard for a rich man to enter the Kingdom of God. Luke 12 v.16-21; The rich fool. Luke 16 v.19-31; Rich man and Lazarus.

11 Luke 12 v.48.

12 Luke 12 v 15.

13 Matthew 6 v.19; compare Luke 12 v.33,34.

14 Acts 20 v.35.

15 Luke 10 v.28.

16 Matthew 13 v.1-9 = Mark 4 v.1-9 = Luke 8 v.4-18; Matthew 13 v.44-50; Luke 5 v.1-11. See also I Corinthians 9 v.8-12.

17 See, for example, 'New Internationalist' March 1997. Whole issue on 'Endangered Species.' 'Who's next?'

18 Organisations mentioned in notes 6 and 9 of chapter 8 are some of many involved in this sort of stimulus. 'Intermediate Technology,' Myson House, Railway Terrace, Rugby CV21 3BR specialises in the development of technology appropriate to the resources available.

19 See Chap. 8, note 17.

20 See, for example Oxfam advice notes of October 1993, on rebuilding after the massive destruction due to the Maharashtra earthquake in India of the same year.

10 Pay the market. Materialism and consumerism; critical comments. A radical Christian response

Note

1 I Corinthians 4 v.7, where Paul writes of spiritual matters; but the question is pertinent over a wide range of gifts.

2 'Research conducted by Oxfam, which in 1995 launched the Clothes Code campaign, indicates that throughout the developing world, where the garment industry is a vital source of employment, a predominantly female work force is forced to work in appalling conditions for wages which barely cover the most basic level of subsistence.'From the 'Observer' © supplement, p.5, in conjunction with the Co-operative Bank, 29th June 1997.

3 Proverbs 14 v.34.

4 See, for example, articles in 'Guardian,' 8th August 1995, tabloid section, 'The Water Bomb;' 15th February 1996, On Line section 'Earth has no substitute for the real thing;' 28th January 1997, 'Word heads for disaster.'

5 See, for example, 'Guardian' articles 25th February 1997, 'Global warming fears add impetues to solar power; 26th April 1997, 'Plague fear from global warming and city sprawl;' 'New Internatonalist' June 1997, Issue on 'South Pacific;' pp.20,21. 'Earth Matters' - Friends of the Earth, Summer 1997.

6 Scene of catastrophic disaster in December 1984. Over 6000 killed by poisonous gas escaping from a chemical plant in India.

7 Location of world's largest nuclear disaster in 1986. Many immediate deaths, with devasting medium and long term human and environmental damage. Note also Kader toy factory fire in Thailand of 1995, when 188 died. (World Development Movement 'Spur' August/September 1995).

8 See, for example, 'Guardian' article 22nd March 1997, 'Those in peril on the sea.'

9 For example 'More middle managers on the fiddle' - 'Guardian' 5th June 1995.

10 Luke 12 v.15, Matthew 6 v.19, Matthew 6 v.24.

11 John 13 v.34, 15 v.12.

12 I John 3 v.17.

13 'A 1988 survey indicated that the average annual income of the Chief Executive Officer of a typical major Japanese corporation was...only three times that of an ordinary white-collar worker nearing retirement...Furthermore, it is often the case in Japan that, before a large company asks the unions to freeze wages, or accept redundancies, top managers take a 10-20% cut in salary.'
(Industry Churches Forum consultation September 1994 - Mr. Sadaaki Numata of the Japanese embassy). The first factor is mentioned by Will Hutton in 'The State we're in;' Vintage '96 p.270. Note also 'Traidcraft,' (Kingsway, Gateshead, Tyne and Wear NE11 ONE) annual review '95/'96, indicating salary ratio of 2.75 between highest and lowest paid employees.

14 'We gave away a fortune,' Magil and Slepian. New Society Publications; Philadelphia, 1992.

15 Kingsley Hall, Powis Road, London E3 3HJ.

16 As in 'Voluntary Service Overseas,' 317, Putney Bridge Road, London SW15 2PN, 'Community Service Volunteers,' 237, Pentonville Road, London N1 9NJ, numerous Christian, and other service organisations.

17 'Traidcraft,' for example, as referred in note 13.

18 Christian, and many other, monastic orders.

19 I Chronicles 29 v.10-14.

20 See Postscript note 3.

11 Personal matters

Note

1 As for example, indicated in Jeremiah 9 v.23,24.

2 For example - Beyond Hatred, ed. Guthrie Moir,

Lutterworth 1969; An Evil Cradling, Brian Keenan, Hutchinson 1992; Uganda Holocaust, Wooding and Barnett, Pickering and Inglis 1980; Long Walk to Freedom, Nelson Mandela, Abacus 1995; amongst many others.

3 Isaiah 40 v.31.

4 Book of Common Prayer; second collect at Morning Prayer.

5 Luke 9 v.24,25.

6 See Galatians 5 v.13, also Philippians 3 v. 17-21, and Luke 11 v.24-26.

7 I Timothy 6 v.10.

8 II Timothy 1 v.7.

9 I Corinthians 6 v.19.

12 Glory

Note

1 Romans 11 v.36. See also Psalm 115 v.1; Daniel chap. 3; Acts 12 v.20-23; I Corinthians 10 v.31.

2 As in Hymns Ancient and Modern, New Standard 240.

3 See CMS Newsletter no. 531 Sept./Nov. 1996.

13 And if not?

Note

1 Church of England Alternative Services Book; Confession at Morning and Evening Prayer and Holy Communion.

2 As in Genesis 18 v.25; Psalm 9 v.16-20; 96 v.13; 98 v.9; 99 v.4; 103 v.6; Isaiah chap.1; Amos chaps 1,2; Micah chaps 1-3.

3 II Samuel 24 v.14; Daniel 9 v.9.

4 Matthew 5 v.48.

5 Forgiveness of sins is a clear Gospel theme, culminating in Luke 23 v.34.

6 As in Matthew 25 v.14-30 = Luke 19 v.12-27; also Matthew 25 v.31-46.

7 See Romans 2 v.4, 6 v.1,2; I Corinthians 10 v.9; Galatians 5 v.13; I Peter 2 v.16.

8 Luke 5 v.8, 19 v.1-10; John 3 v.19.

9 Mark 3 v.6, 12 v.12.

10 Matthew 25 v.31,32; Romans 2 v.1-16; II Corinthians 5 v.10; I John 4 v.17.

11 I Corinthians 4 v.5.

12 Matthew 25 v.1-13.

13 Matthew 25 v.26-28.

14 Romans 14 v.12.

15 Matthew 27 v.11-26 = Mark 15 v.2-5 = Luke 23 v.2-5.

16 John 3 v.15,16.

17 Philippians 3 v.20,21; I Corinthians 2 v.9; Revelation 4 v.1-6.

18 Matthew 22 v.23-33 = Mark 12 v.18-27 = Luke 20 v.27-40; also I Corinthians 15 v.42-50; Revelation 21 v.4,27.

19 Revelation 21 v.9-21; 14 v.10.

20 Whole thrust of Revelation from 4 v.1-6 to 22 v.1-5.

21 Romans 2 v.8; I Timothy 2 v.4; Revelation 14 v.5.

22 Chap. 4 p.31, 32.

23 Hymns Ancient and Modern New Standard 65.

24 Galatians 6 v.7.

25 Matthew 25 v.14-30 = Luke 19 v.12-27; also Matthew 25 v.31-46; Luke 12 v.13-21.

26 For example John 15 v.1-10; Acts 14 v.22; Romans 11 v.22; Colossians 1 v.23; Hebrews 3 v.12-15.

27 I Corinthians 10 v.12.

28 Matthew 7 v.21-23, 24 v.36-51.

29 Leviticus 19 v.1,2 and whole chapter.

30 I Corinthians 11 v.17-22.

31 I Corinthians 11 v.30.

32 For example John 11 v.13, concerning Lazarus.
33 See chap.2 p.11.
34 I Corinthians 1 v.30.
35 Isaiah 64 v.6; see also Romans 7 v.18.
36 Ephesians 4 v.13.
37 James 1 v.7,8.
38 Article by J.K. Galbraith, 'Guardian' 27th August 1991, 'Finding Freedom in a world of Poverty.'

Postcript

1 Philippians 2 v.5-13.
2 Matthew 5 v.24.
4 Romans 11.v36.
3 This suggests taking steps towards changing attitudes and actions. There is nothing hard and fast about what follows; the notes are simply practical suggestions for working on the convictions laid out in the book.
a Have a fresh, or renewed, grip on Jesus Christ, allowing Him to have a fresh grip upon ourselves. This is best approached through contact with a person who has shown such attitudes, with experience, over some time. But it is also vital to have a fresh awareness of at least part of the New Testament, for example, Luke's gospel and the Acts of the Apostles, with one of the shorter letters, for example, Philippians, Colossians or the first letter of John. (See, in this book, chapters 1-3).
b. Keep the renewed vision fresh, by joining with other Christians locally, and in personal reading of the Bible (See chapters 6,12).
c. Work at bringing a spiritual perspective to bear upon everyday life. (See chapters 4,5).
d. Take decisive steps, in however limited ways at first, away from the domination of materialism in personal outlook, and daily life. (See chapters 10, 11, 8 and 13).
e. With renewed vision, and released resources, spiritual, mental and material, make fresh moves in loving your

neighbour as yourself, both spiritually and materially. Starting points for action will open up as steps are taken. Others are suggested in the book. (Chapters 7,8,9,10)

Think eternally; act presently.
Think globally; act locally.
Think humanly and spiritually;
act personally;
and all to be done in the name of,
and to the glory of
Jesus Christ,
who is the same, yesterday, today, and for ever.

THE ENTROPY TANGO

The Entropy Tango

by M. Moorcock

Hermann.

Kosinsky.

I. The Entropy Tango
At the Time Centre
The Birthplace of Harlequin.

2. Pierrot on the Moon
Harlequin's Courtship
Columbine's Song

3. Pierrot's Song of Positive Thinking
The Nature of the Catastrophe
Through the Megaflow

Der alte Moor.

4. Every Gun Plays its own Tune
Pierrot in the Roof Garden
Harlequin and Columbine's Carol

5. Harlequin Transformed
Pierrot and Columbine's Reconciliation
Song of Entropy Tango (reprise)
Columbine's Lament.

Characters:

Nestor Makhno
Una Persson.
Major Nye
Mrs Cornelius
Catherine Cornelius
Jerry Cornelius
Frank Cornelius
Sebast Auchinek
Shaky Mo Collier
Col. Pyat.

MICHAEL MOORCOCK

THE ENTROPY TANGO

A Comic Romance

Pictures by Romain Slocombe
Lyrics by Michael Moorcock

NEW ENGLISH LIBRARY

For Pete Pavli
(who did most of the music)

First published in Great Britain by New English Library, Barnard's Inn, Holborn, London EC1N 2JR, a division of Hodder and Stoughton Ltd, in 1981

ISBN 0 450 04886 1

Design Tim McPhee

Design and production in association with Book Production Consultants, Cambridge

Photoset by Manuset Ltd, Baldock, Herts.
Printed in Great Britain by Thetford Press.
Bound by Pitman Press, Bath.

Contents

List of Illustrations

1

INTRODUCTION

Entropy Tango

My pulse rate stood at zero
When I first saw my Pierrot
My temperature rose to ninety-nine
When I beheld my Columbine

  Sigh, sigh, sigh . . .
For love that's oft denied
  Cry, cry, cry . . .
My lips remain unsatisfied
  I'm yearning so for my own Pierrot
As we dance the Entropy Tango!

  I'll weep, weep, weep
Till he sweeps me off my feet
  My heart will beat, beat, beat,
And my body lose its heat
  Oh, life no longer seems so sweet
Since that sad Pierrot became my beau
  And taught me the Entropy Tango

  So flow, flow, flow . . .
As the rains turn into snow
  And it's slow, slow, slow . . .
As the colours lose their glow . . .
  The Winds of Limbo no longer blow
For cold Columbine and her pale Pierrot
  As we dance the Entropy Tango!

At the Time Centre

Calling in and calling out
Crawling through the chronosphere
Will all members please report
To their own centuries
Where they will receive instructions
As to how to progress

This is an emergency signal
To all chrononauts and
Members of the Time Guild
Mrs Persson calls a conference
Code-name Pierrot—code-name Harlequin
Come in please—this is Columbine

Come in please, this is Columbine
Come in please, this is Columbine
Come in please, this is Columbine
Come in please, this is Columbine
Columbine calling,
Calling
Calling out . . .

The Birthplace of Harlequin

In this ancient time-fouled city discredited gods do brood
On all the imagined insults which down the aeons they've
  received
It is a place of graves and here dreams are destroyed
Dreams are brought from all the corners of the world
To be crushed or ripped or melted down
Into a healthy cynicism
Here are tricksters born
And fools divested of enchantment

This is where Pierrot is killed
And from his flesh Harlequin created
To race across the world, laughing at nothing,
Laughing at everything
Laughing at his pain,
Laughing at the tired gods who bore him
Here in this city, this city of shades,
This city of irony bereft of imagination
This city of suppression
This city of pragmatism
Where the jesters weep
And the tricksters scheme
Parading in motley
Too afraid to scream,
Too wary to acknowledge love
Unless love's made a game.
A game which they can win.

Here, in this city of swaggering fantasticos, of calculated gallantry
Was Harlequin the Trickster born, to go about the world, to win
To attract; to display an easy cleverness; to lie and to deceive
To show what shallow things are dreams, and promises impossible to keep
And should he meet with frankness, unashamed honesty
Back to this city Harlequin may flee
To be replenished, armed afresh by his weary masters,
The gorgeous gods of disharmony . . .

1. FOR ONE DAY ONLY: TWO MIGH-TY EMPIRES CLASH

1

Greta Garbo is here seen in the climax scene of "Queen Christina" after she has forsaken her throne and is sailing away with her dead lover . . . one of the greatest performances of her career, in a story and settings which are sombre and admirably suited to her strong dramatic powers.

Shots from Famous Films, No. 19, issued by Gallagher Ltd, c. 1937

"I STILL BREED and buy a little, but I rarely, these days, kill." Balancing a pink gin in his thin hand Major Nye settled into the light-blue plush and pulled a photograph from his top pocket. Behind him was a wide observation window. He turned to glance through the clouds at what could be Transcarpathia below. There were only four passengers in the airship's lounge and two of them spoke no language known to him, so he was anxious to keep Mrs Persson nearby. As she approached, he said: "What do you make of this couple?"

It was too hot. Una Persson regretted her Aran turtle-neck, and she tugged a little at the top so that her pearls clicked. "Ukrainians." She smiled at them. They were shy. "They'll probably have Russian."

"Russki." The woman responded with an alacrity which dismayed her thick-set husband. "Da." She wore a mixture of national dress (blouse and boots; a brown suit of the rather severe cut favoured east of Warsaw). He wore motley: a short red leather overcoat, tweed trousers, two-tone shoes.

"Then they're anarchists." Major Nye looked curiously at the pair before finishing his gin. "Do you think they'll last?"

Una was amused. They were probably rich emigrants. "What's the alternative? Bolshevism?"

"Jolly good." Major Nye was also feeling the heat. He adjusted the left sleeve of his uniform jacket. "Do you hunt, Mrs Persson? At all?"

"Not seriously."

Nodding at Una, perhaps embarrassed, the Ukrainians replaced their empty glasses on the bar. They offered a muted 'Dasvedanya' to the steward, and climbed up the open oak staircase to the main deck.

"Another half-an-hour and we'll be in Prague." Major Nye was regretful. He had been glad to find an acquaintance aboard. "Have you someone waiting for you? From the Consulate?"

"Do you know Prague?"

"Not since the war." Major Nye smiled like a wistful conspirator. "I change in Dublin for Toronto." He had come from Hong Kong, with a Bradshaw's under his arm, hopping ships after he had missed the *Empress of Canada* on her weekly express run. By taking this flight via China and the Russian Republic he had actually saved himself several hours, since the *Empress* followed an All-Red Route established by sea-going vessels in the century's early years. Now, more than four decades later, big British airships might still moor at aerodromes built on sites of ancient coaling stations. But the Air Ship *Lady Charlotte Lever* belonged to E&A Lines who were concerned less with national prestige than with international competition. Built ten years before, in 1938, she had been one of the first so-called 'China clippers', lifting 31,000 tons and capable of almost 200 mph with a following wind. She stopped at only two British ports, making a six-day round-trip from Nagasaki, via Seoul, Peking, Samarkand, Tiflis, Kiev, Prague, Brussels and Liverpool, to Dublin; challenging the Russian, German and American lines who had previously dominated this territory. Major Nye felt unsafe in her. He preferred more stately, old-fashioned craft.

Mrs Persson sat on the opposite couch.

"I was hoping for a few days leave." Major Nye passed her the photograph. It showed an elderly grey being led from its stall by a smiling, plump young woman. "That's my horse, Rhodes. My daughter, Elizabeth. She runs the stable now. Near Rye. Poor old chap. He's dying. I wanted to be with him."

She was touched. She returned the photograph. "A fine animal."

"He was." Major Nye stroked his white moustache with the tip of a nicotine-stained finger. "Tempus fugit, eh? To the best of us." His pale eyes stared hard out of the airship as if he willed back tears.

Una rose. "I'll have to leave you, I'm afraid. Bags."

"Of course." He stood to attention. "We'll doubtless meet again. That's the Service. Here today and gone tomorrow."

"Or vice versa." Una shook hands. She brushed the short chestnut hair from her face. "Good luck in Canada."

"Oh, it's nothing serious, I'm sure."

When she had left he realised he still held Rhodes's photograph. He tucked it into a top pocket which he firmly buttoned. Moving between empty chairs, glass in hand, he straightened his jacket, looking behind the bland barman at the mirror. As he set his glass on mock tortoiseshell the ship gave one of those peculiar shudders which usually meant unexpected wind resistance and the glass clicked against a chrome railing before Major Nye's bony fingers could close on it. The lounge darkened. They sailed through heavy cloud and the sun and land had been completely obscured. The steward prepared a new drink.

"Not long now, sir, before we go down."

2

ESTONIA obtained her independence in 1918. The colours of her distinctive national flag, a horizontal tricolour: Blue for the sky, mutual confidence and fidelity; black for the nourishing soil and the dark past of the country; white for the winter, hope for the future . . .
National Flags and Arms, No. 16, issued by John Player and Sons, c. 1937

"CAN THIS, AFTER all, be the Golden Age?" Una turned from the first floor window and the bleak Notting

Hill street. She had arrived in England less than three hours ago and had come directly here, hoping to find her lover Catherine, but only Catherine's mother had been in.

"I could do wiv a bit of it," said Mrs Cornelius, mopping sweat, "if, o' course, there's some ter spare." She laughed and looked at the clock. "Sovereigns." On the wireless, briefly, an announcer spoke of chaos in the outskirts of Toronto, but Mrs Cornelius stretched a fat arm and turned the knob to find Ted Heath and his Music who were half-way through *Little Man You've Had A Busy Day*. "Thass an old one." She was nostalgic. "When did that come art? Four? Five years ago? Makes yer fink." She returned to her horrible armchair and lowered herself into it, magazines and newspapers rising and falling around her as if she sank back into some polluted sea. "Bin abroad agin, 'ave yer, love?"

"Here and there," said Una equably. She felt both terror and affection for Catherine's mother. The woman seemed to maintain an ageless decrepitude, utterly at one with her preferred environment. The paint on her face might have been put on that day or ten years before and was flaking to exactly the same degree as the paint on her woodwork. "Had a holiday this year, Mrs C?"

"Nothin' ter speak of. We went ter 'Astings, ther Kernel an' me, fer Easter. It pissed darn." She spoke of her boyfriend, 'the old Pole', who ran a second-hand-clothes shop in Portobello Road. "Spent the 'ole time on ther bleedin' pier. When we wasn't in ther pub." She raised her tea to her lips. "'*E* was dead miserable, o' course. But *I* enjoyed meself."

"That's the main thing." Leaning against the damp draining board Una read the *Manchester Guardian* she had bought at Croydon. Makhno's 'insurgent army', consisting predominantly of Ukrainian settlers, Indians, Métis (pushed out of their homelands), and some disaffected Scots and French, had won control of rural Ontario. The main cities, including Ottawa and Toronto, were still in the hands of the R.C.M.P. It was stalemate of sorts, since Makhno's army was defensive and would only respond to attacks, while the Mounties were unwilling to begin any action which would result in bloodshed. Una found this funny: Anarchism matched against Liberalism in a classic dilemma. But London was upset, which was why she had been ordered home from Prague.

The door opened. Catherine hurried in from the landing. "Oh!" She was pleased. She wiped rain from her beautiful face and tugged off a headscarf to reveal curly blonde hair. "How long have you got?"

"I have to be off tomorrow."

After some hesitation, they embraced.

3

The "Riders of the Plains", hero-worshipped by readers of wild North-West literature as the "Mounties", were formed in 1873 for the purpose of maintaining the law in sparsely populated parts of the Dominion. Recruiting was commenced in 1874, and early in their history their courage and integrity established order and respect in the Indian territory. Although tasks are less picturesque than in the bad old days, diverse activities still include punishment for wrongdoing and the enforcement of Federal Law throughout Canada.

Soldiers of the King, No. 21, issued by Godfrey Phillips Ltd, c. 1937

BY THE TIME Una got there Toronto had capitulated and Makhno's people were everywhere, distributing characteristic anarchist leaflets, informing the citizens of their many rights. Confusingly, numbers of Makhnovischini wore red coats borrowed from disarmed Mounties and a few had even taken the full uniform, though usually with modifications. She went directly to the downtown offices of the Canadian Pacific Airship Company where Major Nye had the responsibility of processing applications from those who had elected to

leave. The building was surprisingly quiet, though long lines of middle-aged men and women stood outside it. In the lobby soft-spoken Mounties patiently kept order, manning desks formerly occupied by CPAC clerks. Una was shown straight through to Major Nye's office. It had been decorated in the clean, stripped-pine-and-hessian style favoured by most Canadian executives, while tasteful scenic paintings had been positioned along the walls at regular intervals.

The large window looked out over Lake Shore Avenue and the harbour beyond, where other refugees were crowding onto boats and ships which would take them to emergency immigration centres at Wilson on the American side. The United States had agreed reluctantly to establish temporary camps, but already, Una knew, they were urging independent Ottawa and Britain to send military ships to the province, to oust the 'illegal anarchist government', as they insisted on terming it. Makhno and his insurgents evidently represented the popular interest and since the Mounties had made no attempt to defend the cities by force of arms (on instructions from London, who were anxious to negotiate with Makhno as soon as possible) there was technically no excuse to send either troops or aerial gunboats. The idea of a Commonwealth in which all were free and willing partners had to be maintained, London felt, above everything.

"I mean Britain has always been the guardian of liberal democracy," said Major Nye, after he had offered her a chair and ordered some coffee. "We can't resort to the methods of Frenchmen or Russians, can we? Or even Americans. We've an example to set. There hasn't been a serious clash of arms in the Empire for thirty years. Everything has been settled by discussion, arbitration, common sense. I can't see what they want with anarchism, can you? I mean, the difference seems so marginal!"

"They think," said Una, "of our democracy as capital's last attempt to survive. In, as it were, disguise."

"There'll always be conflicting interests." He remained bewildered. "Besides, there have been socialist governments for years!"

"Makhno's socialism is a trifle more extreme." Una took the coffee cup with a smile of thanks to the girl who came in. "They want me here, I gather, to parley with the Little Father."

"Not many of our people have had much to do with him." Major Nye returned his attention to the lines on the quays. "You know him well, don't you?"

Una came to stand beside him. "We're always looking out of windows, you and I, aren't we?"

He had not heard her. "This is what comes of giving autonomy to Quebec," he said. "Canada simply isn't India."

4

DRUMMOND. Motto "Gang warily". Badge, Wild Thyme. The ancestor is said to have been Maurice, a Hungarian, who accompanied Edgar Atheling into Scotland, and obtained from Malcolm III the lands of Drymen. This patriotic clan fought with distinguished bravery at Bannockburn.

Highland Clans, No. 3, issued by John Player and Sons, c. 1920

HALF TORONTO SEEMED deserted now. Named like Ontario's towns and villages for their nostalgic associations with Britain, the quiet streets of the suburbs, with big shady trees and pleasant lawns, were almost wholly taken over by the insurgents to whom the references—Albion Road, Uxbridge Avenue, Ballantrae Drive—were all but meaningless. Certain self-conscious Métis and Indians, who occupied houses on their own farms, had pitched wigwams in the parks and were holding councils with local inhabitants. The smiling residents still found it hard not to be eagerly condescending to those now regarding them with cheerful contempt. The majority of Torontonians remaining behind were the same nationalist sympathisers who had elected the provincial government which had so quickly disappointed their hopes. In reaction, the rural people had made the ageing anarchist their spokesman.

The shirt-sleeved driver of the Rolls landau pointed ahead to a large timber-built house at the end of the road and said in Ukrainian: 'Batko Makhno headquarters. See.'' A black flag had been stuck in a chimney and was visible over the surrounding pines and birches. Una was delighted by the introduction of so much incongruity into this Home Counties dream of Utopia.

Makhno was leaning on the veranda frame as she walked up the crazy-paving towards him. He was greyer and thinner than when she had last seen him during his successful campaigns against the Russian Republic in the thirties, but he had the same alert, sardonic eyes. He wore a jaunty astrakhan cap, a dragoon jacket in blue and gold, civilian jodhpurs and soft Ukrainian boots. Almost as a concession to his past he sported two large automatic pistols and a sabre. Although cured of TB he retained the slight flush often associated with the disease. He burst into laughter as they embraced. "We've done it again. Only this time it was easier!"

"That's what I've come to see you about," said Una.

They entered the cool open-plan interior, full of woollen scatter-rugs of Indian design, polished boards and low furniture in muted colours. A well-fed blonde Canadian girl with a smooth skin which needed to be tanned to look agreeable said brightly: "Hi! I'm Nestor's new wife."

"My twenty-first," said Makhno. He put an arm about her upright shoulders. "This," he said of Una, "is my oldest friend and closest enemy."

"We've heard of you, Miss Persson," said the girl, "even in Toronto."

With a slightly studied display of carelessness, Makhno dropped into a beige armchair near the rough granite fireplace. "Have you come to bargain, Una?"

"In a way. You know you've upset the Americans."

"Certainly. Is that difficult? And the Russians. Our Alaska raid."

"Exactly. Two airships. But London's under a lot of pressure."

"We've already been promised autonomy. The same terms as agreed with Montreal. Everyone is happy."

"The Russians are claiming that by recognising you Canada has violated the Alaskan treaty. Therefore they feel entitled to retaliate. The US would see such a move as the first step in an attempt by Russia to gain further North American territory."

Makhno laughed. "What are you suggesting? Some sort of second Great War?"

"You know there are tensions."

"But no one would risk so much over one tiny event!"

"They see it as the spread of anarchy. First the Ukraine.

Then Andalusia. Argentina. Kwan Tung. You know what emotions are involved. Perhaps if you appeared initially to modify your programmes, give them a 'liberal' slant . . .?"

The girl spoke, smiling earnestly, with self-conscious passion, as she tried to persuade Una to a point of view unfamiliar only to herself: "You have to see, Mrs Persson, that this 'liberalism' is the same sentiment people reserve for the beasts they keep for food. Their love of the masses is love for the lambs they shall one day slaughter! The impulse remains authoritarian, no matter what it pretends to be. Bolsheviks and capitalists. They're identical."

The phone rang. Makhno went to it. He listened, his smile growing broader as his eyes became sad. He shrugged, replacing the receiver. "There you are, Mrs Persson. British ships have been sighted over Winnipeg. A large fleet. Evidently on their way here. It's the finish. Obviously. Is it my fault do you think? Have I fallen into the trap I always warned you about? The fallacy of 'history'. The myth of 'precedent'?"

"What shall you do?"

"Oh, I shall avoid bloodshed at all costs. I shall advise the army not to fight in cities, where civilians will be hurt. We shall have to do our fighting in the countryside." He sighed. "Where we belong."

"But you'll continue to defend the revolution?"

"If people wish it. If not, I'll make a run for it. Not for the first time."

The pale girl was confused. She squatted on her haunches in the middle of the room, holding her long hair away from her ears. "Oh, my god. This is *Canada*! We've gone too far!"

Una was much harsher than Makhno. "Your problem came when the Mounties changed their motto from *Mantien Le Droit* to *Mea virtute me involvo*."

Makhno interposed. "If only it could have been *Omnia vincit amor, et nos cedamus amori*." He looked regretfully down at the blonde. "It'll be good to be on horseback again. I hate machines."

"It's your one weakness, I'm afraid," said Una.
The silence became uncertain.

5

CORONATION OF WILLIAM IV AND QUEEN ADELAIDE.

The Coronation of William IV took place on Sept. 8th, 1831, and was celebrated with less magnificence than usual on the ground of economy. The Queen's silver crown was set with jewels which were her own property, and were afterwards returned to her, as she desired that there should be no unnecessary expense incurred.

The Coronation Series, No. 31, issued by W.D. & H.O. Wills, c. 1936

THERE WAS, IT seemed, to be no consolation in England. Over tea in Derry and Toms roof garden ('their' place) Catherine told Una of her engagement to Mr Koutrouboussis, the ship-owner. "His naturalisation came through last week and he popped the question."

"You don't love him." Una was bleak.

"I love what he represents."

"Slavery!"

"Freedom. I shan't be his only interest."

The sun shone on large mock-silver cutlery, on sturdy china, on rock-cakes and scones. Beyond all this, in tiny artificial pools, marched fastidious pink flamingos against a background of box and privet.

"And anyway," Catherine continued, "I need the security."

"I'm giving up the Service."

"I think you should." She realised she had missed the implication and melted. "You know how much I love you."

"Going back into the profession," Una said.

Catherine put a hand on Una's hand. "You'd still be away a lot, dear. But now we can go on meeting—having lovely secret times. You already have more men-friends than I do. That anarchist was one, wasn't he?"

It was true. Una removed her hand in order to open her bag.

"I really do think men are our superiors in almost every way," said Catherine. She smiled. "Of course, we are their superiors in one area—we can handle them without them realising it. But don't you feel the need to give yourself up to a man? To think you could die for him, if necessary? Oh, Una, there's nothing like self-sacrifice!"

"Jesus Christ," said Una flatly. "He's done it again."

6

MEADOW BROWN (Epinephele ianira). This species is the most abundant of all British Butterflies, occurring throughout the British Islands as far north as the Orkneys, and frequenting every meadow, lane, wood and waste land, from the middle of June until the middle of October. The Meadow Brown is one of the few butterflies that appear regardless of the weather, flying during dull stormy days, as well as in the hottest sunshine. At night it roosts amongst the foliage of trees, and also on low-growing plants. The life of the caterpillar of this butterfly extends over a period of about 250 days. Expanse of wings 2 inches.

British Butterflies, No. 15, issued by W.D. & H.O. Wills, c. 1935

EXACTLY A WEEK after she had had her meeting with Makhno, on Sunday 27th June 1948, Una Persson accepted Major Nye's invitation. She took a train to Rye and a cab from the station to the Jacobean house whose ornamental gardens had been almost entirely converted into fruit and vegetable beds and whose stables were now run as a commercial enterprise by Elizabeth Nye, one of the major's two daughters. His son was away at school. His wife had been confined to her rooms for three or four years.

It was a very hot day. Summer flowers, arranged in dense clusters and grown for profit, gave off a thick scent which brought Una a trace of euphoria as well as sad memories of Makhno's fall. The nurse who looked after Mrs Nye directed Una to the stables. Elizabeth had taken a group of children for a trek. Major Nye, in a worn tweed hacking jacket, darned pullover, moleskin trousers and old wellingtons, stood outside a stall over which the name 'Rhodes' had been engraved in poker-work. He was feeding an ancient grey horse handfuls of grass from a bucket at his feet. The horse had watering, bloodshot eyes and its nostrils were encrusted with mucus. It laid its ears back as Una approached, causing Major Nye to turn.

''Mrs Persson! Wonderful! This is Rhodes.'' The smell

from the stall was strong, tinged with sickness.

Una, who had no special fondness for horses, stretched a hand to stroke its nose but it moved, refusing contact. "I'm afraid he's a one-man horse. I'm so glad the Canadian business is over. Have you heard anything of our friend, Makhno?"

Rather closer to self-pity than she would have liked, Una said: "He's gone where the Southern cross the Yellow Dog."

"Eh?"

"On his way to South America, I heard."

"Best place for him. Plenty of room for political experiments there, eh?"

"Not according to everyone's thinking."

"At least we avoided a Big One. You see I remember the Great War. I was at Geneva in 1910. Eighteen years old." He smiled and patted Rhodes's nose. "We don't want another, do we?"

"Perhaps the cost of peace has become a bit too high?"

"It's never too high, my dear. I speak as an army man." He handed her the bucket. "Rhodes can't graze for himself any more. Shaky on his pins. Come and help me pick some grass on that bit of lawn over there." He reached down to pluck a muddy *Telegraph* from a pile near the stall's gate. "Kneel on this. Have you got any older clothes?"

"Not with me."

"We'll find you something. You're staying a week or two?"

"If that's all right."

"All right for me." He chuckled. She realised that she had never seen him happy before. "They've allowed you some leave, have they? You've earned it. Makhno would never had given in to anyone else."

"Possibly." Una was reluctant to continue this line. "But I'm not on holiday. I've resigned. I've decided to go back to the stage. I'm tired of diplomacy. It's a bit depressing. Or perhaps I'll try films."

"Brave girl," said Major Nye. "You've sacrificed too much already."

For a moment she rebelled, resenting his approval. Then she walked over to a lawn already practically bare, and began to tug up grass.

Major Nye joined her. He bent with difficulty. There was a tearing sound as he pulled roots and earth. "They all say I should have him shot. But I can't do it, you know. I love him. Elizabeth," he smiled with some pride, "says he'll be the death of me."

The shadow of an airship, going from Croydon to the continent, passed over them rapidly. They heard the distant drone of engines.

"It's the beginning of the end," murmured Major Nye.

"It always is," said Una.

2

DEVELOPMENT (a)

Pierrot on the Moon

They didn't tell me
That breathing was so difficult.
I can't say I think
much
Of the scenery
I wish I was back
in my home again
—They've left me behind . . .

It seemed a good
idea at the time
Just me—Harlequin and
Columbine
—But they slipped off soon
And here I am
Stranded on the bloody
moon . . .

Next time things will be
different
And I'll know the score
I'll bring at least an
oxygen tent
And a good deal more
besides
Bacon, eggs and bread
And a telescope . . .

And I'll buy returns as well
There's no bloody ticket office
Or a gentleman's lavatory
Or a deck chair to be had
And every time I take a step—
I bounce . . .

They said it'd be just like
Brighton beach
Dodgems and roundabouts
Candy floss and sticks of rock
Though not so many crowds
Try and get a donkey ride
That's all I've got to say . . .

Harlequin's Techniques of Courtship

If I let her see my love
Will she also see my pain
And flee from it
As I would flee?

And if I pulled my domino
From my eyes
Would she then know
How much of Pierrot's
Left in Harlequin?

And if I told her of my yearning
Would her body
Cease to burn for me
Instead would she give me
Only sympathy
And mistress turn to wife?

And if I swore eternal love
In anything but
A tone of insincerity
Would I alert her
To involvement
Turn her thoughts
Away from lust?

And if I wept upon her breast
And spoke of fears
Of ghosts and death
Would she withdraw
Her favours from me
Choosing silly Pierrot
For a husband
And shunning me?

No, I can only speak of bright lies
Offer only flattery
Tell her that there are no others
But let her think that many follow
That I may be gone tomorrow
Insecurity is all she wants
From me.
Madam, I present myself:
Sir Harlequin—
I bring you Sin . . .

Columbine Confused

On the banks of Time's river
Two lovers await me
As the flood takes me by
They reach out their hands
Pierrot and Harlequin
Weeping they greet me
The stream bears me onward
Future and Past . . .

Which shall I choose?
Oh, I am confused . . .
Often amused and
Constantly torn . . .
Down the long centuries
They have pursued me
Courted and cursed me
For what I am

Gravity holds me
In sweet indecision
Between Sun and Moon
To each I'm attracted
Pierrot and Harlequin
Loser and Trickster
Laughing they beckon
As the years flood away

Future and past
Future and past
Future and past
Future and past

As the years flood away
As the years flood away
As they years flood away
Future and past . . .

2. THE KASSAND – RA PENINSULA

1

In which his torment often was so great,
That like a Lyon he would cry and rore,
And rend his flesh, and his owne synewes eat.
His owne deare Vna hearing euermore
His ruefull shriekes and gronings, often tore
Her guiltless garments, and her golden heare,
For pitty of his paine and anguish sore;
Yet all with patience wisely she did beare;
For well she wist, his crime could else be neuer cleare.

Spenser, The Fairie Queene, 1. x. 28.

UNA CONSIDERED HER compact. It was silver, with delicate enamel-work by Brule; one of his last pieces.

"Una."

She shook her head. She refused his confession. His eyes were agony.

"Una."

She replaced the compact, unused, in her patent leather purse. His voice brought her the image of a dark, motionless sea. She drew breath. Makhno had gone on. It had been necessary. His success—what little he expected—depended on the speed of his strategies. Here there was only defeat.

"Una."

He lay in the shadows, on straw. Through the barn door came the hard air of the New Hampshire winter. She could see across the deep, undulating snow the flat outline of a Dutch farmhouse, black against a near-white sky: the isolated birches, the clustering pines. She could hear the muffled sounds of work. It would be dawn in a moment. They would discover him soon. Freezing her face, Una forced herself to look at her ex-comrade. He had seemed so powerful.

"Una." It was like the sound of a dying albatross she had heard on Midway Island in the early 1940s.

One of his hands moved a fraction. To stop her? To beg?

She glanced beyond his head, at the disused harness, the rusty implements: mementos of simpler days. She smoothed the silk of her skirt and swung the purse by its strap; then she placed it carefully on her shoulder. She battled against her particular curse, against mindless altruism. But was it a curse or merely her permanent dilemma?

"Una. They'll kill me."

"No, Jerry." He would probably be interned until after the primaries. She was close to offering reassurance when happily there came a scream from the sky and snow thudded from the roof of the barn as a pirate Concorde passed overhead, pursued by angry Freedom Fighters. It was so cold and she, like him, had no appropriate clothing. "Montreal." she said. "Try to get to Montreal. I'll see you there." She stepped in black, high-heeled court-shoes into the snow. She shuddered. It had been stupid of them to trust the old Kamov.

2

'I'm ready when you are, Senor . . .'

Bob Dylan

"WE BEGIN WITH ambiguities and then we strive to reconcile them through the logic of Art," said Prinz Lobkowitz. "Though these chaps often begin with some simple idea and then try to achieve ambiguity through obfuscation. It won't do." He threw the composition paper on the floor beside the piano and got up. "I blame the academics."

Something rumbled underfoot.

"Well," she said, "it's easy."

She leaned back on the piano stool and swung round to peer at the half-built auditorium. She could see the night sky through the gaps in the tarpaulings covering the shattered glass of the dome; another publicist's broken dream. Lobkowitz, in evening dress, loped forward, tall and thin, looking less well than usual. His attempt, at the invitation of the United States provisional government, to form a cabinet had failed, as he had predicted it would. As a result both he and Una were out of their jobs. She was relieved; he was contemplative. The meeting, which had been held earlier that evening, in the light of candles and oil-lamps, had taken on the air of a funeral reception. Then, gradually, the distinguished old men had drifted away. All but a few of the lamps were out. It was a shame that the damp had affected the murals, from Mozart to Messiaen, on the hastily emulsioned walls. She appreciated the peculiarities of Gregg's style, with its muted colours and shadowy outlines. She had particularly liked the portrait of Schoenberg, on stage for *Pierrot Lunaire* in Berlin, 1912. Now, however, only the composer's raised hands were perceivable, as if he conducted the invisible crowd, here muting the antagonistic shouts, there bringing up the applause. Una wished she could explain her sudden feeling of well-being. She swung to smile at Lobkowitz who shrugged, grinning back at her.

"Ah, well."

"We search so hard for these intense experiences. Then we reject them almost at once."

"Is it because we are frightened?"

3

'There are jewels in the crown of England's Glory;
And every jewel shines a thousand ways
Frankie Howerd and Noel Coward and Garden Gnomes
Frankie Vaughan and Kenneth Horne and Sherlock Holmes
Monty and Biggles and Old King Cole, in the pink or on the dole
Oliver Twist and Long John Silver, Captain Cook and Nellie Dean
Enid Blyton, Gilbert Harding, Malcolm Sargeant, Graham Greene
Gra-ham Gree--ne!'

Max Wall

RELUCTANTLY SHE PICKED up the Ak-47 as Petrov pushed pouches of ammunition across the table at her.

"It suits you," he said. "It's elegant, isn't it?" He lit a thin Danemann cheroot. "You know the rifle?"

"Oh, yes." She checked its action. "I was hoping I'd never see one again." The smoke from his cheroot made her feel sick.

"There's the M-60 . . ." He made a movement towards the rack.

"No, no." She clipped the pouches to the webbing of her lightweight camouflage jacket. She wished that she did not feel quite so comfortable in the gear. It was suspicious. Another cloud of smoke reached her face. She turned away.

"You have everything else?" he asked. "Plenty of mosquito oil?"

"Plenty. Can't you tell?" She wiped her fingers over the back of her greasy wrist.

He stood up.

"Una."

"Oh, no you don't," she said. Helping the wounded was no longer any part of her brief.

"It's you I'm thinking of." He sat down again, staring beyond her at the veldt on the other side of the border. He brightened, pointing. "Look. Vultures."

She did not turn.

He was grinning. "They're a protected species now!"

Carefully she closed the screen door behind her and stood on the veranda, looking up the road for her transport. It was already half-an-hour late. She wondered if something had happened to it. If so, it would mean a long wait while they radioed back to Kinshasa for instructions. She glanced at her watch without reading it. She had never been over-fond of Africa. Somehow, in spite of everything, they had continued to look to Europe for their models. Just like the Americans. And here she was, Britannia Encyclopaedia, returned for the shoot-out.

"You 'ave ter larf, don't yer, miss?" said the black

cockney corporal, holding up the water-can in which someone had shot two small holes. His heavy boots made the veranda shake as he went by, entering Petrov's office to request an order.

She sat down in a khaki deck-chair, placing the rifle at her feet. She stretched her body. The corporal came out again. "Seen anything o' that Captain Cornelius, miss?" he asked, to pass the time. "'E was 'ere before the real trouble started."

She laughed.

"He usually is."

4

In the event of a Sonic Attack, follow these rules:

Hawkwind

AS THE RIVER broadened, she became alert, releasing the safety catch, crouching in the front of the motor launch and studying the jungle.

She gave particular attention to the thicker clumps of reeds on both banks. Soon she had made out the funnels and the bridge of an old steamer which had been ambushed here two years before. *The Little Madam* had keeled over so that she was almost on her side; she was rusty and plants clung to her. As Una watched, a small crocodile emerged from one of the funnels and wriggled into the water. *The Little Madam* had been the last of her kind. She had been carrying missionaries back to the coast when a handful of Eritreans, lost and on the run, had mistaken her for a military vessel and used the rest of their mortars on her.

There was a horrible silence in the jungle, as if every bird and insect had been blown away. Yet the foliage itself was lusher than ever; fleshy and dark green. They approached a bend. A huge stretch of dirty detergent scum came swirling towards them and passed on both sides of the labouring launch.

In the stern Shakey Mo Collier, watched by a listless Makhno who had drunk at least twenty cans of local beer, was jumping up and down throwing carved wooden idols into the scum. "Fuck you! Fuck you!" He drew the idols from a bulky sack, almost as large as himself. He had been upset to learn that his loot had become valueless since the falling off of the tourist trade.

The jungle on the right bank ended suddenly, to be replaced by the great grey terraced complex of Durango Industries' protein processing plant. Una tried not to breath any of the sweet air until they were past. Nearby were the white buildings of the hospital, identified by their red crosses, looking remarkably like reception buildings for the plant. It could have been one of the sleazier suburbs of Los Angeles, with huge, unhealthy palm trees growing all around. Workers on the roofs and gantries paused to watch the launch. Collier waved at them but lost interest when nobody waved back.

"Surly buggers." He threw the last of his idols in their direction.

Makhno was asleep. Una was relieved. If he slept, there was not so much danger of his being sick over the seats. They were already slimy with a variety of filth.

Mo moved along the boat to stand beside her. He lit a papyruska lifted from the tunic pocket of some fallen foe. "There won't be trouble here, will there?"

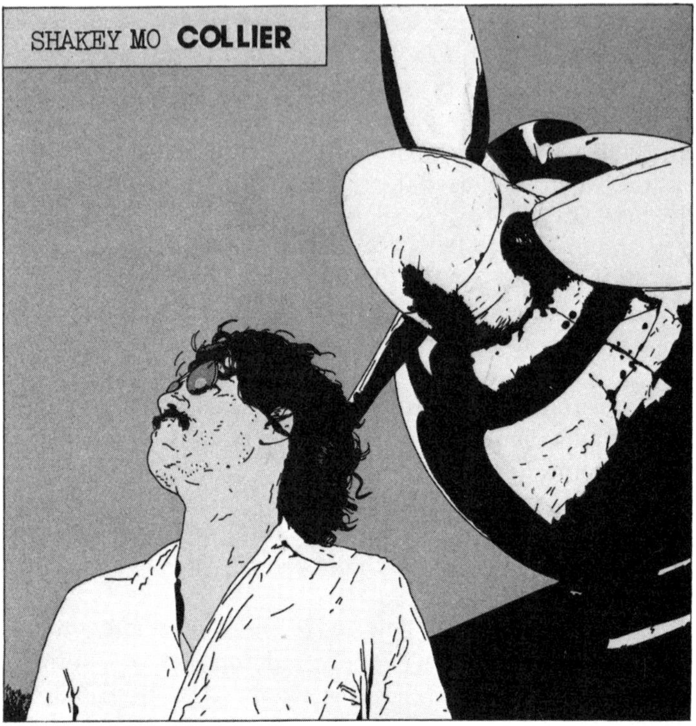

"Unlikely." She wiped her forehead. "The worst is over. It seems we'll be slipping this shipment through, at least."

"I'm making bloody sure I get my bonus in my hand next time." Mo scowled. "In gold." He patted his belt pouch. It bulged. From under the tightly-buttoned flap a few fair hairs emerged.

Una still marvelled at Mo's ability to adopt enthusiastically the ideals and ambitions of any employer. A day or so earlier she had asked him about this. He had replied: "I enjoy being loyal."

He had earned his high reputation. He had even earned his Russian scalps (he would pass them off, of course, as Rhodesian).

For all his awful habits, Una enjoyed his company and she would be sorry to part, but with the successful delivery of their cargo her mission would be over. She was glad the journey had been relatively swift. No amount of disinfectant or perfume could disguise the smell from the hold. It was the last time, she promised herself, that she took over one of Cornelius's jobs. He had only taken this one on so as not to lose face, to protect a reputation for ruthlessness which he had never really deserved.

Collier could continue with the load to Dubrovnik and get a plane home from there if he wanted to. But she would take her chances at the ports. She had had enough.

5

'Isn't it delicious? There's a red sun in the sky! Every time we see it rise, another city dies . . .'

The Deep Fix

"OF COURSE, I remember him from the early, carefree days," said Miss Brunner, smiling up at the crystal ball which turned in the centre of the ceiling of Lionel Himmler's Blue Spot Club. "He was much better company, then." She seemed to imply that that had been before he had met Una. There was nothing superficially attractive about the woman, in her severe suit; her awkward, almost self-conscious way of moving; but Una experienced a strong desire to make love to her, perhaps because she sensed no hint of resonance, no sympathy for Miss Brunner. She tried to suppress the desire; she had a good idea of any consequences resulting from even a brief affair. "When he was still idealistic," continued Miss Brunner. "Weren't we all?"

"I still am," said Una. "It's silly isn't it?" She was shocked at herself. That last remark was unlike her. She admired Miss Brunner's power to produce it.

Miss Brunner gave her a smile which might have been of sympathy or of triumph. "When you're as old a campaigner as me, dear, you won't have time for that sort of thing." She signed to the sour-faced Jewish waiter. As he approached, she pressed a coin in his hand. "Bartok's String Quartet No. 1," she said. She watched him shuffle towards the juke-box. It was her turn to display embarrassment. "I'm feeling a bit reflective. You weren't about in the old days, of course."

"It depends what you mean," said Una.

"Our paths hadn't crossed, at any rate."

"No." Una wondered how, with so many wounds, the woman could continue to function.

Miss Brunner sipped her B&B. From the fur collar of her jacket came the smell of artificial hyacinths. "It's nice to know someone's prepared to fill in for him."

"I'm not exactly filling in," said Una. "I think you have the wrong impression."

"That's what they told me at the Time Centre."

"Auchinek?"

"No, the other one. Alvarez."

"He only enjoyed working with Cornelius."

"That's true."

"Of course you move about more than any of us ever did, don't you?" Miss Brunner continued.

"I suppose I do."

"I envy you your freedom. I'm afraid I'm very old fashioned."

Una was amused by the series of ploys. "Oh, no," she said.

"A terrible reactionary, eh?"

"Not at all."

"I came out of a very different school." Reminiscently Miss Brunner smacked her lips.

"It's just a question of temperaments," said Una.

"Well we each of us see what we're looking for. Especially in a man. That's what 'knowing' someone means, doesn't it?"

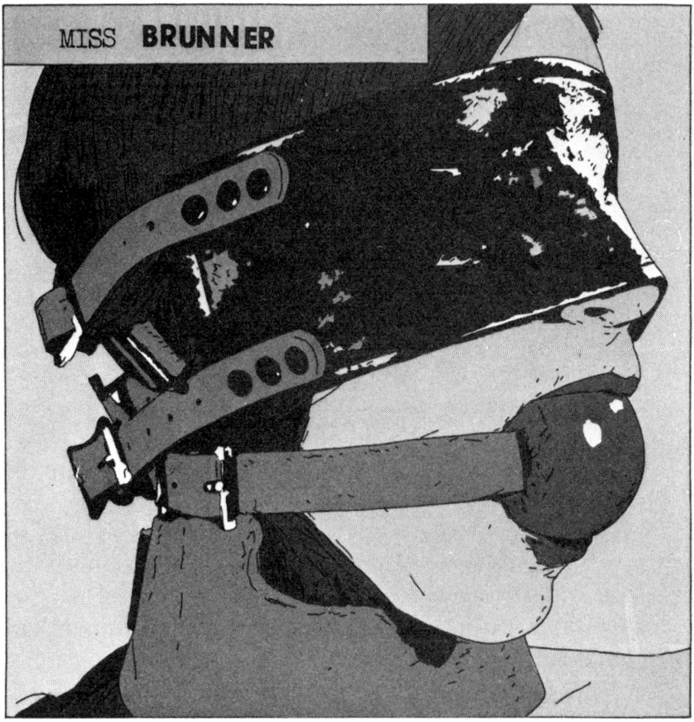

The waiter returned, just as the scratched record began to play.

"I hate Bartok." Miss Brunner picked up the menu. "I find him empty. Vivaldi's what I really like, but the selection's so limited here." She peered savagely up at the waiter. "I'll have the *moules* to begin."

"They're Danish," said the waiter.

"That's right. And then the jugged hare."

"Just an omelette." Una made no attempt to read the menu in the dim light. "And some mineral water."

"Plain omelette? Perrier?"

"Fine."

"Anyway," said Miss Brunner as she handed the menu

to the waiter, "Collier got through with that last consignment. Which about wraps Africa *and* South America up."

"It's a relief."

"It must be for you. I'll be going back to Sweden tomorrow. It's where I live now."

"Yes."

"You know Sweden?"

"Oh, yes."

"Kiruna?"

"Yes."

"It's so peaceful."

Una could not bring herself to confirm any of these desperate affirmations. As a result Miss Brunner became agitated and cast about for another weapon.

"He was never straightforward," she said at length. "That's what I couldn't stand."

"Well, some of us need to create an atmosphere of ambiguity in which we can thrive." Una hoped the response wasn't too evidently direct.

"I don't quite follow you, dear." Miss Brunner had understood all too readily.

Una dispensed with caution. "While others of course try to resolve something from the ambiguity they sense around them. As I say, it's a matter of temperament."

"It's obvious which kind of temperament meets with your approval."

Una smiled. "Yes."

"Speaking for myself, all I want is a quiet life. You didn't get that with Cornelius. He'd foul anything up."

"I probably didn't know him as well as you did."

"Very few people could have done."

Miss Brunner's mussels arrived. She bent her angry head over the bowl.

6

'Their snakeskin suits packed with Detroit muscle . . .'

Bruce Springsteen

IT WAS A relief to enter the car and stuff Ives's First Symphony into the player. It wasn't that she had objected to the Bartok, but Himmler's ancient recordings, always too heavy on the bass and worn and scratched, made everything sound awful. Of course Himmler regarded even this as a concession. When he had opened the nightclub there had been nothing but Phoenix records to play—a label devoted entirely to Hitler's speeches and National Socialist songs. It had been founded by Arnold Leese, best remembered for calling Mosely a 'Kosher Fascist'. This description was more appropriate to Himmler himself who had, in 1944, changed his name from Gutzmann. It was amazing, she thought, as the music began, how she was warming to America since it had rejected her.

She drove through a cleaned-out Soho, her body filled with sound from the quad speakers in the AMC Rambler Station Wagon she currently favoured. She had never been happy with non-automatics, and though this car had seen more exciting days it provided a secure environment in a world which, at present, she preferred for its chaos. The alternatives to chaos were all too suspect. With the volume as high as possible it was impossible to hear either the engine, the air-conditioning or the few other noises from the streets. This and her sound-proofed flat helped her keep herself to herself. Just now, she had no time for civilians or casualties. The abandoned strip-joints and casinos behind her, she made for Hyde Park as the second movement began. It was hard to believe that this was the conception of a seventeen-year-old. She yearned for her lost youth.

Studying her hands as they rested casually on the large steering wheel she almost crashed into the pack of dogs crossing the road in front of her. The dogs were the reason why it was now only safe to drive through the park.

Mongrels, greyhounds, alsatians, chows and poodles ran erratically, snapping at one another's necks and flanks, and disappeared into the shrubs. She turned out of the park into Bayswater Road, passed Notting Hill Gate and the ruins of the apartment buildings blocking Kensington Park Road, made a right into Ladbroke Grove then, eventually, another right into Blenheim Crescent, stopping outside the seedy terraced house she feared so much, even though it sheltered at least one of the people she loved.

She disembarked from the car and locked it carefully, putting the keys into the pocket of her long black trench-coat. She turned up her collar, mounted the cracked steps, found the appropriate bell and pressed it. She leaned on the door, watching the Co-op milkman as his van moved slowly down the other side of the street making deliveries. Una pressed the bell again, knowing that there was bound to be someone up. It was almost seven o'clock. There was no reply. The milkman came back along the other side of the road. Una pressed the bell for the third time. The milkman climbed the steps with five pints in his arms. He set them at her feet. "You're up early," he said. "Who you after?"

"Cornelius," she said.

He laughed, shaking his head as he went away.

Una found his attitude irritatingly mysterious and would have followed him to question him had not she heard a cautious movement on the other side of the door. She stepped out of view, huddling against the broken pillar of the porch. The door rattled. It opened a fraction. A red hand reached for the milk.

"Good morning," said Una.

The hand withdrew, but the door did not shut.

"Mrs Cornelius?"

"Not in," said an unmistakable voice. "Bugger orf."

"It's Una Persson."

The door opened wider and Mrs Cornelius stood there, in curlers, her woolly dressing gown drawn about her, her bleary eyes blinking. "Ha!" she said. "Thort you woz ther

bleedin' milkman.'' Now Una knew why he had laughed. It was why there had been no answer to the bell—the combination of bottles rattling and the doorbell ringing sent Mrs Cornelius automatically to cover. ''Wotcha want?''

''Actually I was looking for Catherine.''

''Actcherly, she ain't 'ere.''

Mrs Cornelius relented. ''Orl right, luv, come in.'' She took two pints from the step, darted a look along the street, admitted Una, closed the door.

Una followed Mrs Cornelius, ascending stone stairs still bearing traces of broken linoleum; they reached a landing and a half-open door. She entered a room full of unattractive smells—cabbage, lavender water, beer, cigarette smoke. It was immediately evident that Catherine had been here recently, for the flat was tidier than usual. The piles of old weeklies were stacked neatly beside the sideboard which, though cluttered with Mrs Cornelius's cryptic souvenirs, lacked the bottles, cans and empty packages she allowed to accumulate while her daughter was not in residence. Mrs Cornelius made for the gas-stove in the far corner, picked up the dented kettle and filled it at the tap over the sink. Una could see through to Mrs Cornelius's small, dark bedroom, with its huge wardrobe, its walls covered with photographs, many of them cut from magazines and newspapers. The other door was shut. This was the door to Catherine's room.

"She's not up yet, lazy bitch," said Mrs Cornelius. "Cuppa tea?" She relaxed and was friendly. Of her children's acquaintances Una was one of the few Mrs Cornelius actually liked. It did not stop Una being afraid of the woman as of nobody else.

"Thanks." Una hated the prospect.

Mrs Cornelius shuffled to her daughter's door and hammered on it. "Wakey, wakey, rise an' shine. 'Ere's yer mate fer yer!"

"What?" It was Catherine.

Mrs Cornelius laughed. "It'd take the 'Orn o' Fate ter get 'er up!"

Suddenly the whole flat smelled of rose water. It was wonderful; a miracle.

"Bugger," said Mrs Cornelius, picking up the fallen bottle.

7

'In the heart of the city, where the alligators roam, I'm a little lost lamb. Ain't got no place to go . . .'

Nick Lowe

SHE FOUND LOBKOWITZ where she had last met him, in the ruined auditorium. Through the speakers of an inefficient tannoy came the familiar last passages of the *Browning Overture.* Then there was silence.

"Browning was a prose Wagner and so was Ives," said the Prinz as he dusted down his tweed fishing suit.

"You've been seeing Cornelius. Is he back?"

"With a vengeance. Though not a very big one."

"Anything I'd recognise."

"You know his penchants . . ."

"I'm not surprised, though I felt he'd crack."

Prinz Lobkowitz seemed to tire of this exchange. He leaned against the warped piano. "There's rarely any danger of that. He just goes dormant."

"I was right to trust my instincts, then?"

"Always, Una."

"They're so hard to rationalise."

"We waste too much time, trying to produce quick resolutions, when usually they're on the way and we don't know it."

She was amused. "The voice of experience!"

"I hope so."

"Anyway, he's better?"

"Yes, he's better. The usual fever. We all suffer from that."

She was not sure this was true of her, but she said: "I was never any good at instant decisions."

"Maybe because you had more to lose than anybody else."

She shrugged.

"Anyway," he continued wistfully, "you received his message?"

"It was unmistakable."

"You didn't have to fulfil all his obligations. He was grateful when he heard."

"There were other people involved. It wasn't his ego I was worried about. He was stupid to have tried for the Presidency. Then, of all times! He was never what you'd call a convinced republican, or a democrat, in the accepted sense."

"Surely, though, that's why he tried?"

She nodded. "I'm glad America's pulled a couple of decent chestnuts out of the fire."

"You couldn't say they deserved it. But I'm sentimental about George Washington, too. Chile, Brazil, the Argentine—their worst crime was a kind of naïve complacency. Admittedly that attitude leads to excesses of brutality in the long run." Lobkowitz yawned. "I've never seen so much jungle on fire. And whole mountains. The

apocalypse. I wish you'd been here.''

''I had to go back to England.''

''I know.'' He was sympathetic. He put a white hand on her shoulder. ''Will you stay for a while now? In New England? You have a place in the Appalachians, haven't you?''

''A couple, at different ends. But there's a sub-tenant in one. He must have been there forty years or more. It would be interesting to see how he's getting on. I haven't aged that much. Not superficially.''

He shook his head. ''You can be very vague at times. Feminine, eh?''

''Is that what it is?'' She bent to kiss his hand. ''Have you got the map? I'd better be going.''

8

''YOU'RE STILL LOOKING ill.'' She tried to disguise any hint of sympathy. She forced her mouth into disapproving lines.

''They don't treat you very well. But I'm grateful, really. It kept me out of the war. I always wondered how I'd do it.''

''You thought you could stop it. You remember?''

He was bashful. ''Oh, yes. So thanks again.''

All his old charm had returned and it was hard for her not to warm to him, as she had first warmed, long ago. The self-pity was gone, for the moment, and he had a good deal of his old style. He fingered the collar of his black car coat, turning the lapels so that they framed his pale face. ''It's cold for spring.''

''The long range forecasts are predicting an Ice Age again.''

''Always a bad psychological sign. And the computers?''

''That we'll all be dead in a year or two.''

He grinned. ''Acute depression often follows a period of frenetic activity. You'll see—in a few months the weather forecasts will give us brilliant summers, plenty of rain for the crops, mild winters, and the computers will be going on about a Golden Age.'' He put his arm around her shoulders. It was awful how quickly her resolutions disappeared. Her struggle lasted less than a second. ''Stick with me, baby,'' he promised, ''and it will always be a golden age somewhere.''

''That's not what you were saying the last time we spoke,'' she reminded him.

''We all suffer from depression occasionally.'' He dismissed the creature he had been. Probably he didn't remember. She began to think that his attitude was the healthiest.

She climbed into the driving seat of the Rambler. He sat beside her, watching her with approval as she started the big car. ''It's a good thing petrol's cheap again. Where are we going? Concord?''

''Yes. First.'' As she started the engine the tape she had been playing came on. He reached to remove it. ''Enough of that classical stuff,'' he said. ''Let's have something romantic and jolly.'' He sorted through the box of cartridges on the seat between them. ''Here we are.''

He slotted the *Holiday Symphony* into the player. ''Much better.''

He leaned back in the car as she drove it down the bumpy track to the empty highway.

''That's what I like about you, Una. You know how to relax.''

3

DEVELOPMENT (b)

Pierrot's Song of Positive Thinking

I'm glad I'm not dead
I'm glad I'm not dead
I'm glad I'm not dead
I'm glad I'm not dead
I'm glad I'm not dead
I'm glad I'm not dead
I'm glad I'm not dead
I'm glad I'm not

The Nature of the Catastrophe

Can anyone suggest an explanation
Can anyone please suggest an explanation
Can anyone suggest an explanation

Through the Megaflow (Waltz)

Oh, Columbine
I'm lost in Time,
There ain't a sign
Of ho-o-ome . . .

Where is—where is—
My lovely Columbine?

She took a trip
On an old time ship
There was a slip
And now she's lost
Alone . . .

She could be
In Nine O Three
Or Twenty Million and Six
She told me
That she'd be free
But now she's lost her fix . . .

Oh, Columbine
Sweet love of mine
I missed you so
On the megaflow

Where is—where is—
My lovely Columbine?

She said we'd meet
In a place so neat
Say June of Fifty Seven,
But catastrophe
She could not beat
So maybe she's in Heaven . . .

Where is—where is—
My lovely Columbine?
Where is—where is—
My lovely Columbine?

3. REVOLUTIONS

1

GET CRACKING ON KELLOGG'S

Barnie stacks bricks as quick as some people talk, and he never drops them. 'Course it's simply a case of cause and effect. You see, his Missus knows that at least a quarter of a man's daily output of energy must come from his 8 o'clock intake of calories. So she gives him Kellogg's Corn Flakes for energy and warmth. Food needn't be hot to warm you. Human beings take their fuel from energy-giving foods (chiefly carbohydrates) that are burned up in the body. Kellogg's are extremely rich in carbohydrates—so they give you energy and keep you warm.*

**Calories are units of heat that measure the amount of energy different foods provide.*

ADVERTISEMENT: Picture Post, 1 March 1952

"THOSE POOR DEVILS," said Colonel Pyat, "they cannot survive in the world of the imagination. They are afraid of it. They reject it as vulgar, or over-coloured or—what? And then they offer us their threadbare language, their worn-out images as—" he sniggered "—poetry."

"If I were you, colonel, I would be concentrating on the immediate problems." Nestor Makhno shifted his weight as best he could. At least the truck was moving fairly rhythmically now and the swaying could be anticipated. They must be on one of the pieces of autobahn which had been extended into Bohemia in the days before the war. The men were tied to each wheel of a huge, old-fashioned 120mm field-gun. "I'm not impressed by your sudden discovery of the romantic agony."

"Particularly since it was our money which helped you make it." In the corner, near the only place where the canopy was loose enough to let in a breeze and the occasional light from a passing vehicle's headlamps, Una Persson looked up from the rope which bound her hands. She had been trying to gnaw it but her mouth kept growing intolerably dry. She referred to the cocaine Colonel Pyat had bought with cash set aside for bribing their way out of

Bohemia. At Passau, on the Danube, they had been changing trains with the other passengers when several militia-men had stopped them. At that time Colonel Pyat had been even more euphoric than now. He had addressed the soldiers as comrades and tried to appeal to their sense of liberty. Consequently he and the others had been searched and their weapons discovered. Now they were on their way back to Prague. Una knew that there was every possibility of treating with the new authorities and getting free again, but she was worried in case someone should link her name with that of Lobkowitz, who would be arriving on *The Kansas City Whirlwind* the next day, brought back, once more, from exile in America. Lobkowitz's peculiar mixture of anarcho-syndicalism and despotism had an appeal to all the factions involved in the Slavic Border Wars. Everyone was tired of the present cant, all of which denied authoritarianism and displayed it in every action. With a bit of luck the Czechs and Slovaks and Poles and Galiceans and Bylorussians and the rest would see some virtue in the example of Ukrainia, whose anarchism had given the country stability, relative wealth and security from outside attack, and had since Istanbul had been razed by the so-called suicide fleet of Cypriot airships five years before, turned Kiev and Odessa into the most vital cultural centres of Europe or the Middle East. She turned her face against the cold stream of air and wet her lips. She was half-way through the rope and congratulated her captors for their contempt of her femininity when they had casually tied her hands in front of her. Makhno and Pyat were much more secure. If she used all her strength now, she might even snap the rope. But she continued to chew. In the meantime Nestor Makhno was rubbing fruitlessly, trying to find a suitably sharp place on the field-gun, while Colonel Pyat's voice rose higher and higher as he elaborated his indignation, expressing cosmic disgust at their plight, offering cosmic solutions, the broadest of comforts.

Una sympathised with him. The tight, worried, stupid faces of the local authorities, who had sneered at them and sent them back to Prague, were still in her mind. There was nothing more depressing than those faces: men and women who, through expediency and fear, served a revolutionary cause they could not understand. She had seen so many of them. They continued to depress her. For some reason there were always more of them around railway stations than anywhere else. Perhaps the tracks and the timetables offered less ambiguity than the rest of the world. Wristwatches were important to them, too, she remembered. And tightly-buckled coats. It was interesting to note how in the early, wild and enthusiastic days of the Revolution the characteristic costume was a great-coat flung open, a hat askew, a hand spread outwards; later the representations of leaders became identified with neatly-buttoned uniforms, well-set caps and firm salutes, and only the Cossacks, as in Tsarist times, had been allowed to display a certain 'freedom', to represent the glories of irresponsibility. The new Tsars, in Muscovia, favoured the casual-bourgeois style of middle-aged German businessmen on holiday: cashmere pullovers, well-creased grey slacks, plaid sports-jackets and straight-stemmed briar pipes. It was what they felt, Una assumed, the people wanted—middle-class monarchy, armchair imperialism. She feared those people almost as much as she feared the police-caste Pyat still raved against.

"They destroy so much in the name of safety. They destroy those who have enabled their kind to survive for millenia. Without us, they would die out!" Pyat continued.

Makhno was amused. "Us? Your Zaporozhian Cossacks were not the most liberal and pacific of people."

"The Cossacks held liberty to be their most prized possession!" Pyat had long-since revealed, by his mistakes, that he had no Cossack background at all, but had been born in the slums of Minsk, probably of half-Jewish parents. He had fled Ukrainia in the uniform of a Zaporozhian Cossack colonel and for a while had benefited from the deception. But Makhno enjoyed pretending to believe the lie.

"And were prepared to kill every Jewish baby to defend their liberty!" The anarchist laughed.

"Don't blame the Cossacks for that!" said Pyat with heat. "It was all the fault of the Polish landlords who leased their Russian lands to Jews. A lot of Jews said so themselves."

"You mean the Jews blamed the Poles for letting them bleed Ukrainians?" Makhno flexed his arms. "My God!"

"You're as anti-semitic as the rest of them." Pyat spoke in that peculiar, detached tone he always affected when the subject of Jews was raised. He thought the tone lofty. Sometimes it deceived and angered a less perceptive hearer. But it aroused Makhno's sympathy. The

Ukrainian did his best to change the subject, in order to lose his temptation of baiting Pyat. "I could do with a drink," he said.

"You usually could." Pyat disapproved of Makhno's habits.

Una was pleased with Makhno's self-control as he resisted any further mention of the twenty-five grams of cocaine found on Pyat while the militia was searching him. The soldiers had accepted his explanation that these were headache powders and had carefully set them aside, doubtless for their own use. Makhno and Una had been amused by such a turn of events but, for a while, just after they had been tied up in the truck, Pyat had wept. He still had some five grams hidden in the collar of his English shirt: just under his nose, as it were, but at this moment totally unattainable.

"The Cossacks aren't cowards, at least!" Pyat returned grumpily to the earlier point.

"No," said Makhno. "They seek out the highest possible authority and then fight for it to the death." Actually, he shared a great deal of Pyat's romanticism where Cossack ideals were concerned. A number of renegades had fought with him at Ekaterinburg and elsewhere, though at least half his officers had been Jewish intellectuals who had recognised in him a tactician of almost preternatural genius. Because Makhno had objected to Grigorieff's pogroms the anarchist had shot down Grigorieff while the nationalist hetman's followers looked on. A little later he had gently disbanded the nationalist army as being of no use to him because it had 'absorbed inhumane habits of thought and action'. That had been the day before he had carried the black banner against the combined forces of Trotsky's reds and Krasnoff's Don Cossack whites, when the anarchist army, outnumbered four to one, had scattered its enemy so thinly along the banks of the Pripet, and later the Donets, that since then neither Reds nor Whites had ever considered a further strike against the Ukrainian heartland. Nowadays, of course, Makhno was *persona non grata* in Kiev. His sense of history gave him an ironic perspective on the situation. He had expected nothing else. For the past twenty-five years he had lent his energies to half-a-dozen successful revolutions and a dozen failures, such as the recent ones in Canada, Yucatan and Somalia. It had only been to please Una, who had looked him up in Paris during one of his three-month benders, that he had become involved in supporting the Bohemian anarcho-communists who only a week before had threatened Prague under his leadership. But the whole army had been betrayed, in classic manner, by authoritarian socialists. Bolsheviks had all destroyed the anarchists in an ambush in the Ruthenian Carpathians, near the Veretski Pass. There had been nothing for it but to try to take what was left of their light armour through Hungary and seek refuge in Vienna, but the Bolshevists had somehow found an airforce and seven aerial cruisers and had bombed the rest of the army to bits. About fifty survivors had split up in order to cross the Austrian border, but Una, Pyat and Makhno had been recognised and turned back, having to take the train via Brno to Passau, where the Bolshevists, temporarily in control, had caught them. Una knew that their return to Prague as prisoners was bound to embarrass someone, so there was a chance that they would be 'lost'—shot or let go. It was a fifty-fifty chance. And if Lobkowitz was given the opportunity to save them, it would embarrass him and put him in an extremely difficult position, if he appeared to favour them.

Una freed herself at last. Lobkowitz hardly knew Makhno or Pyat and so their chances were better than hers. Travelling alone she would have more flexibility and therefore more hope of escape. She stood up. She spoke a little shakily as she peeled back the canopy, waiting for the truck to slow.

"Good luck." She unhooked her tape-player from her belt. She checked the batteries. It was still surprising that the militia had left the unfamiliar-looking machine with her. Perhaps they had decided it was a booby-trap. She

switched on. Richard Hell was singing *You Gotta Lose*. "It's painful unless it's loud," she said. But she failed to get the volume very much higher. It served its purpose, however, drowning out Pyat's protests and causing the truck to slow.

She slipped through the curtain.

Time for a new temporary role, she thought.

2

KITTY-KOLA: A CORRECTION

Our attention has been drawn to an article entitled Sudan in Ferment in your issue of Dec. 29. In this article you refer to 'Egypt's plagiaristic Kitty-Cola.' We would point out that 'Kitty-Kola' has no connection whatever with Egypt. 'Kitty-Kola' is a speciality soft drink marketed by this company, and licences for its preparation and sale are granted to bottlers after their application has been approved. The Kitty-Kola Co. Ltd., of London, is associated with another English company which has now been established over 100 years and there is certainly no connection whatsoever with Egypt.

'Kitty-Kola' is a drink formulated here in England which is rapidly gaining acceptance on world markets. It is all part of this country's export drive and of our efforts to keep overseas markets which have been traditionally this country's for many, many years.

LETTER: Picture Post, 1 March 1952

IT WAS 1952 according to Una's newspaper and 1976 according to Nick Lowe, who was singing *Heart of the City* on her Vidor portable radio as she raised its lid and slid back in her deckchair, positioned to face Bognor's doubtful ocean. Jerry, that eternal spirit of seaside holidays past, came limping over the shingle towards her, his scrawny body bright red and peeling, his peculiar trunks threatening to slip over his hips.

"Blimey! Hot enough for you?"

Una pushed her sunglasses onto her forehead. "You didn't get burned like that on any British beach. Not in May you didn't."

"I'm not burned!" He was indignant. "I'm tanning. What's that row?" He nodded at the Vidor.

She turned it off. "The future. Do you want to get me an ice-cream? What flavours do they have?" She reached into her beach-bag for her purse.

"Flavours? They might have strawberry. But it's probably only vanilla."

"The newspaper was right."

"Eh?"

"Get me a wafer, will you?"

He was glad to go. He returned with two hard blocks of ice-cream sandwiched between wafer biscuits. Austerity, she thought, took some getting into. She wished she was back in the Balkans where life, at least, was interesting. She looked to left and right at deckchairs and British bathers. This was Jerry's nightmare, not her own.

He kneeled beside her, licking the ice-cream, looking craftily out to sea.

"Well," she said. "What is it? You arranged to meet, don't forget."

"Oh, yeah." He was looking younger and weaker, as if time were running backwards in him and draining him as it did so. "My mum said I ought to join the Home Guard."

"You want me to get you out of some sort of domestic row? Or military service?"

"I'm stuck here, Una. I've lost all my old power. I don't think you realise . . ."

"I can't change the megaflow."

The word was only dimly familiar to him. "It's ever since mum died."

"Your mother's still alive. I saw her over near the entrance to the pier."

"That's what's wrong."

"Retrogressive tendencies, eh?" She shook her head. "You always had them. But you never came this far back before—and not on this line. Do you know there's never been a second world war here?"

He was disbelieving. "Then why are we putting up with all this bloody austerity?"

"We never got over the General Strike. There's nothing much wrong with the economy. It's supporting the Empire. This is a sort of punishment on the working classes."

"No!"

"There are pros and cons," she told him.

"Cor!" He was impressed. "What can you do to get me out of it?"

"I don't think you've got the moral rigour to do it," she said. "You're not even a force for Chaos any more. You've become a victim, Jerry. Once . . ."

He smirked.

It made her laugh. "I'll do my best. Is your mate Collier around?"

"In London. His mum and dad aren't going anywhere this year."

She closed the lid of the Vidor and fastened the catches, replacing it in her bag. She took out a strange Baedeker and turned to the timetables at the back.

3

WILL THE FRENCH HOLD?

There is therefore grave danger that the French, losing every year the equivalent in officers of a complete promotion from their military college of Saint Cyr and 5,000 boys from every corner of France, deserted as they think by their natural allies, the British and the Americans, threatened as they think by a revived Wehrmacht, may pull out of Indo-China and bring their battle-trained divisions home to watch the Rhine. But if they do, Korea will look like a tactical exercise, and Malaya a piece of boy-scouting. Indo-China, as de Lattre told the Americans, is as important as the Battle of the Bulge in 1944. If it falls, Communism within a few short months could be battering at Suez and Australia. The Diggers might hold out: how about Farouk?

ARTICLE: Picture Post, 1 March 1952

THERE HAD TO be an alternative, thought Una, to Disco Fever on the one hand and the Red Army Ensemble on the other. She drove the hearse as fast as she dared; up past the West London Crematorium and round the corner into Ladbroke Grove. Behind her something in the elaborate coffin grumbled and squeaked. Jerry never

travelled well, even when she was trying to help him through the early seventies and into the middle of that decade where, everything being equal, he could rest up for a bit. Most likely, she thought, he was objecting to the fact that the hearse was a converted Austin Princess and not the Daimler he had asked for. If he went on like this, however, she would have to give up all her promises and bury him in the country. Somewhere near Godalming, she thought viciously. But she hadn't the heart for it.

Or the sea, she thought. Not for the first time.

She groped on the seat beside her for her half-eaten apple. There was nothing harder, she reflected, as she speeded up past a march of Radical Social Workers, for the imaginative person to imagine than an unimaginative person. Consequently the paranoid ascribed every Machiavellian motive to the dullest, least inventive people. Those least capable of subtle malice were those most often credited with it. The time dwellers had to learn such things early. Too often metaphysics got you and then you were lost. It was very much like a drug experience, she supposed. But that was more in Jerry's line than hers. She would have to ask him when he woke up.

She went past Ladbroke Grove tube station, past the Kensington Palace Hotel on the one side and The Elgin on the other, past the new housing development standing on the site of the Convent of the Poor Clares, past Blenheim Crescent, where Jerry's mum had lived, and parked near the corner, just before Elgin Crescent. From the house opposite came Shakey Mo Collier and three of his ageless friends, in black leather, studs, silver, and street ephemera, members of the pop group Motorhead. In the lead, his features beaming with somewhat generalised good-will behind mirror shades, was Lemmy. He pushed his hair back from his ears and lit a cigarette. "Bloody hell," he said. "Is this it, then? Is it?"

"It's all yours." Una found herself warming to the musician. He reminded her of Jerry. "Is the hole ready?"

Mo interrupted. "I dug it myself. Are you sure he won't—you know—cough it?"

"He can't," said Una. "Can he?"

4

LINER TO MARS

We've seen how short-sighted these particular prophets were. Is the same story going to be repeated when, some time during the next fifty years, we begin the exploration of space? Most scientists who've made a serious study of 'astronautics' agree that we'll ultimately be able to build spaceships, but probably few consider that they'll be of much more than scientific value. We'll be able to send small expeditions to the Moon and planets, at very great expense—but as for large-scale space-flight and the colonisation of the planets, that belongs strictly to the realms of 'science-fiction'. So say the pessimists—and we propose to ignore them. It may take a hundred years, it may take a thousand—but, ultimately, men will lift their commerce into space as they've lifted it into the air. The liners of the future, homeward bound from Mars or Venus, will link our Earth with the new worlds that now lie waiting for the first human footsteps.

ARTHUR C. CLARKE: Picture Post, 1 March 1952

"EVERY FUTURE WE inhabit is someone else's past," said Una as she and Catherine unpacked the picnic. "God, how I yearn for the mindless present. When you were a kid. Do you remember?"

"Do you? I've got a lot of different memories. It's what happens to you."

Una nodded and began to peel the sealing strip from the small jar of Beluga caviar they had brought, while Catherine buttered slices of Ryvita. They had parked their orange Mobylette-50s by the gate of this Cumbrian field and were seated in the long grass by the river. Overhead was a willow. To their left was a small stone bridge, thick with weeds and flowers and scarcely ever used. Behind them and ahead of them were rolling, vari-coloured summer hills, their contours and buildings unchanged since the 17th century. The women took deep breaths of rich air and swatted at midges and wasps. As often happened in this part of England, summer had come early and would be short. They were making the most of it. It was one of the few parts of the world where both of them could feel completely at ease. Fifty miles or so away, on the coast, the great nuclear reactors seemed to guard their security, as timeless as the rest of the landscape. Una, so used to impermanence, to plastic vistas, to all kinds of physical and social permutations, found herself incapable of imagining any radical change to this world. They had built a six-lane motorway through it, and that had only enhanced it, added a dimension. She smiled to herself. She had thought the same of the Sussex downs, once, without realising that that was where she was. Was it a state of mind which imposed tranquility upon a landscape, after all? Was it the only salve offered to the wounded romantic imagination? She had always preferred hills and mountains to valleys and plains. When she was in low country she always felt the urge to run off someone's cattle.

"There's an inevitability to linear thinking that sometimes brings me down a bit." Catherine mused. "Do you remember that time in Bombay? Or wherever. The future. No, it couldn't have been Bombay? Angkor Wat? Anuradhapura? One of those old cities. They had created a huge future and then it had deserted them. Is that what happened? A divergence of some kind? Where did they go? All these mysterious monuments scattered about the world. Monuments to literal-mindedness."

"And the literal-minded, in turn, think that people from space built them." Una was amused. "There's an irony."

"They'd never get it." Catherine pulled back her blouse and bared her breasts to the sun. "Ah. That's better. The only invasion from space I care about is the one that turns me nice and brown."

"It's a very simple form of pragmatism," said Una. She hitched up her summer frock and put her feet in the water. "But that's fair enough. We are on holiday."

"Which reminds me. How's Jerrry?"

Una wished that Catherine hadn't raised the subject. "Lying low."

"In cold storage is he? That makes a change."

Una had forgotten how little disturbed Catherine could be where Jerry was concerned. Catherine believed Jerry to be immortal.

Her feet still in the water she turned at the waist and laid a lip on Catherine's nipple.

Catherine stroked Una's hair.

"You must be tired of playing Jerry's role," she said sympathetically.

Una rolled on to her back. "Shall we buy a place here? A retreat?"

"There's no such thing, love. Once you own it, it stops being a retreat. You know that as well as I do." Catherine found her friend's hand. "Sorry if I upset you. I didn't mean . . ."

"You don't understand," said Una.

"Does one have to? I can't believe much in understanding. I do believe, though, in sympathy and comfort. In enthusiasm. What is understanding? It's translation. And you always lose something when you translate. Don't you?"

"But you have a rough idea of what I'm going through."

"Sort of," said Catherine. She laughed. "No."

Much to Una's own relief, she laughed in return.

5

"IF ONLY MY NAME WAS DENIS"

To score double centuries, to man a frontier-post in Mexico, to pilot a Space-fleet to Mars—these are games popular with every boy of every age. And it is natural and right that this should be so. Tales of sport and adventure and excitement fire a boy's imagination; they help him to see the world in a fresh and vivid way; they enlarge his horizon, and inspire his ideals. Yet—it cannot be denied—a boy's longing for adventure and excitement may often cause great and reasonable anxiety. Adventurousness may be turned to violence, excitement to cruelty by a variety of vicious influences. And here cheap second-rate comic-strips are much to blame. They warp and distort a boy's sense of values and give him a false outlook on life; under their influence he fancies himself a hero, a superman; someone who escapes responsibility and seeks refuge in fantasy. It remains the prime object of EAGLE to change all that; and (adapting the famous phrase) to see that 'the Devil does not have all the exciting comics'. Here no creed of violence is preached; no tawdry morality or cheap sensationalism or worship of the superman ever appears. For

EAGLE is edited by a Clergyman; and underlying the tales of Space Exploration, the exciting strip cartoons and articles on sport, the colourful features on Science and Nature and the World, there is a Christian philosophy of honesty and unselfishness. And in EAGLE it is shown in a form which every boy can understand and respect.

ADVERTISEMENT: Picture Post, 1 March 1952

MAJOR NYE SAT on a stool outside his shed, grunting as his daughter Elizabeth grew bright red and tugged at his left gumboot. "Sorry about this," he said.

Una and Catherine said in concert: "Can I help?"

"It's okay," said Elizabeth. "Awkward buggers, wellies. Sorry, dad." She winked at her friends. "He hates me swearing."

"I shouldn't," he said. "Do enough of it myself." He rose in his thin socks. "What do you think of the patch now?" He regarded, with some satisfaction, his vegetable gardens. "We're almost entirely self-sufficient, you know. Apart from tobacco. But that's not really any good for you, anyway, is it? Come the revolution, we'll be okay."

Una remembered a thousand famines and gasped.

"You all right, Mrs P?" He put his hand on her arm. "Trod on a stone? Put the kettle on, Liz, there's a good girl. We'll have some tea."

Elizabeth shrugged. "Come and help me, Cathy."

Una and Major Nye stood alone in the garden. From an upstairs window a pale, forgotten face regarded them with miserable and imperfect knowledge. "I had planned to retire completely," said the major. "But what with kids to educate and the wife's doctors, and the value of the pension going down every year . . ."

"We're the only ones Prinz Lobkowitz trusts," said Una. "If you can get Makhno out of prison in Australia I think it would do a lot of good. The charge was trumped up, wasn't it?"

"I wouldn't go as far as that. But I've looked at the file. A lot of circumstantial evidence, certainly. We could re-open the case.''

''And release him.''

''I think so.'' Major Nye sat down on the stool again and put his feet into carpet slippers. He lifted a boot and began to bang it against a nearby step. ''I saved some radishes for you.''

''Lovely. The conference is to be held in September. In Trieste.''

''Best time of year for Trieste.'' He began to roll himself a cigarette. ''I should think the Jugoslavs are happy about that. Not so far to go for them.''

''They're hardly playing an important role. They've been more or less neutral, along with Ukrainia. Lobkowitz hopes for a Pan-Slavic Treaty, to include the Russian states.''

''They've always been a bit stand-offish, haven't they?''

''But it isn't important. Makhno is still very much respected in Ukrainia, even if he isn't liked. He was never a natural politician.''

''That's obvious. Fancy trying to start an anarchist uprising in Queensland!'' Major Nye lit his cigarette, puffing vigorously. ''That's what I call Quixotic, Mrs P. Eh?''

''Well, optimistic, anyway.''

''I've heard that Makhno wasn't too pleased with you, however.'' Major Nye squinted back at the house, but the face had withdrawn.

''Not Makhno. You're thinking of Pyat.''

''You know my nick-name for that one?''

''No.''

''Squash.''

''Swede?''

''What? Oh, not the turnip sort. The game. Fives. Get it? Why does he call himself by a number? Is it an old code-name? Those Russians change their names at the drop of a hat.''

''I don't know what his real name is.'' Una smiled. ''It's strange I never wondered. Colonel Five. Five what?''

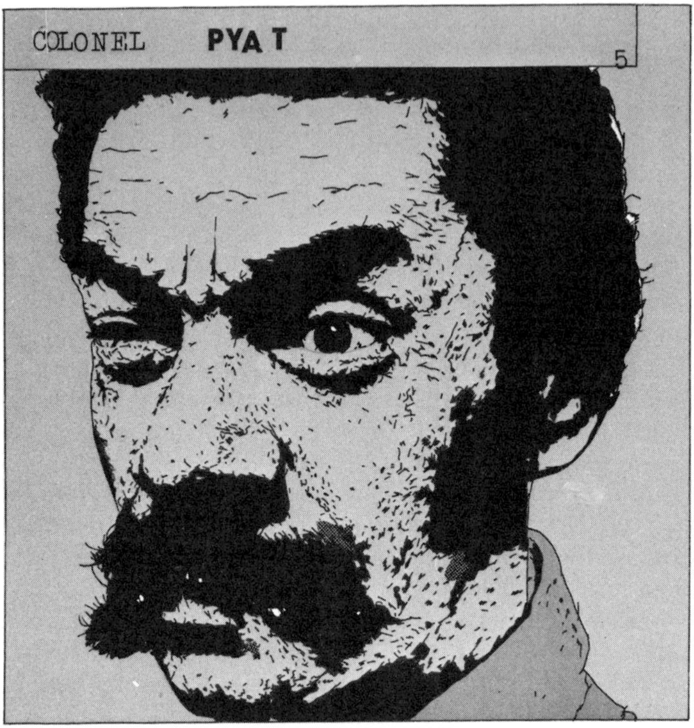

"Five lives," he said, "at least."

"Five lies, in his case. He's not a colonel, of course. I don't think he's ever served in a war. Not voluntarily, at any rate. He's from Kiev. An engineer or something. Born in Minsk. His family—his mother, at least, went to Tsaritsyn where he spent his early childhood. Later the pair of them turned up in Kiev. I think that's where he met Makhno."

"A funny pair."

"He doesn't like Makhno a bit. But he sticks close to him. Familiarity is a form of security, after all."

"So Makhno is still friendly to you."

"As always. That doesn't mean he listens to me. And

I'm not going to represent you this time, major. I did it once, for reasons of my own."

"Oh, quite. No. All I want you to do is brief him. I'm sure he'll support Lobkowitz. They're both anarchists."

"Lobkowitz is a pacifist. Makhno isn't."

"I suppose it was simple-minded of me to link them in that way."

From the house Elizabeth called that tea was ready. Major Nye guided Una towards the side door, past the empty stables. "You must come in June. It's the best time to see our place."

"Maybe it's a diminutive," she said. "Of fifty. Pyatdyaset."

"Why fifty?"

"No reason. It's just associations of my own. I'm rambling. Mozart sonatas. God, I hate the fifties."

"You'll be out of them soon." They reached the kitchen. "Think of me. Stuck in 'em for God knows how long. Borderland years for me. For you they are merely the badlands. To be crossed quickly and forgotten about. They've done me in, Mrs Persson." He reached to open the door into the sitting room. "I assure you I don't like them any more than you."

For the first time, she realised the extent of his dignity.

It was these old men she admired most. Those who had suffered so much and still kept their faith. They were braver than Makhno in many ways. But Makhno was one of them. And perhaps more attractive.

In the old couch Bishop Beesley leered at her.

"I don't believe you've met our vicar," said Mrs Nye from her invalid chair.

6

S. AFRICA SEEKING LEG IRONS

Tenders have been invited by the South African Police for the supply of 200 leg irons, apparently as the result of a ban imposed by the United States government last month on the export of 'torture' equipment to the republic. The exact specifications of what the police need are on file with the Director of State Purchases in Pretoria. They are to be marked 'SAP'—South African Police—and supplied with two keys. Emphasis is placed in the tender document on a 'secure system'.

Daily Telegraph, 20 July 1978

"THE FRENCH CAN'T help their Classicism any more than the Italians can control their Romanticism. Look at those poor French horror comics. Their sex magazines. Look at Le Drugstore! And so it is with politics. They must always embrace some classical, unambiguous cause. They become Marxists." It was autumn in the Luxembourg Gardens and, as always, the only time they were at all atmospheric. A few leaves disgraced the orderly paths or lay, willy-nilly, on the gravel. Makhno stiffened his back to gain height, but he remained significantly shorter than Una. On the other hand; his girl-friend, Maxime, was diminutive. She wore her camel-hair coat as if it were a uniform. Her small, fierce face peered at Una from beneath a defiant orange 'punk' coiffure. She gave exactly the same attention to Una as she did to Makhno. And she said nothing. Occasionally she would light a cigarette with an old-fashioned Polish petrol lighter, using energetic, economical movements. If Una smoked a cigarette, Maxime would light it. Makhno was smoking papyruska cigarettes from a box inscribed with a representation of Ilya Moromyets and other Kievan legendary heroes. They were a commercial Russian brand called Vogatyr, made in Moscow. He was completely grey now and his face, although a little corroded from his drinking, was still humorous and attractive. He had the same sardonic manner, the same look of stocky integrity. He was nearly seventy, in exile in Paris again, having found the role of Bohemian diplomat too much at odds with ideals which, as he said, had become physical as well as mental habits, so that his very presence in conferences made other people uncomfortable. He wore an old-fashioned Norfolk jacket, plus-fours and his favourite pair of English riding boots which he had picked up in some South American war. He held the tube of the Russian cigarette upwards and at an angle away from his hand. The smoke, drifting through the clear air, made Una feel at once nostalgic and wary. Her romance with the various Slav revolutions had brought her too much pain. It had been a century full of fire and she would look on it with nostalgia, if the memory lasted at all.

"Pure, classical Marxism," murmured Makhno. "Not the rough-edged vulgar Russian kind. Closer to the Chinese, of course, with whom the French have such an affinity. And they have made me a hero!" He dropped the cigarette. "They have almost convinced me that I am 'really' a Marxist. Poor old Kropotkin. He wasn't quite mad enough, was he?"

"You're becoming a racist," said Una.

"I'm Ukrainian. All Ukrainians are racists. Racism is an honourable form of logic pre-dating psychology as a useful way of rationalising prejudice."

Bishop Beesley, in gaiters and frock-coat, and Miss Brunner, in severe St Laurent tweed, approached them through the stiff, Parisian trees. The co-conspirators were arm in arm. They waved when they sighted Makhno's party.

"Hi," said the bishop, perhaps not sure where he was. "How goes it?"

Maxime slowly turned her eyes on him. Then she regarded Miss Brunner. It was as if she absorbed their essence. Miss Brunner looked uncomfortable and then curious. She smiled at Maxime. "Hello, dear. I don't know you, do I?"

Maxime looked to Makhno.

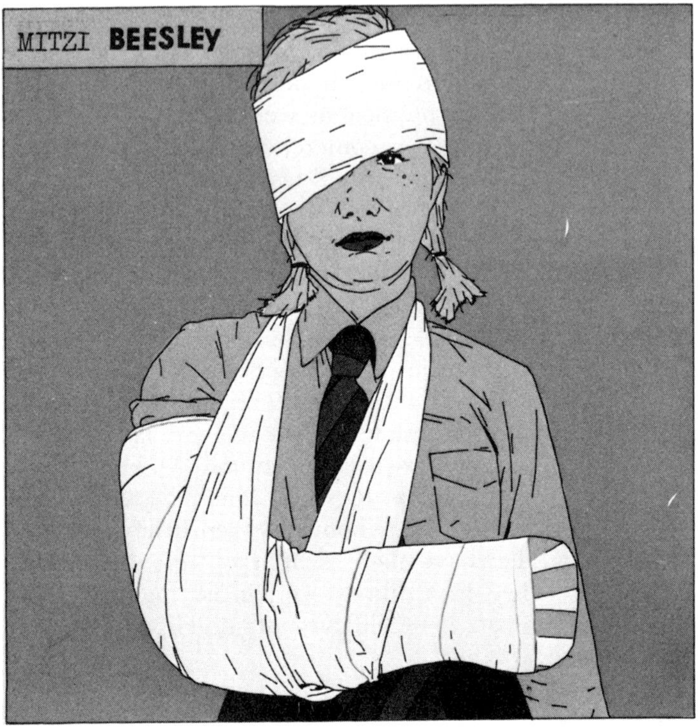

"This is Maxime," he said. "We are married."

"Oh, congratulations." Bishop Beesley put a fat hand towards the girl, who flinched. He looked at it, perhaps detecting a trace or two of chocolate on the pink flesh, and began to suck it before he drew a red and white spotted hankerchief from the pocket of his coat and wiped the hand carefully. Meanwhile Miss Brunner appeared to have sidled between Makhno and Una and threw a cloud of some Gerlaine or other about them all. "Darling Nestor!"

"What?" Makhno coughed. "Are you emissaries from the Germans?"

"Certainly not. We are tourists."

"Trapped," added the bishop, "like you."

"We're not trapped." Makhno grinned. "We're communards, all of us."

"Splendid," said Miss Brunner. "We were hoping you were." She bit her lip; looking up as a flight of Prussian Starfighters came honking and wailing through the misty morning. "Bombers?"

"They only observe us. We're an independent city. Technically, we're not even under siege. Technically, there's no German blockade." Una watched Miss Brunner who hefted her handbag on her arm and glanced at Bishop Beesley who drew a small Browning automatic from his pocket and pointed it at Makhno. Miss Brunner produced her old Smith and Wesson .45 from the bag.

Nestor Makhno took out his cigarette case and offered a Vogatyr to the company. "Is this an assassination?"

"Justice," said Miss Brunner.

The scene fractured and Una, Makhno and a frowning Maxime stood at the crest of a hill, looking down on the white road winding across the yellow Ukrainian steppe. There were no houses to be seen. Behind them, three ponies, furnished for war, cropped at grass. Makhno returned his field glasses to their case. "We had best make for the railway station," he said. "It's too far to ride."

They mounted the ponies, but, even as they began to trot forward, the scene melted and became a town in flames. Nationalist bandits were looting it. It was the time of the retreat from Minsk. Makhno drew his revolver, firing into the air. "Stop!" He moved round in his saddle and shot a looter wearing an army greatcoat and a sailor's cap. The man began to cough and searched for his own gun amongst the knives and swords and cartridge belts hung about his chest and waist. He fell on his knees and collapsed to one side before he had sorted through the collection and discovered that his holster had moved round to the small of his back.

Two armoured cars moved through the smoke and the crowd. A green flag waved from a mast on the leading vehicle. The street was mud. The noise of mortars and

human beings mingled into one appalling scream. Una was about to wheel her mount when a silence fell and the ponies were plodding knee-deep through snow. Una shivered. The fracture had saved them from Miss Brunner and Bishop Beesley but it could have sent them into stasis. In this primordial snow they must soon freeze. It would mean the end of a whole cycle of consequences. She began to feel the familiar lethargy and prepared herself for the fate which must sooner or later befall all temporal adventurers.

"Mush!"

It was Jerry, driving a team of dogs, a corpse-shaped bundle before him on his sleigh. He was dressed in white furs and looking his most handsome. "Want a lift?"

Makhno put fresh shells into his revolver. "Where are you going?"

"Does it matter?" Una dismounted and plunged through the snow towards the sleigh which became a small boat in which Jerry and Catherine, dressed as seaside Pierrots, manned two sets of oars and at the same time stretched to where she stood waist-deep in the sea, trying to get to them. Una herself was dressed as Harlequin and her vision was impaired by her mask. She felt a strange, melancholy lust.

"Quick," said Catherine. "There's still time, Una. Quick."

But Una was losing it. She knew. Memories dissipated. Identity failed. She was still in her Harlequin set as she stumbled up the yellow beach of some Indian Ocean island, weeping for rest. Desperate for consolation.

7

COMPUTERS PICK LIKELY 'SUICIDES'

Computers can predict suicide attempts much more accurately than human therapists because they have no hesitation in asking blunt questions, according to a series of experiments by two psychiatrists at Wisconsin University Medical School. When hundreds of depressed patients were interviewed by a computer . . . three suicide attempts were accurately predicted. The two doctors had failed to predict any of them . . . In the first part of the interview, the computer would win their confidence with such morale-boosting remarks as: 'You're a pro at using the terminal.' Then it became blunter with such questions as: 'What are your chances of being dead from suicide one month from now?'

Daily Telegraph, 20 July 1978

"WHAT ARE THESE new Americans who have made of tautology a substitute for literature? Who celebrate the euphuism as an art-form? Who take crude peasant prejudice and elevate it, placing it on par with Emerson or

Paine? What are these babblers, so free to debase the Word? Who employ the corrupt terminology of the encounter group in all their dealings?'' Professor Hira held the board against the window and reached for the hammer Una passed him. ''Eh?''

''I'm sure I don't know, darling? I'm not a great reader,''

''Do you have to be? You should wear something more practical.''

''I like satin. It's cool. Do you think the Dacoits will attack before help comes?'' She adjusted a pink strap.

He scratched his hair-line, just where his turban touched his forehead. ''We can't take chances. There is nothing worse than an Indo-Chinese pirate. You must shoot yourself, of course, if they land.'' She turned back to look out to sea. The sails of the junks seemed no closer and the smoke of the white steam yacht which appeared to lead them was, if anything, closer to the horizon. The little Brahmin knocked an inexpert nail into the board and then made his way cautiously down the ladder. The main settlement of Rowe Island was below them: a group of stone and stucco buildings which had housed the mine-managers, their employees and the few traders who had found it worthwhile to set up shops and hotels here. Professor Hira's house had once been the control shack for the airship field. The steel, triangular mast was still there, but no ships had called in years, since the mining of phosphates had become unprofitable. The Malays and Chinese labourers had been the first to go. There had been some attempt by the mine-owners to turn the place into a resort, but it was too far from anywhere else in the world to attract more than a few of those who genuinely sought a remote haven. Now it was a sort of R&R base for members of the Guild, being away from all shipping routes. The one hotel was run by Olmeijer, the fat Dutchman, who for some reason found it convenient to serve Guild people, but Olmeijer had made his annual journey to Sarawak, to see one of his several families, and would not be back for two

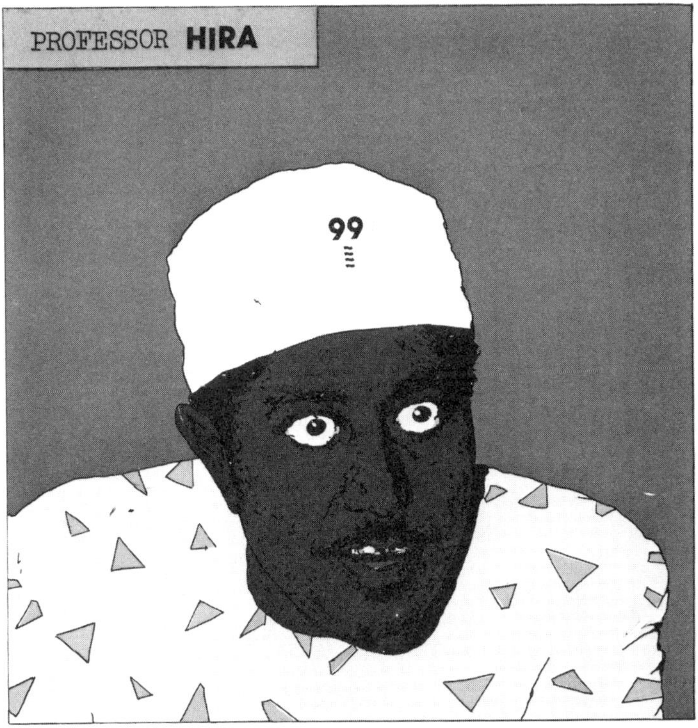

weeks. Hira and Una were presently the only inhabitants.

"There's nothing at all here for them." Hira squinted out to sea. "Could they be after us?"

"What would they want?"

"They could be linears, out to destroy our base. It wouldn't be the first time. Remember what happened in 1900, at the Centre?"

"It was one of the very first and oldest bases. We never made the same mistake. That Centre was shifted into the Palaeozoic. Or was it the Devonian?"

"Don't ask me. We have different terms for the time cycles. But they're about as vague as yours." He heard a familiar coughing from the sky and looked up to point

towards the silhouette of a cream-coloured Dornier DoX banking over the top of a cloud and heading clumsily towards the island. "We all know who that must be."

"I wish to god he'd get a better bloody plane."

"It suits his sense of history."

The huge white aircraft floundered lower, only half its engines firing at any one time. It had a grubby, under-used look to it.

"I suppose," said Una, hitching up her long dress,

''we'd better get down to the harbour before the pirates.'' She had noticed that the yacht had picked up speed. She heard a distant rumble. ''They've got a Bofors. They're firing at the plane.''

It was impossible to tell if the plane were hit. From somewhere near its tail, a Browning M1917-A1 began to fire. The junks retaliated, with every kind of light weaponry, but principally, if Una's ear were in, with near-useless Ingram M10s.

"At least they're a bit more up to date," said Una. They had reached the ramshackle outskirts of the settlement and were running over distorted flagstones towards the harbour. "But at least we can be certain of one thing. We're in a fault of some sort. Maybe even a loop."

"It's better than being frozen," said the Brahmin.

Una's memory became vague again. At least she still knew enough to understand that there were no such things as paradoxes and that ambiguities sustained and enriched the basic fabric of human life; that Time was a notion and nothing more; and therefore could neither be challenged, nor overwhelmed: merely experienced.

Death, of course, was real enough, when it came. She looked nervously towards the yacht which appeared to be sporting a Hudson's Bay Company flag. She could easily spot the Dacoits on the deck. They were training the Bofors towards the harbour itself. She thought she saw the glint of a bishop's mitre on the bridge.

Whining and grunting intermittently, the DoX flew low overhead, its wings swaying, turned almost directly over the yacht and came in to land on the oily waters of the harbour, bouncing dangerously on its heavy floats. The engines continued to miss as a figure emerged from the cabin and stood on the float, signalling to them.

"We're going to have to swim for it," said Professor Hira removing his beautiful silk coat.

"Bugger," said Una. She stripped off her pink satin evening dress and in nothing but her camisole returned gingerly to the water.

Shakey Mo Collier helped her crawl onto the float. His long hair fell about his yellow, seedy face. There was a black Burmese cheroot in one corner of his mouth. He wore huge mirror-shades which gave him something of an insectile look. He was dressed as Captain Fracasse, although the costume was filthy and so torn as to be barely recognisable. "We were on our way to Australia," he explained, "when we got your call. Is that the Teddy Bear firing at us?"

"It must be," said Una. "The last time I was on it was for the concert party. Do you remember?" Dripping, she climbed into the cabin. Frank and Jerry, in identical flying gear, sat at the twin controls.

"Remember?" said Mo, reaching out a hand towards Professor Hira. "I haven't had a moment to bloody change, have I?"

Frank looked round at her and licked chemically-reddened lips. "Cor! Me first," he said appreciatively.

Jerry's voice was remote. "No time." An automatic arm stretched towards the throttle. "Taking her up." There was flak now, and spray, as shells struck the water near them. The plane lurched, bounced, slewed round and had to be straightened out. Then they were taking off, the sound of the inefficient engines drowning the sound of maniac gunfire which burst from every ship in the pirate fleet.

They were back in the political arena with a vengeance.

8

SIX LIFE SENTENCES FOR ANTI-ABORTION BOMB STUDENT

A 'brilliant' science student, who carried out fire bomb attacks on people whose pro-abortion views 'sickened' him, was given six concurrent life sentences when he appeared at the Old Bailey yesterday. (He) made 'lethal and beautifully designed bombs which, by the grace of God, did not kill anyone,' said the Recorder of London Mr James Miskin Q.C. 'He took the view that those who support abortion are wrong. He has exhibited no remorse or any concern for his intended victims . . .' In a workroom at his home police found 'a mass of bomb-making equipment' and a diary in which he recorded his crimes. He had written about his urge to 'purge the land of evil' and of his 'noble mission' against abortion. Of the bomb intended to maim Mrs Lord, he said: 'I laughed to think of my own cunning in constructing it . . . I believe strongly that something should be done to remedy abortion. I am sickened by it and decided a campaign against those who preach the unwarranted murder of innocent children.'

Daily Telegraph, 20 July 1978

"IT ONLY COSTS about £16.00 for the whole round trip," said Una as she followed Catherine into the back of the Daimler limousine. "Hardly any more than a taxi, these days." She smiled at the chauffeur who had turned his head and was giving both of them the eye. She smoothed chiffon. "Derry and Toms," she said. "In Kensington High Street. Do you know it?"

"Well . . ." He shrugged. "I know what you mean." he put the car into gear and drove round the corner into Campden Hill Road. "Is that where you want to go? I mean, the only place?"

"And back," said Una, "when we've done some shopping and had our tea. Isn't it lovely today?"

"Lovely," said the chauffeur.

"I'm so glad to be back." Una giggled at Catherine. "So much has happened!"

Catherine, looking a little wary, said: "Yes?"

"You think I've changed?"

"Sort of."

"I've given up everything. I've decided to be more feminine."

"You're always deciding that," said Catherine. She looked soberly at her own blonde frizz in the little mirror provided. Her make-up was fashionably extravagant: imitating the naïve almost as successfully as a Lowry, but with much more passion. She put her red lips together. "And usually at the wrong time."

Una's enthusiasm waned. She crossed her legs. "It's the only escape they leave open."

"They leave it open because they want you to take it."

"Fine. I want to take it."

"Fine." Catherine spoke cheerfully, frustrating Una.

"Well, what else can I do? I need the rest."

"You ought to find another way, dear. Or another chap."

"He's lovely, Major Nye."

"He's married to that poor old bag. And then there's Elizabeth. I mean, she'd be pissed off to say the least, if she found out. You can't screw fathers and daughters and get away with it." Catherine laughed coarsely. "Bloody hell!"

"It's not really like that." Una was offended. She regretted suggesting the trip.

The Daimler reached Kensington High Street and turned left. "I need to combine ideals with sex, that's my trouble."

"It's because you're so puritanical."

Una nodded.

"That's it," said the chauffeur. "Isn't it?"

"God help us!" Una was terrified as she stared out at the department store. "I hoped I was safe!"

"It changed ages ago. To Biba's first. Then to this." Catherine was sympathetic. "I thought you knew. I thought you were being satirical."

"How do you get to the roof garden?"

"You can't any more, I don't think. It's private."

"Get anything in there these days," said the chauffeur.

Una continued to stare in silence at the pale green, the faded gold, of the new Marks and Spencers.

9

GIFT FROM QUEEN

Seven deer, two stags, and five hinds—the Queen's jubilee year gift to the Canadian province of Nova Scotia—will be flown from Heathrow today.

Daily Telegraph, 20 July 1978

BENEATH THE GREY Westway motorway, in the gloom of the half-ruined People's Theatre, peering out of

the rain through wire-netting, sat Jerry Cornelius, a crest-fallen white linen Pierrot. He hugged his cold, thin body. He whimpered as, from another bay, further west, came the giggling and wheezing of his half-cut mum enjoying an afternoon gin with Bishop Beesley in some corner or other. He knew Una was standing at the back of the stage, behind him. She sniffed. The railway sleepers used for seats had been set on fire and partially burned. The theatre was useless, filthy, incredible. The Pierrot suit was wet, as if Jerry had tried to run home through the rain and then turned back. This Sunday they had all been due to make their appearance here, in a version of the role made famous by Sarah Bernhardt almost a century before, as *Pierrot Mort.*

Jerry's white make-up had the flaky look of salt-flats suddenly inundated. It made him look infinitely aged as he eventually turned reddish eyes to acknowledge her. "I thought they'd turn up anyway," he said. "Did you bring your costume?"

"I left it at your mum's. Cathy's there."

"I know. She wouldn't come."

"She said."

"Thought it wasn't worth it. There was no cancellation announced. I mean. Are we troopers or aren't we."

"Troopers." Una offered him a packet of Black Cats as she came towards him. "Of some sort or other."

"What's the point of doing a play to celebrate the spirit of the theatre and then showing none of that spirit yourself." He took a cigarette.

"Do you want to put it on?"

"There were only about six people turned up and they went away when they saw what had happened. Bloody vandals. Who was it?"

"I think it was a rival political theatre group," she said. "That's what I heard. Marxists. They're very concerned about reaching the people in the correct way."

"Bloody communists. Worse than the church."

"Well, so they say."

"And they're bloody right."

"Why can't they leave us alone."

"It's not in their nature."

"Sod them all."

"No point in sulking, Jerry. Not if you're a trooper."

"I'm not going to be brave about it. That's unhealthy. It's better if I sulk."

She sat down at the hacked-about piano and played a chord. The sound was primaeval; terrifying. She couldn't stop it. It grew in the bay; it echoed through all the other bays, right down to the end, in Ladbroke Grove. It joined the noise of the cars above, the trains of the Metropolitan Line to the south; there was a sense of eternal syncopation. Jerry's face cleared. Una shook the piano. The sound continued to swell from it.

"That's great," said Jerry.

"It's cacophony."

"No it's not. Listen."

"I don't want to listen."

"Everything intersects."

"We all know that."

"This is the music of the lines. Not the spheres. Like knitting. Like a vast cat's cradle. Can you hear it all, Una?"

"Nothing but a horrible noise."

He sighed. "Maybe you're right. All we have is imagination. And that lets you down so often. Everyone has a different explanation."

"Can you suggest a universal one?"

"Music."

"What?"

"Nothing."

The smell of damp charcoal was getting to Una. "Shall we go and have a cup of coffee in the Mountain Grill? We'll be under cover most of the way. You won't get much wetter."

"If you like." He had stopped sulking and had become artificially compliant. He got up at once and followed her through the gap in the wire, round the corner into Portobello Road. The windows of the Mountain Grill were steamed up from the inside. Within, the usual cast looked at the newcomers. There was a row of tables against either wall. Each row contained five tables. At the end of the café was the counter with the till on it. Behind the counter was the kitchen. In the kitchen were the Cypriot proprietor, his wife and his father. They were cooking the food. A little boy and a little girl, the proprietor's children, were serving it. There was a smell of boiling potatoes. It dominated all the other smells. At the furthest table on the left row sat Miss Brunner, Bishop Beesley, Karen von Krupp, Frank Cornelius. At the next table down sat Shakey Mo Collier, Nestor Makhno, Maxime and Mrs Cornelius. At the third table were Major Nye, Elizabeth Nye, Pip Nye and Captain Nye. At the fouth were William Randolph Hearst, Orson Welles, Alfred Bester and Zenith the Albino, all in evening dress. The fifth was empty and Jerry and Una sat down at it, facing one another. On Una's right (her back was to the moist window) the tables were occupied thus:

Table One:	Nik Turner, Dave Brock, DikMik, Del Dettmar
Table Two:	Simon King, Bob Calvert, Lemmy, Martin Griffin
Table Three:	Pete Pavli, Adrian Shaw, Michael Moorcock, Simon House
Table Four:	Steve Gilmore, Douglas Smith, Wayne Bardell, Graham Charnock
Table Five:	Phil Taylor, Eddy Clarke, Catherine Cornelius, Harvey Bainbridge

"It's bloody full this afternoon," said Jerry. "It's a wonder there's any empty chairs at all."

"They're for absent friends."

"What is this? A private party?"

"We're just waiting for some transport." Jerry began to feel a comforting sentimentality.

"You'd better get something inside you," she said.

10

VISCOUNT'S SON 'PAID £70 FOR CHILD SEX'

A Viscount's son, on a 'fantasy bandwagon' fed by child pornography for several years, told Manchester Crown Court yesterday that he had paid £70 for an introduction to 'child prostitutes' at their mother's flat. (He) was giving evidence at the trial of a mother of three who is accused of inciting one of her daughters to commit gross indecency with him. (She) pleaded not guilty to three charges—encouraging an indecent assault on a girl under 16, indecent assault, with two men, on a girl under 13; and with a man, inciting a girl of 10 to commit gross indecency with (him). (He) claimed that he was 'revolted and horrified' by the reality of seeking out child prostitutes and reaching the point where he actually saw 'these little girls' and went to bed with one aged 10 . . . He had amassed a considerable quantity of 'child porn' over a number of years and 'a fantasy had been built up in my mind but it had not crashed at that time. That is why I went on.'

Daily Telegraph, 20 July 1978

THEY WERE STILL in their uniforms as they left the tiny theatre and climbed into the back of the Ford Transit. Una crawled through to the driving seat and pulled off her Harlequin mask. Jerry and Catherine lay face forward on the mattress while Catherine unscrewed the top of a thermos. Una got the engine going and backed the van into the midnight street. Even as Catherine handed her the plastic cup of sweet tea Una said goodbye to Harrogate and took the A65, heading north. "Never again," she said.

"They were awful." Jerry held out his own beaker and let it be filled. "What did they expect."

"Follies," said Una. "I knew it."

"There's no audience for the traditional *Commedia dell' Arte*," said Catherine dutifully, dabbing some tea-stains from her frothy costume. "And Harrogate's where people retire. They're nostalgic for the seaside pierrots. That's what they were expecting. That's why they left, you know. They were disappointed, all those retired people. We have ourselves to blame."

"Old farts," said Jerry. "You can keep bloody Harrogate. Where to next?" He remembered. "Kendal?"

"We're booked in at the Community Hall, but I'm not sure we should carry on." Una handed the cup behind her. "London was okay because people are into that sort of thing now. But we're ahead of our time up here."

"That's not hard." Catherine was grim. "I'm pissed off and no mistake. I never wanted any part of this pretentious crap. I thought it was going to be like those old people expected—songs and dances and that." She had given up duty.

"There *are* songs and dances." Una was aggrieved. It was she who had talked them both into the venture.

"Not proper ones." Catherine turned over on her back and tried to get comfortable with her head on her suitcase. "This is worse than rep."

"It's what rep's all about." Jerry, who had had less theatrical experience, still found the whole travelling part of it romantic.

"But it isn't rep. It's—God knows what!" Catherine sniffed and shut her eyes.

"It's how rep started. This."

"It's self-conscious." She opened her eyes again. "Has anyone got a cigarette?"

Jerry went to his own grubby bag and found a tin. "Only these rotten Russian ones."

"They'll do." She lit a papyruska. "I like 'em." She was enjoying herself, testing her power. She knew that they were both trying to placate her. She continued her role. "Couldn't we try to pep it up next time. With some more contemporary material—or at least some nostalgia stuff—vo-di-o-do—you know. This is so old nobody can feel nostalgic for it!"

"That's the point. It's genuine rediscovery of dramatic ideas disused for a couple of hundred years. Well, a hundred—if you count Debureau and Les Funambules—"

"Which I do," said Catherine, taking an entirely different but equally aggressive tack.

"Some Good Companions we are," said Jerry unhappily. "This ain't rock and roll. It's Leonard Merrick."

"Who?" they said.

He smiled smugly. He began to remove his make-up. He seemed to be the only one who was enjoying himself.

They made their way into the Dales, down the dark, empty road towards Cumbria.

Somewhere beyond Ilkley, a Banning began to sound for a few seconds. Then the noise died.

Jerry was asleep. Catherine crawled into the passenger

seat and handed Una one of her brother's Russian cigarettes already lit. "Was that fighting?"

"There's an army near. Of some sort. But I don't think we should worry too much. I'm going to try to make for the old road, once we're past Kirby. Get into safe country."

Catherine nodded. "Good idea."

She began to doze.

She was wakened by the dawn and looked to see a disturbed, red-eyed Una, looking dreadfully pale in her red, green, blue and gold lozenge motley. "What's the matter?"

"I can't find the bloody road. I've looked and looked. It's not blocked or anything. I just can't find it."

They were on the motorway. "But we're in it." said Catherine. "It's over there. And there."

"We're going through it. But I can't get into it. I don't know what's wrong."

"Where are we heading?"

"Where else?" said Una. "The Lake District."

They had reached Grasmere and had stopped in the deserted car park next to Dove Cottage before Jerry woke up, looked out of the back windows of the Transit, saw grey stone and turned pale. "Oh, no."

"Don't blame me," said Una. "All roads lead to Wordsworth."

"What?"

"That's how it seems."

"I hate this bloody place."

"Why do you keep coming back to it then," said Catherine sardonically. "And you do, don't you?"

"Not voluntarily. I thought—Weren't we heading for Kendal? We've passed it."

"By-passed it, actually," said Una. She was grim. "We can't go back and we don't want to stay here. Where shall we head for?"

Catherine said: "Keswick's better than this."

"Yeah," said Jerry. "Keswick."

"Why not Scotland?" Una leaned on the steering wheel

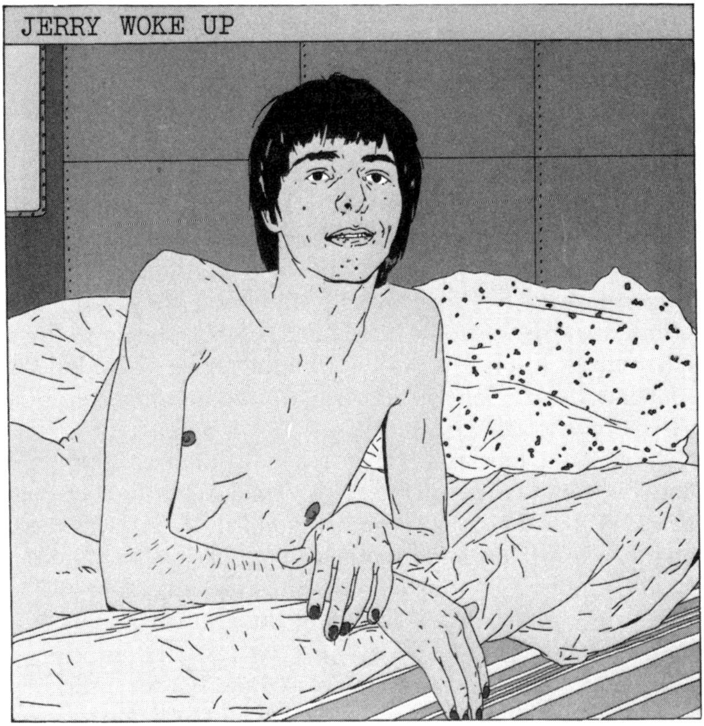

and peered at the ruins of the Prince Charles Hotel beside the lake. "It's a free country, at least. And peaceful."

"Sort of peaceful. Is your pal still there? The anarchist?"

"There are lots of anarchists in Scotland now," said Una.

"You know the one I mean."

"Makhno should still be there. I'd like to look him up. He's getting on now, you know. Must be at least eighty."

"You wouldn't think it would you?" said Catherine salaciously. The older they got the more she fancied them.

From the lake emerged a peculiar submersible vehicle. It paused on the bank, throbbing. Its conning tower turned as if to watch them. A Browning M2 .50 took their range. Una started the old engine. ''We can outrun that bastard if we're quick.''

''Better do it, then,'' said Jerry. He unwrapped their only gun and wound down the side window even as he pushed Catherine into the back. The heavy Thompson .45 made him feel much better than it should have done.

The Transit lurched and Jerry fired a burst at the submersible more to startle it than anything else. The Browning did not fire back. Only when they were two hundred yards down the Scotland road did it begin to fire a few rounds, but it was evident that the crew—some kind of renegades—was conserving ammunition for defence rather than attack.

Jerry looked around him at ruined romance. The place had been the scene of five or six major battles between Black Watch divisions trying to establish themselves fresh territory since they had been driven out of Scotland and the local Cumbrian bandits who resented the incursion all the more since the Black Watch had little worth looting but their weapons.

By that afternoon they had crossed the border under the gaze of a small black patrol ship which had dropped to a few feet above their heads to inspect them and then risen swiftly as a sign that they could proceed.

By evening, after resting and eating, they could see sanctuary ahead as Glasgow's solid towers became visible above the mist.

''Shall we be staying?'' asked Catherine of Una.

Una shook her head. ''Not for long. The war is endless, you know. Someone has to carry on.''

''You're sounding more like your old self,'' said Catherine approvingly.

''Well, one of them, at least,'' said Una.

Jerry rolled onto his side and began to snore.

4

RECAPITULATION

Every Gun Plays Its Own Tune

The Bishop and Mitzi
  Were on the rampage
She full of lust
  He full of rage
Looking for victims
  They hoped to convert
Stopped in the fifties
  And there found a cert . . .

They got me again
They got me again
Oh, shit, they got me again
I was holed out in 'fifty
And having some fun
When I heard Mitzi coming
Caught the sound of her gun

Bang-bang-bang
Here come the gang
Bang-bang-bang-bang-bang!

The Bishop and Mitzi
  They found him at last
Stuck in a time-slip
  On his way to the past
He cried out for mercy
  But they only laughed
As they took him in
  To remind him of sin . . .

They got me again etc.

Pierrot, poor Pierrot
Must become Harlequin
Learn about sin
Drugs, whisky and gin
Such a bad convert
That's the thing about him
He'll forget all his
Lessons in time . . .

They got me again etc.
Bang-bang-bang etc.

Pierrot in the Roof Garden

I've climbed so high
I can't climb higher
I've reached the top
And have to stop
Sitting on the steeple
Like a silly little fairy
Goodbye Tom and Goodbye Derry
Goodbye sahib, hello effendi
Biba's bust and I'm so trendy
Marx and Spencer's fails to send me
I've a hole in my trousers
And a boil on my nose
But they won't catch me
With my teeth round a rose
My time's run out
I'm a senile ghost
Run-down loony
Who never signed up
Music box
They can't wind up
You should see
What I had lined up

It was sweet
And it was tasty
Lost the lot
By being too hasty
I don't care
I've reached the limit
You can keep the world
There's nothing in it
I'll just sit here
And eat my spinach
Waiting for
The thing to finish
Up above the moon
Is shining
As I squat here
Quietly whining
For Columbine
I still am pining
My reel is spinning
But I can't get
The line in
So I think I'll just
Crawl under this bush.

Columbine's Carol

Sing for joy, we've met in time
Harlequin and Columbine
Praise the jolly myth of Yule
May good cheer forever rule
Fire doth blaze and snow doth fall
Peace on Earth for One and All
Holly shines and Ivy glows
Bunting from the roof-tops flows.
Sing for joy, we've met in time
Harlequin and Columbine.

In the bell-tower Pierrot kneels
Surrounded by the merry peels
Now they're singing ding-dong-dell
Send the sinners down to hell
Snow doth fall and fire doth blaze
Numbering poor Pierrot's days
Down the bell-rope he descends
Knowing he must face his end
Out into the graveyard white
Pierrot must embrace the night.

Sing for joy, we've met in time
Harlequin and Columbine
Sing for joy, we've met in time
Harlequin and Columbine

Surrounded by a Christmas throng
Pierrot sings a silent song
(Goodbye me and goodbye time
Goodbye lovely Columbine)
Falling snow and blazing fire
This is Pierrot's funeral pyre
Gone is laughter, gone is light
Pierrot must embrace the night.

Sing for joy, we've met in time
Harlequin and Columbine
Sing for joy, we've met in time
Harlequin and Columbine . . .

4. THE MINSTREL GIRL

1

WHO TURNED THE COURTESY CAR INTO A HEARSE?

ISIS provides accurate gyro-stabilised weapon-aiming for guns air-to-air and guns, rockets and bombs air-to-ground . . . The D-282 has the added facility of airspeed computation in the air-to-ground strike role. A unique feature of this equipment is roll stabilisation of the aiming mark, reducing tracking time by 50%. Incorporated within the single optical lens system is a fixed cross standby sight. ISIS is also designed to integrate with laser rangefinders and inertial navigation systems.

Ferranti

"NUCLEAR FUSION WILL return our birthright to us. Melting our cities into the softer contours of our original hills; restoring our caves, our safe places, bringing back the radiant landscapes of the world before the Fall." Jerry Cornelius stepped carefully over the huge blown-up photograph of the three murdered killers covering the middle of the studio's floor. It was black and white. He was a ghost. She was surprised that she could still see him.

"If you could only guarantee it," she said. In the far corner of the studio Una shivered beside one of the old-fashioned floodlamps. She extended her palms towards the warmth. She wore a military greatcoat, spangled tights. He, on the other hand, wore a huge black fur coat, some kind of shako, jackboots, as if he hoped that these rather more substantial clothes would hold him together long enough to do whatever it was he had come here for. Sinuously, with all that was left of his old self-conscious grace, he came to a stop beside a tank of developing fluid. He pushed back his coat and eased his needle gun into the heavy holster at his hip. The outline of the holster spoiled the otherwise perfect symmetry beneath the fur. "Dusty roads," he murmured nostalgically.

Her shoulders slumped. "Why not?" Would he want her for his next victim?

There was a four by eight picture of a child pinned to the wall to her left; a naked blonde of about ten. He shrugged at it. "We bring them into the world and then they die."

She glanced at him in surprise. "Die."

He continued his approach. "Love can be found nowhere, these days, except in the ruins." His hands reached out.

"We're not there yet," she said.

His hands fell.

As if to apologise she said: "I cannot lose my belief in original sin. That is, I do think there are those who carry sin with them, who infect the rest."

"What would you do with them?" He seemed to be sulking.

"Them? I suspect I'm talking about myself."

"Why not."

It was twelfth night and he was on his way, he had told her, to the Hunt Ball. He had a pair of antlers in the parcel he had left by the door as he had entered to rescue her. Through the glass roof she watched the sky grow cold, yellow, and then black. She thought of sex and sighed.

She sighed again, regretfully. She could see his body trembling beneath his clothes. They were worlds apart.

(The girl's face came closer. He saw the eyes narrow and the mouth twist. She began to weep. He backed away, raising his hands defensively and shaking his head from side to side. The music started and the dance went on.

Let the good times roll.)

2

WHERE IS THE KILLER WHO HATED REDHEADS?
The Royal Air Force is currently undertaking studies on the use of the Hawk as a frontline operational aircraft in addition to its basic role as trainer. As Air Vice-Marshal Gilbert, Assistant Chief of Air Staff (Policy) put it to Interavia: 'We are well aware that the Hawk has an operational capability, in addition to training, and we are conducting studies to see to what extent the capability can be

exploited under the operational conditions of the 1980s.' Among the tasks being looked at are ground attack, self-defence and air defence. A compact easily-maintained aircraft like the Hawk would clearly be an asset in any breakthrough situation in the NATO central region. It would be particularly effective against vehicles and thin-skinned armour columns which had advanced beyond the heavy anti-aircraft weapon support available in the existing front line.

Interavia

"WE DO WHAT we do. We are what we are."

Maxime glanced up when she heard this. Her expression was one of amused irony. "Your voice has altered. It's deeper. Almost negroid, hein?"

"Oh shut up." Una freed herself from the grubby sheet and struggled towards the side of the vast Louis XIV bed. She reached it at last, rolled off, then crawled through the tangles of the sheepskin carpet to the mirrored wall to look at her seedy, youthful face. She stuck out her bruised red tongue and inspected the tiny sore on the tip. Naked, she turned and sat cross-legged with her back to the mirror, staring across the room to where Maxime, her faintly Asiatic face frozen in a frown, smoked a cigarette and smoothed her thin fringe down over her forehead. Behind the heavy yellow velvet curtains the dawn was breaking.

"Fuck!" said Una.

"Die," sighed Maxime. She stretched her muscular arms. "Is the world still there, this morning?"

Una got to her feet and, hunched with cold, padded for the door. "I used to enjoy it all. I used to love it."

Maxime's tight mouth smiled. "First the romance goes, then the love, then the lust. The innocent! The gangster!"

When the door closed, Maxime leapt from the bed and ran to the chair on which, last night, she had flung her party uniform.

Una watching her through the keyhole, experienced a faint stirring in the region of her pelvis. She had begun to develop a fear of individuals. Nowadays she could only

embrace causes. She knew it was a weakness, but history was not, at present, on her side.

3

CAN TOO MUCH SEX PLAY LEAD TO MURDER?

One of the largest potential military markets during the next decade will be that for subsonic trainer/ground attack aircraft. While estimates vary from source to source, a reasonable assessment of the demand is that about 6,000 aircraft will be needed to replace existing types in countries outside the United States and the East Bloc.

Interavia

"IT IS THE disordered mind which detects order everywhere", Prinz Lobkowitz held her tightly in his grey arms, looking down at her head through fine, fading irises as he stroked her hair. "The schizoid brain seeks desperately for systems, the paranoid produces patterns from the most unlikely sources. The mad eye selects only what it wishes to see—proof of political plots, evidence of interstellar visitation, moral corruption in any given society. The evidence is not presented to us in linear form, you see, and cannot be read as we read lines of print. The secret is to make no specific selection."

"And go mad," said Una.

"No, no, no. And learn to love the world in all its aspects."

"Even cancer?"

"Love and cancer are scarcely compatible. But you could say that what we call 'cancer' has a perfect right to exist."

"We'd all die," she said. She broke away from him.

"Nonsense. We'd all experience miracle cures." He was hurt by her action. He began to roll down his sleeves, glancing round him at the abandoned surgery in the hope that she would not see his tears.

She moved a step or two towards him. His body was stiffer than it had been, his tone was over-controlled. "Shall I see you tonight, Una?"

"No," she said. "I can't come."

The room shook. An explosion somewhere. The first for a long time. A tray of instruments tumbled to the floor. He picked up his jacket from the threadbare carpet, holding back a leaning screen with his other hand. She sat on the edge of the leatherette inspection couch and combed her hair. "What about art?" she said. "That orders things, surely? At best."

"But at best it doesn't deny the rest of the evidence." He buttoned his jacket and found his homburg where it had fallen behind the doctor's desk. The doctor's skeleton lay clean and slumped, skull back against the chair's headrest, resembling another piece of analytical equipment. "You're staying here, then?"

"I said I'd meet a friend."

"Cornelius?"

She blushed. "No. His sister."

"Aha." He drew in his breath and headed for the door. "The world's turned topsy-turvy!"

"That's only how you see it," said Una. Then she regretted the irony. She had no wish to hurt him.

4

IS IT TRUE THAT THE SECRET OF S.S.P. HAD TURNED MEN INTO GODS AND CAN SHOW YOU HOW TO PROGRAM AND RECEIVE EVERYTHING YOU'VE EVER WANTED IN JUST SECONDS . . . INCLUDING RICHES, LUXURIOUS POSSESSIONS, POWER OVER OTHERS, AND EVEN A LONGER LIFE?

In a deal worth £180 million, Iran has selected the 'tracked' version of the Rapier low-level air defence system which is based on the FMC M548 armoured carrier. Iran already operates the standard Rapier version.

Interavia

UNA AND CATHERINE were completely out of ammunition by the time they hit the IBM building. They were disturbed to find that the building had not been defended at all and suspected a trap. They proceeded warily across the campus, but it seemed the remaining students had fallen back to the great hall. The two women ducked into the low concrete entrance and ran along the corridor, bursting in on the computer room. The machine filled all available wall space on four sides. But it was dead. None of its indicators flickered, none of its lights glowed and its tapes no longer rotated.

"We've been done," said Catherine. She threw her carbine butt-first at a battleship-grey panel. It bounced back towards her so that she had to skip aside. It rattled across the floor. "This bugger isn't controlling anything. There's no power."

"I wonder why Maxime said she thought it was the centre of operations." Una lit a thin brown cigarette.

"Because she couldn't bear the idea of being in any way responsible herself," said Catherine spitefully. She patted at a blonde Marcel wave. "What a cock-up eh? What a bloody waste of time!"

"That's the trouble with computers," said Una. "They do confuse things."

"And take a lot of heat away from those who deserve to get it," said Catherine. She bent down wearily to pick up her M16. "Come on. Let's see if we can find any ammo outside."

"Wait," said Una. She opened her arms to her friend. "I feel so lonely suddenly, don't you?"

Catherine shook her head, but she came to Una. "Not here," she said.

5

WILL YOUR JOB BE NEXT TO GO?

Fixed armament on the General Dynamics F-16 consists of an internally mounted M61A1 Vulcan 20mm gun installed aft of the cockpit and avionics bays. External stores can be carried on nine stations: one central underfuselage, six underwing and two wingtip. A Pave Penny laser tracker pod hardpoint is also provided . . . A potential world market for the F-16 is seen as 4,800 aircraft; the conservative programme basis is put at 1,500. Based purely on the F-16 replacing the F-104. General Evans has said that there is a potential market for some 2,000 aircraft. (Almost 2,500 F-104s were built and over 2,200 of these were exported.)

Interavia

CATHERINE SEEMED TO have settled down nicely so Una left her in Kiev and took the night train for Warsaw. From Warsaw she went to Dubrovnik, a roundabout route but the safest (if her instincts were to be trusted). Large

movements of men and equipment were taking place everywhere and she walked up the gangplank of the S.S. *Kao An* with a deep sense of relief. By the next morning they were making steam, heading for the less cluttered environments of Darwin and Sandakan. They had scarcely made it into the Timor Sea, however, before the ship was commandeered by a South Korean gunboat and Una and a selection of passengers were packed off back to the West with stamps on their passports forbidding them ever to

cross beyond Lat. 30 or Long. 40 again. Paranoia was settling in all over it seemed. Una had tried to make friends with one of the Korean officers, to find out what their complaint was. The man had struck her lightly across the mouth, refusing to speak English; he found that he had enjoyed hitting her and slapped her again until his commander had reprimanded him, not from any humane motive but, as Una interpreted it, because he would lose face.

Arriving in London, which had been 'cleaned up', she was subjected to an investigation into her movements over the past three years. Since she had begun to suffer from amnesia it was difficult for her to answer the questions but, knowing that they would be satisfied with any information so long as they could make it jell with their preconceptions, she invented a life-story for herself which was not only acceptable to them but suited her. She regretted that it was fictional.

Prinz Lobkowitz, the new Minister for Controls, heard that she was in England and sent an invitation for her to join him for dinner, but she was too frightened to accept. She headed for the cotton wool zone, eventually settling near Box Hill until one evening the telephone rang. Since it had never been connected at her request she saw this as a sign and returned to London and the Convent of the Poor Clares in Ladbroke Grove where a cell was held in readiness for this sort of emergency. She was convinced however that she was not going to escape. Her lovers were closing in on her.

She became desperate in her search for an ideal, a cause, a focus, but nothing presented itself to her. She refused to find what she wanted in an individual. She wanted, she said, something bigger. She regretted that her mind refused to manufacture fresh evidence for her researches.

Eventually, rather than face the more familiar dangers, she gave herself up to the nuns who had been begging to help her since her arrival.

6

THE STRANGE CASE OF THE PANTY-CLAD COED AND THE NIGHT-RIDING MONSTER

Financial restrictions are pushing Western aircraft development in one direction, while the East Bloc nations, spearheaded by the Soviet Union, are moving in another. The most remarkable point is that the latest Soviet aircraft display a sophistication that was almost unthinkable only a few years ago. During the 1950s and 1960s, the tendency was for all but the most specialised combat aircraft (e.g. reconnaissance and anti-submarine warfare) to be simple and robust, and produced in large numbers. The MiG-21, for example, was described by one Western analyst as a 'throw-away fighter', scarcely more than a piloted projectile.

Interavia

SOMETHING WAS HAPPENING in the lower back section of the left-hand side of her brain. Memories of childhood disguised the deeper issues. She tried to trace the association. A flicker of hope. A few more cells began to die. She settled the expensive Koss headphones more comfortably over her ears and listened to the music with desperate concentration. Humour? Love? A sense of relish? The images of demolished streets and overgrown parks got in the way again. Perhaps if she adjusted the balance a fraction? She felt for the control, fingered it, moved it. Her face ached as she squeezed her eyes still tighter. All her heroes and heroines were dead. Those she had met had proved to be unworthy of what she had to give.

. . . *I swear the moon turned to fire red. The night I was born* . . .

She focussed on the appropriate section of the cortex. Drugs could produce a terrible self-consciousness, particularly when coupled with psychiatric research. The brain scanned the brain, scanned the brain.

Surely it must be possible to awaken sections of the mind just as one could sensitise areas of the body? She was right inside now. She slipped out. Her sense of yearning became even more painful. Inside again. Out. She increased the volume. Inside.

A question of proteins. They were being manufactured. But would they be the right ones?

The tempo of the drumbeats increased.

Inside.

The memories of childhood began to dim. Now she was sure something lay behind them. Deeper. She had isolated

THE IMAGES OF DEMOLISHED STREETS ...

the cells at any rate.

The music stopped.

She screamed.

7

THE QUESTION WITHOUT AN ANSWER

The RBS70 missile system has been designed to provide extreme mobility and rapid deployment with a very short reaction time against high-speed aircraft flying at the lowest possible altitudes. The RBS70 missile system has recently been ordered by the Swedish Army, in an order worth nearly SKr-500 million. First deliveries, mostly of training equipment, will start in 1976, with series production by 1977. Bofors is also looking at future developments, including a possible nightfire version using electro-optical sensors for target detection. At the moment the visibility limitation on the use of the weapon is the ability of the crew to see the target. The laser guidance system is able to provide guidance under any conditions in which the target is visible.

Interavia

WITHIN THE SKULL the universe was at war.

Maxime and Catherine, Jerry and Lobkowitz stood on each side of the white hospital bed, their eyes fixed on the tragic face.

"She was looking for love," said Maxime.

"I loved her," said Jerry a little shiftily.

"So did I," said his sister.

"We all loved her," said Lobkowitz. "She was Life. She was Liberty. She was Hope."

"She was Future," said Jerry. "Fusion and fission, the glowing, rolling obsidian ranges of the post-war landscape." He sighed.

"But she was trying to love us, you see," continued Lobkowitz. "She wanted what we saw in her—she looked for the same things in us and could not find them. This is a good hospital. They will do what they can."

Maxime nodded. "Our people specialise in such complaints. *Tout cela vous honore/Lord Pierrot, mais encore?*"

Jerry glared a little resentfully at his rival.

"She thought she experienced it so many times," said Catherine, "but she was always disappointed. And yet she continued to seek that love, against all the odds."

"She loved it all," Maxime shrugged. "All of it."

"The data became confusing towards the end." Lobkowitz was sad.

"I could have simplified it." Jerry pouted. "Only nobody would let me." Then he laughed spontaneously. "Too much!"

And for a moment the electrodes protruding from Una's skull quivered in sympathy with the sounds from her mouth.

5

CODA

Harlequin Transformed

3/4 (A sort of carousel tune)

Destroyed by a comedy I did not devise
I've reached the limit of my changes
Repeating tricks solely for my eyes
Now, at last, my legend ages
And reveals the structure of my lies . . .

And my body alters as I watch
Black mask fades
My skin is pale
The colour leaves my costume
And I'm no longer Harlequin
—I am defeated from within

4/4

Say goodbye to Harlequin
Poor Pierrot now replaces him . . .

3/4

By a legend I sustained
Sardonic gaze and vicious brain
By mythology I maintained
The posture that I feigned
Inevitably my pose dissolved
Entropy has left me cold
And Harlequin is slain—
Again . . .

4/4 (rep. tune Every Gun)

Drip, drip, drip, drip
Here come's the rain

(Plink, plink, plink, plink—plucked on violin) *Abrupt End.*

Pierrot and Columbine's Song of Reconciliation

Divided I love you
And united become you
Columbine, Columbine
We are one at last

Rejecting all armour
Thus we are conquered
Conquered, we vanquish
All that we fear

Pierrot and Columbine
(Harlequin with them)
Conquered, we vanquished
All that we feared . . .

(This leads into the tune of the Entropy Tango, acting as an introduction for the reprise, which is up-tempo, cheerful . . .)

The Entropy Tango (Reprise—The Ensemble)

For a while at least it's all right
We're safe from Chaos and Old Night
The Cold of Space won't chill our veins
—We have danced the Entropy Tango . . .

So we'll love, love, love
One another like two doves . . .
And we'll hug, hug, hug
We can never have enough . . .
The power of love has won this throw
—We have danced the Entropy Tango . . .

And it's kiss, kiss, kiss
Fear and hate we have dismissed
And it's wish, wish, wish . . .
For a better world than this . . .
So say goodbye to pain and woe
—And we'll stop the Entropy Tango . . .

5. HARLEQUIN'S LAMENT

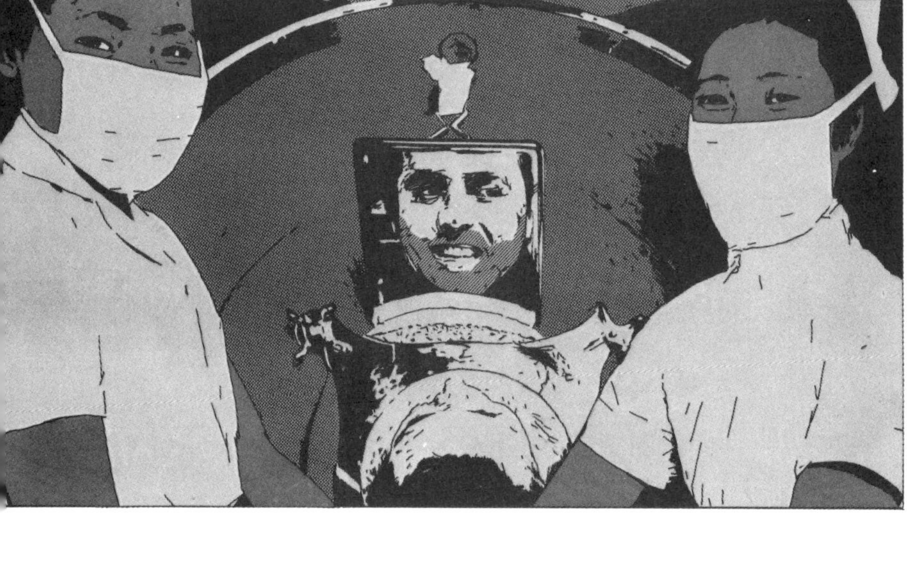

1

This is the personal flag of the Sovereign, and a symbol of the tie which unites under one monarch the British Dominions throughout the world. The three golden lions represent England, the red lion rampant Scotland, while the golden harp stands for Ireland—the three states from which the Empire grew. Royal personages have the right to fly royal standards, members of the Royal Family having their particular standards. This flag should only be hoisted when H.M. the King is actually present, and ought never to be used for purposes of decoration.

In the Royal Navy, by special privilege, the King's health is always drunk sitting.

Flags of the Empire, No. 1, issued by W.D. & H.O. Wills, c. 1924

AT SUNSET, WHEN the beggars in Chowringhee settled themselves into doorways for the night and the kites and vultures on the lamp-posts and telephone poles roosted, reconciled that they must wait for a fresh day to bring them their share of death and garbage, Mrs Persson would climb into her rickshaw and let the ageless coolie, in his turban and his loincloth, run with her to the Empire where she was starring as Diana Hunt in the musical comedy *Wonderful Woman*. She played a Greek goddess transported to 1930 (with hilarious misunderstandings) who eventually gives up all her powers to marry the hero and become an ordinary housewife. Una considered the role ideal. It was the sensation of Calcutta.

Through the mobs of cyclists, pedestrians, rickshaws; past the trams, bullock carts, limousines, trucks, taxis, buses which blared and flared in the twilight, darted Una and her coolie, until at last they reached the marble face of the Empire (with her name in electric lights above its Graecian portico) round to the stage entrance, a little bit late as usual. Una got out and the rickshaw was off (she paid it weekly) and she, in silks and chiffon, in her Reynolds hat and veil, briskly went through nodding to the

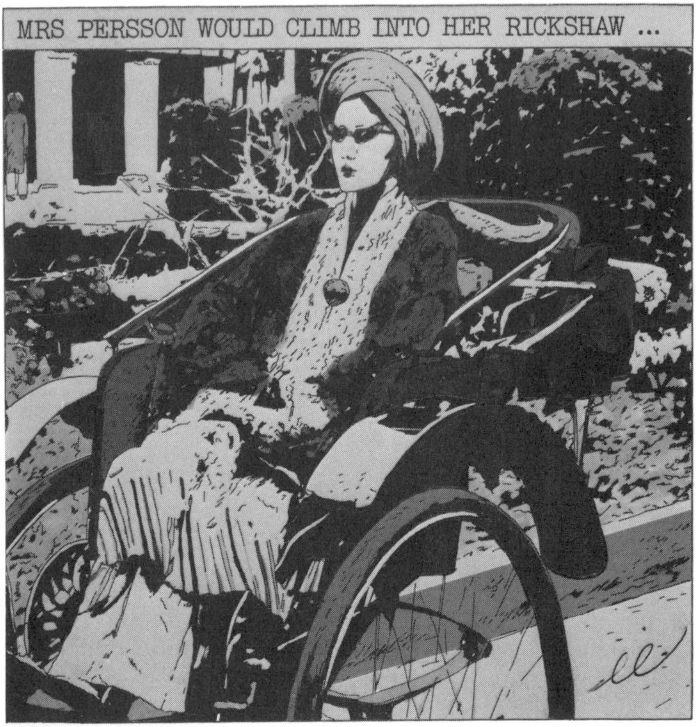

Bengali stage-door keeper, who smiled and nodded at her. He was trusted by the management. He was one of the very few natives they employed at present. So many young Bengalis were anarchists and might be expected to attack the theatre.

Una got to her dressing room and became suddenly wary, for the door was open and voices emerged. She recomposed herself and entered. She vaguely recalled the couple who waited for her—the fat clergyman with his hat in his fingers, the thin bluestocking in pale linen. Her dresser began to speak rapidly in her lilting English. Una smiled. "It's all right, Ranee. Bishop Beesley and—?

"I'm Miss Brunner. We met, I believe, at Mrs Brightsett's garden party. Last week."

"Oh, yes. And I promised you tickets!"

"No," said Bishop Beesley. "We are from the local Moral Rearmament Committee."

"This play is objectionable? Surely not."

"The play is fine. There's one scene, that's all." Bishop Beesley brightened as Ranee offered him some of Una's Turkish Delight.

"Which one?"

"The . . ." he mumbled the confection, ". . . second act. Scene one."

"Where I have my first drink?"

"Yes." Miss Brunner spoke significantly.

"The audience love it. It's the funniest."

"It's very good." Miss Brunner seemed baffled. "But we wondered if you could accommodate us. Accommodate the residents of the city, really. Anywhere else, I'm sure it would not be important—but there are Bengalis in the audience, and Anglo-Indians and so on, as well as English people."

"Yes."

"And we feel the scene could—" Bishop Beesley wiped sugary lips "—corrupt some of them."

"Because of me getting tipsy? I would have thought there was a moral there—not to drink."

"You could see it as that," Miss Brunner agreed, "but when it is combined with your costume . . ."

"A bit flimsy?"

"Exactly," said Bishop Beesley in relief.

"And the language," said Miss Brunner. "I mean—what you say."

"What do I say?"

"Something about crime and anarchy?"

"Ah, yes: Here's to crime and here's to anarchy! I'm showing my frustration. I come round in the end."

"Not the best-chosen line, given the current political climate."

"I don't know anything about politics," Una told them.

Ranee brought over some tea. "Tea?" added Una.

"Thank you. Even you, Mrs Persson," continued the bishop, "must realise there have been bombings of white people almost daily. In the name of the anarchist cause." He unrolled a copy of *The Englishman* and pointed out its headline: ANARCHY: A CHALLENGE TO THE EMPIRE. "It's in the leading article. And you should read the Bengali papers. Full of such stuff."

"What stuff?" asked Una.

"Anarchy," said Miss Brunner, lifting her cup. "They get it all from France, I believe."

"Aha," said Una. She sat down at her mirror and looked at her face. She gave herself a wink. "Well, I'll bear it in mind, of course. Thanks for pointing the problem out."

"You'll change your lines? And your costume?"

"I'll certainly give it some thought," Una promised.

2

What man that sees the eur-whirling wheele
Of Change, the which all mortall things doth sway,
But that therby doth find, & plainly feele,
How MUTABILITY in them doth play
Her cruell sports, to many mens decay?
Which that to all may better yet appear,
I will rehearse that whylome I heard say,
How she at first her selfe began to reare,
Gainst all the Gods, and th'empire fought from them to beare.

Spenser, The Fairie Queene, 7. vi. 1.

AS THE TRAIN pulled out of Odessa, leaving the warmth and the ocean behind, Una swayed on her feet, attempting to freshen her face in the mirror above the opposite seats. Her lipstick dropped from her hand and fell onto green plush. She said: "Damn!" and bent to look for it just as the compartment door opened and a man holding a carpet-bag entered and raised his straw hat. He wore rimless glasses and had the kind of goatee beard which hid nothing of his face, added no character and was perhaps a badge to make it clear that he was an intellectual. The casual Norfolk, the unpressed trousers, the peasant shirt, all proclaimed his chosen role and, of course, he addressed her in French rather than Russian. "Excusez moi, mademoiselle."

Una had recognised him. It was the old butcher himself. He couldn't see past her heavy make-up.

"Bronstein!" she laughed. "Are you back in favour?"

He relaxed, at the same time displaying his embarrassment. "It's you, comrade. Dressed up like a bourgeois whore. What are you doing? Going all the way?"

"Hoping to. Kiev?"

"I change there. I don't like this part of the world much. The people are lazy. Too rich, all of them."

"All?"

"By my standards. What have you been up to?" He offered her a Sobranie which she accepted because she liked the feel of the gold tip on her mouth.

"I've been resting," she said. "I'm too tired, darling."

"And why are you in Russia?"

"I'm not in Russia. I'm in Ukrainia."

"You have a pass?" He pulled a card from his pocket. He seemed to be proud of the distinction. "Like this? It's a special pass. Everyone must help me."

"You're not posing as an anarchist now!"

"What's the difference? We're all socialists. I shall represent Kiev in Moscow and resume my position as head of the Bureau. In time." He opened his bag and took out a large notebook. "I have agreed to put the South Russian case."

"They don't need it put. They're strong—and rich. You said so yourself." The train began to move faster. They were in Odessa's new garden suburbs. The light was perfect. Una stared out of the window, back at the misty sea with all its ships, inland at the green steppe ahead. "You've conned them. You'll use their strength to help you get your job back! You cunning old bastard."

Trotski sniffed. "I have a case to put. I must have an effective power-base if I am to put it properly."

"And Stalin?"

Trotski pursed his lips and smiled. "Didn't you know? He's dead."

"I'll never understand politics." Una looked out at golden fields and saw horsemen riding along the nearby white road. They were racing the train, waving their caps as they spurred their ponies. She was reminded of the old days, of Makhno and his riders. She waved back. They were past. She returned her attention to Trotski. "Maybe that's why I find them so eternally appealing."

He leaned forward and put a familiar hand on her knee. "Where have you been for the past five years? This time I want the truth.'' He attempted joviality.

''You'll have it,'' she said. ''But you'll never appreciate it.''

''Don't be mysterious.'' He leaned back and picked up his book. He took a fountain pen from his inside pocket. ''It irritates me.''

''I can't be anything else. I'm Una. I'm the truth. Eh?''

''You're the very antithesis. You've gone back to acting, I see.''

''I had. But I've given it up again. I'm on my way to see a friend in Kiev.''

''Makhno, that hooligan?''

''No. Quite another hooligan. He's not fond of you.''

''Few are,'' he said smugly. ''Who is it?''

''Jerry.''

''Cornelius. Bah! He's no threat at all. Except to himself. I thought he was liquidated. Or in a coma or something.''

''It's not his turn.''

He removed his glasses. The gesture was meant as a warning signal. He drew heavily on his cigarette as he leaned forward. ''Stop it! Una!'' He wagged his finger. He was pretending to joke.

Una felt the familiar terror. She drew in a breath and was defiant. It was just what she had needed.

3

THE RIVER

It is during the Diwali festival, when the darkest night in October is illumined by myriad bonfires, each symbolising a life sacrificed in the conflict between good and evil, that the girl, Harriet, falls in love with a young captain, lamed in the First World War. Lacking beauty, she hopes to win his heart by writing a poem for him about the legendary Radha, whose love for the god Krishna made her a goddess . . . In India all rivers—symbols of Eternity—are sacred . . .

ARTICLE: Picture Post, 1 March 1952

BEHIND THEM, THE Golden Gate Bridge sagged and squealed as the explosive took it out. It was dawn. There were fires all over San Francisco, particularly in the suburbs. From the harbour the pirate ships continued to shell the city. They were retreating now. On the bridge of the submarine liner *Seahorse* Una, her face blackened by smoke, her hand on the butt of her holstered revolver, looked at their hostages—almost all young men and women—totting up their value in her head. They would be ransomed.

The fleet, mainly a mixture of commercial and naval submarines stolen from half the countries in the world, had arrived at midnight, surfacing in the bay to begin its attack. It had fought off the few defending airships, and, in the time gained while Washington hesitated, had been able to loot the city of most of what they had come for.

Makhno, in a long leather coat and riding britches, an M60 in his left hand, joined her on the bridge. His men were hauling boxes aboard. "There it is, Una. All the gold of Sacramento."

She was a little dismayed at his tone. "You sound like a bandit."

"Don't be moralistic now you've had your fun. There's something Victorian about you, Una. Always washing your hands. I am a successful bandit!" He touched her arm gently. He was very old. The white hair was growing thin. His movements, however, were those of a ballet dancer—imitating youth from training and habit.

He went below, making some noise, and greeted the Pole, Captain Korzeniowski, who had inadvertently inspired this raid with his tales of gold and who had commanded the *Seahorse* ('For safety and comfort in troubled times, these luxurious hotels of the deep will get you where you want to go in the condition you'd wish to arrive!') before Makhno had requisitioned her. Korzeniowski was contemptuous. "How many hundreds of innocents has your raid destroyed?"

"There are no innocents in this struggle." Makhno spoke automatically and Una felt sad. The years had at last succeeded in coarsening him. It had been almost inevitable. She leaned down towards where the hostages still stood watching the gold being lowered into the special hatches. "Let them go. Give them boats." She told the guards. She would not take any more responsibility.

In a dinghy coming alongside from their own wrecked sub, Shakey Mo and Jerry called out to her. They were filthy and jubilant. Cornelius at least was drunk. It was always hard to tell with Mo what sort of condition he was in.

"Mrs P." Jerry raised a bottle of wine in a salute. He began to get up but the rocking boat made him sit down again. "Ready to leave when you are!"

"Not long now," she said. She searched the sky for dawn, but the flames obscured it.

"This is what I call effective political action," said Mo. "We need our course. We had the chart on the bridge when that bloody destroyer got us. Dropped a fucking great torpedo, didn't it."

She had seen them leap into the sea just before the destroyer had, in turn, been blown out of the sky.

Could she hear screaming from the city? Smoke clogged her nostrils, stung her eyes. The suburbs were on fire, now. Many wooden houses were burning and they sweetened the otherwise acrid air.

Mo scrambled over the rail. "Better than any earthquake," he said. "Better than any Indian raid. Where are we headed? My guess was Mexico."

"You're not far out," said Una. Mo clinked and looked embarrassed. "What have you got this time?" she asked.

"Nothing much." His grin was sheepish. He reached into one of his several sacks and pulled out a coin. "Pieces of eight. Doubloons. And that . . ."

"Where on earth did you get them?"

"The museum. I always hit the museum first. You know me. An incurable bloody romantic. I love old things."

She felt affection for him. More than she felt at that moment for the others.

"This did used to be called the Barbary Coast," he said defensively.

"Wasn't that in Africa somewhere?"

"No," he said. "You're thinking of the Mountains of the Moon." He vanished into the liner's enormous hull.

Una saw that Jerry was helping some of the girls into the boat he had abandoned. He looked as harmless as they did. He was being very gentle with them. She drew a deep breath and controlled her tears.

"It all seems a bit self-indulgent, really," she said.

Fisherman's Wharf exploded suddenly and she was blinded.

4

HOOLIGANISM ON SOCCER TERRACES "HARMLESS RITUAL"

Soccer hooliganism provides a harmless outlet for aggression which could take more violent forms, says an Oxford psychologist in a book published today. Battles between rival groups on soccer terraces are an artificial form of violence rather than the real thing, and few people really get hurt, says Mr Peter Marsh, of the Oxford University Department of Experimental Psychology. In 'Aggro: the Illusion of Violence,' he appeals to people to learn to live with 'aggro'—fights between rival gangs of youths at football matches, dance halls and public houses—rather than trying to stamp it out. 'By trying to eradicate aggro we end up with something far more sinister. Instead of social violence we get non-social violence that manifests itself in random, gratuitous injury . . . By learning to live with aggro . . . we begin to see that illusions of violence are much preferable to the very real violence which maims and kills . . .' Mr Marsh sees 'Aggro' between rival gangs as an equivalent of tribal warfare in less developed societies.

Daily Telegraph, 20 July 1978

ALTHOUGH THE HOSPITAL was virtually silent, it seemed to Una that there was a threat in the air. She tried to move her eyes a little further than they would comfortably go. The metal cage keeping her head in position (she had a broken neck) allowed her no flexibility. Major Nye was still there, holding her hand. He was half asleep, his gaze fixed on the opposite bed. He attempted to carry on the conversation where it had stopped, five minutes before. "Yes," he said. "It's the vermin."

"Rats?"

"Mainly."

"Models, metaphors—even examples, I suppose." Una was glad that they had taken the screen away and she could see at least part of the ward with its privileged beds. The hospital was run by nuns and was private. There was no vermin here to speak of.

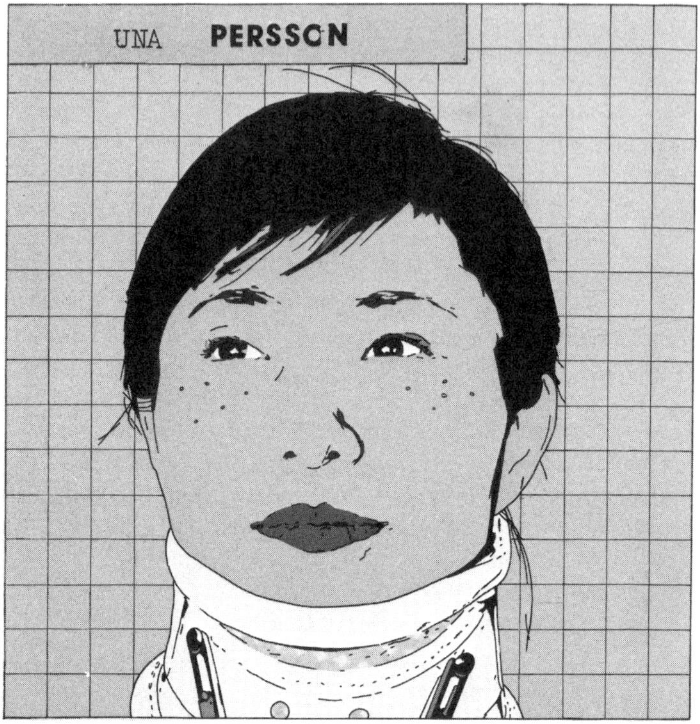

"I see what you mean." He smiled. "You're too imaginative."

"I live in a world of poetry," she said. "Or rather, of poetic images. Everything seems significant to me. Everything has meaning. It's what gets me into trouble. And I never listen. I only watch."

He patted her hand.

She heard very soft sounds and thought at first that she was listening to his hand on hers, but they were footfalls. At the end of the bed stood Prinz Lobkowitz. "They haven't moved you yet?"

"Not yet." Major Nye answered for her. He got up and brought a chair to place next to his own. "Sit down, old boy. You look very tired."

Lobkowitz's back was stooped. His grey hair fell over his face. The skin of his face had become baggy with care. Una felt frustrated. She wished she could be of help.

"Makhno?" she said.

"Dead. The Americans caught him at last. He was electrocuted three days ago. In Oregon, I believe."

"The Californians gave him up."

"Californians are like Greeks. They talk themselves into things and then they talk themselves out of them again. It must be the sunshine. No, he's buried in some Portland cemetry. Shall I get you the details?"

"It's pointless," she said. "I'll be in this thing for six months."

"Yes."

"He made a name for himself, at least," said Major Nye. "There's no one in the world hasn't heard of Nestor Makhno. He's a hero and a martyr in six continents. And his example lives on." He was trying to console her, but he could not fail to register a little disapproval. She gripped his wrist.

"Don't worry," she said. "It's a victory for your sort of rationalism, major."

"I've never much cared for my sort of rationalism. Not in isolation, anyway. I see myself as a balancing force—not as a positive one. Makhno represented all I envied. It was the same sort of balance which controlled the Empire for so long—we all admired the Bengalis, you know. And the Pathans. It's a terrible sort of paternalism, I suppose, but it had certain simple virtues."

"Are you sure there are such things as simple virtues?" Prinz Lobkowitz's accent had grown a shade stronger. "I would say that only vice was simple."

Major Nye hadn't followed him. "You sound as if you've come to preach the last rites," he said. "I don't think you'd make a very good clergyman, Prinz."

"Oh, I'm not so sure!" He strove for levity and failed miserably. "A couple of hundred years or so ago I could have filled the role you see as your own, major. A temporiser. Mm?''

''Church and State stuff. There's a fair bit to be said for the ideas of the middle-ages. We've complicated them rather, haven't we, without improving on them.''

''I wouldn't say that,'' said Una. She attempted to move and failed. The harness was firm.

''We're taking you by airship to the coast,'' said Prinz Lobkowitz. ''And then, perhaps when you're whole again, a cruise.''

''I might have had enough of cruises.''

''We'll see.''

''Do you good,'' said Major Nye with weary mindlessness.

''I'll happily take over.'' Prinz Lobkowitz smiled at his old friend. ''You could do with some shut-eye, eh?''

''About as much as you.'' Major Nye appreciated the thought. ''But I haven't any travelling in the morning. I'll carry on here.''

''You should both rest.'' Una hoped they would not take her seriously. She was terrified of being left in the hospital. She needed one of them there at least, to comfort her.

''Well,'' said Major Nye, ''perhaps you're right. Will you sleep now, Una?''

''Oh, yes. Of course.''

They rose; two tired ghosts. ''Goodbye.''

5

Buf if he sees a sad face staring through the glamour of light, the face of a girl who is thinking of a lover who comes no more to her Christmas parties, of an old mother whose children have gone about their business in the world, Pierrot will go on tiptoe to them, and lay a hand lightly on their shoulders, and say, 'It is not good to remember too much. Play the game of life. I have suffered too; but listen to my laughter on this Christmas night. Come, play the fool with me! Why, there is little Columbine who flouted me three hundred years ago! Bless her sweet heart; I will steal a kiss tonight.'

THE SPIRIT OF PIERROT by Phillip Gibbs, The Graphic, 27 November 1911

THE WHITE STEAM-yacht moved slowly through the drifts of ice. Steam curled from her deck as she gave her heat to the Arctic. The blue sky was like thin ice enclosing them. It was as if they sailed through the semi-fluid remains of some frozen confection, under glass. This was no place, thought Una as she pulled her huge white furs around her, for *The Teddy Bear*. It was no place for her, for that matter. She coughed and more heat escaped her to be absorbed by that unambiguous continent. The yacht bumped against a few small floes and the engines stalled for a second, then started up again, firmly pushing the ship on, heading closer and closer to the Pole.

From below came the sound of a piano, thin and brittle, and the applause of the guests. They had already had their turkey. They had opened their presents. Now the party was to begin with an entertainment.

Una turned from the tranquility of endless ice and made her way to the louvred door which would lead her down. The ship, though strengthened in her hull, had been designed for warm weather cruising.

In the saloon the audience had gathered. "All our old chums," as Bishop Beesley had said. He had handed over control of the ship only after he had been locked up for an afternoon without sweets. He was in the front row now, with a plate of cake and candy on his knees. Miss Brunner, wearing a paper hat on her violent red hair, sat next to him. She held a tiny piece of marzipan between the finger and thumb of her left hand. Her right hand rested against Maxime. The bishop's blonde daughter, Mitzi, glared at them from the other side of her corpulent dad.

Una removed her coat and revealed herself as Harlequin. She put on her mask and her cap. She bowed and was cheered. Mrs Cornelius, behind the bishop, blew a friendly raspberry. Major Nye began to vamp a 4/4 tango. He looked a little incongruous in his clown costume. Columbine (played by Catherine) curtsyed on the tiny stage. Behind her, wistful as ever, stood Pierrot, pretending to play a guitar.

The audience began to clap in time to the music, so loudly that the words of the song could not be heard at all.

Outside, the ice grew thicker and it seemed it must soon stop the ship completely. The steam from the white decks was growing denser, almost hiding her from view, as the passengers put their hearts and souls into their enjoyment of the show.

A little faint music found an echo in the distant mountains; the ancient ice.

If it was to be a farewell performance, none of the actors had yet guessed. They sang louder and louder above the steady drumming of the applause, which took on the nature of a gigantic heartbeat. They sang as loud as they could. They sang with gusto. They sang for all the world.

THE END

Also by Michael Moorcock

The Cornelius Chronicles
The Final Programme
A Cure for Cancer
The English Assassin
The Condition of Muzak
The Lives and Times of Jerry Cornelius
The Aventures of Una Persson and Catherine Cornelius in the Twentieth Century
The Great Rock and Roll Swindle
The Entropy Tango

The Dancers at the End of Time
The Hollow Lands
An Alien Heat
The End of All Songs
Legends from the End of Time
The Transformation of Miss Mavis Ming [Return of the Fireclown]

Hawkmoon: The History of the Runestaff
The Jewel in the Skull
The Mad God's Amulet
The Sword of the Dawn
The Runestaff

Hawkmoon: The Chronicles of Castle Brass
Count Brass
The Champion of Garathorm *
The Quest for Tanelorn *

Erekosë
The External Champion
Phoenix in Obsidian
The Champion of Garathorm *
The Quest for Tanelorn *

*interconnected series

Elric Series
Elric of Melnibone
The Sailor on the Seas of Fate
The Sleeping Sorceress
The Stealer of Souls
Stormbringer
Elric at the End of Time

The Books of Corum
The Knight of the Swords
The Queen of the Swords
The King of the Swords
The Bull and the Spear
The Oak and the Ram
The Sword and the Stallion

Other titles
The City of the Beast
The Lord of the Spiders
The Masters of the Pit
The Warlord of the Air
The Land Leviathan
The Steel Tsar
The Winds of Limbo
Behold the Man
Breakfast in the Ruins
The Blood-Red Game
The Black Corridor
The Chinese Agent
The Russian Intelligence
The Distant Suns
The Rituals of Infinity
The Shores of Death
Sojan the Swordsman (juvenile)
The Golden Barge
Gloriana [or, The Unfulfill'd Queene, A Romance]
The Time Dweller (short stories)
Moorcock's Book of Martyrs (short stories)
Heroic Dreams (non-fiction)
The War Hound and the World's Pain
My Experiences in the Third World War
Byzantium Endures